How To Build Your Own Working Microcomputer

Other TAB books by the author:

No. 935 *Build-It Book of Optoelectronic Projects*
No. 1015 *A Beginner's Guide to Computers & Microprocessors—with projects*
No. 1299 *Master Handbook of Microprocessor Chips*

How To Build Your Own Working Microcomputer

BY CHARLES K. ADAMS

TAB BOOKS Inc.
BLUE RIDGE SUMMIT, PA. 17214

FIRST EDITION

THIRD PRINTING

Printed in the United States of America

Library of Congress Cataloging in Publication Data

Adams, Charles K.
How to build your own working microcomputer.

Includes index.
1. Microcomputers—Design and construction—Amateurs' manuals. I. Title.
TK9969.A3 621.3819'5 80-23630
ISBN 0-8306-9684-9
ISBN 0-8306-1200-9 (pbk.)

Preface

A computer is a fascinating device. It is an extension of the operator, capable of doing many intriguing things. It is under complete control of the operator, ready to do what is commanded. Recent advances in semiconductor technology have made it possible to build a computer on a single circuit board. This computer is not the complex monstrosity normally considered as a computer. Instead, it is a relatively simple device with a versatile, yet easily used instruction set. One person, with the desire, can build and program such a computer.

This computer, called a microcomputer, can be assembled with a handful of chips at a very reasonable cost. These microcomputers are based on the microprocessor, which is a very complex circuit, integrated into one large scale integrated circuit. Yet, all the chips required are readily available.

This book is about building and programming a computer. The computer is a relatively simple microcomputer by todays standards, but when compared to computers of twenty years ago it is very advanced and more than capable.

The computer is an expandable, usable computer, complete with programming instructions. This book is designed to take the reader through the hardware step by step so that a thorough understanding of the hardware is gained. In addition, the instruction set and the mechanics of programming are detailed to allow the user to program the computer. This is to assist the user in obtaining a working knowledge of both the hardware and software.

This book may be used in one of three manners. First, it can be used as a general reference book, to obtain general information. Second, it may be used as an aid to the designing and building of a computer. Third, and most important, it may be used as a guidebook to build and program the computer described here.

Charles K. Adams

Contents

Chapter 1
Introduction

The early electronic computers, built in the late 1940's and early 1950's, were monsters created by research and development laboratories, and by the large universities. These computers required several cabinets of equipment, several people to maintain and operate them, a lot of air conditioning to keep them cool, and a lot of power to keep them running. Costing several hundred-thousand dollars, they were affordable only by the government, large corporations, and universities. These computers could perform complex mathematical operations which required many man hours to solve manually.

An increase in reliability and operating time, along with the decreasing costs, brought large computers to the commercial market. Companies came into existence solely to lease computers, or sell computer time to users. Such services increased the commercial world's exposure to the compuuter, and it soon became apparent that the computer could do several things better and faster than its human counterpart.

COMPUTERS GET A JOB

It wasn't long before companies began transferring billing and accounting to tasks to computers—the public started getting computerized bills. This introduced the public to the computer; and the public soon found out that the computer does only what it is told.

The early computers fulfilled their obligation—the handling and sorting of large amounts of data— but in turn created another requirement. Business required a small, inexpensive computer that was simple to program and operate. Such a computer was needed to replace the increasingly complex logic arrays required in some of the current logic designs.

It was the advent of a microprocessor— the heart of the microcomputer — that changed things. That this computer is simple, inexpensive, and easy to use, is proven by its tremendous popularity. There are thousands of hobbyists making, programming, and using microcomputers in addition to the millions in use in the commercial world. Microcomputers now control almost everything from toys to automobile-combustion efficiency. From games to microwave ovens. From stop lights to numerically controlled machines.

The microcomputer boom is just beginning. Advances in the microcomputer area almost daily. There is even a microcomputer which operates on analog inputs or outputs, along with the digital functions. Large quantities of preprogrammed single—chip microcomputers are available which cost less than $10 each (in volumes of several thousand).

The advent of semiconductor theory and solid-state technology led to the development of the transistor. This device virtually replaced the vacuum tube for a large percentage of electronic applications. The transistor led to such things as the transistor radio, stereos, and the cassette recorder.

Manufacturing techniques that were developed to make the transistor, along with an increase in knowledge about solid-state theory and semiconductor applications led to the development of the digital integrated circuit (IC). The IC comprised several transistors, diodes and other components on one small piece of semiconductor material. This piece of semiconductor material (the chip) was encapulsated into a package with leads. Such simple digital ICs each replaced several discrete components.

MAKING COMPUTERS EVEN SMALLER

Improvements to process techniques and the development of photographic reduction processes and equipment led to increasingly complex circuits in the ICs. This led to medium-scale integration (MSI) and eventually to large-scale integration (LSI); more and more components were incorporated into one IC. A typical LSI circuit requires about 7 masks for its deposition and doping operations. The photographic masker, from which the masks are made, is 200 times real size, and may be 10 to 20 feet square. This is the technology that generated the microprocessor. Now there are third and fourth generation devices available, which obsolete the early devices. The new devices can equal 450 standard digital ICs (or 110 MSI devices), and yet come in a standard 40 pin dual in line package (DIP). Most of their area is devoted to connecting the chip to the package pins for connection to the outside world.

Processor	Number of pins	Data word size	Addressing capability	Number of instructions
4004	16	4 bits	4K bytes	46
4040	24	4	8K	60
8000	40	8	1K	48
8008	18	8	16K	48
8080	40	8	64K	78
6800	40	8	64K	72
2650	40	8	32K	75
Z80	40	8	64K	150
6100	40	12	4K	81
9440	40	16	64K	42
8086	40	16	1M	97
68000	64	16	16M	61

Fig. 1-1. Comparison of some of the popular microprocessors.

There are several microprocessors available. These range from simple 4-bit devices to complex 16-bit devices. Some of the devices contain all that is required for a small, simple computer. Figure 1-1 shows the sizes of some of these devices, and lists some of their important characteristics.

As the microcomputer becomes more versatile and capable of doing more things, the line differentiating a minicomputer from a microcomputer becomes fuzzier—their applications and capabilities overlap. The microcomputer is usually defined as a computer with a single-chip central processor unit (CPU); the minicomputer covered the range from the simple-computer applications to those of the large computers before the days of the microcomputer.

Figure 1-2 shows the block diagram of a test set that detects opens in cords for a production-repair facility. The computer used to control the test set has a program of less than 500 words, and a temporary memory of 256 words. Yet it controls several analog switches and provides several LED indications of the cord's status. This is the first of many computers that the author built. It is a small computer, and could today be replaced by a single-chip computer, cutting the required number of circuit boards from two to one.

HOW TO USE THIS BOOK

That's what this book is all about — building, testing, and programming a simple microcomputer. This microcomputer is a small device, with 1k of temporary RAM and up to 3k of permanent memory. But you can expand it up to 8k of memory. Hardware read and load, and single step circuitry assist in troubleshooting and bringing the system up. Keyboard read load, and a 7-segment display allow the operator to talk with the computer. An EPROM programmer is included to allow the operator to commit programs to permanent memory.

The individual computer sections are explained in an effort to acquaint the reader with the hardware which makes up the system. To efficiently utilize a microcomputer, both

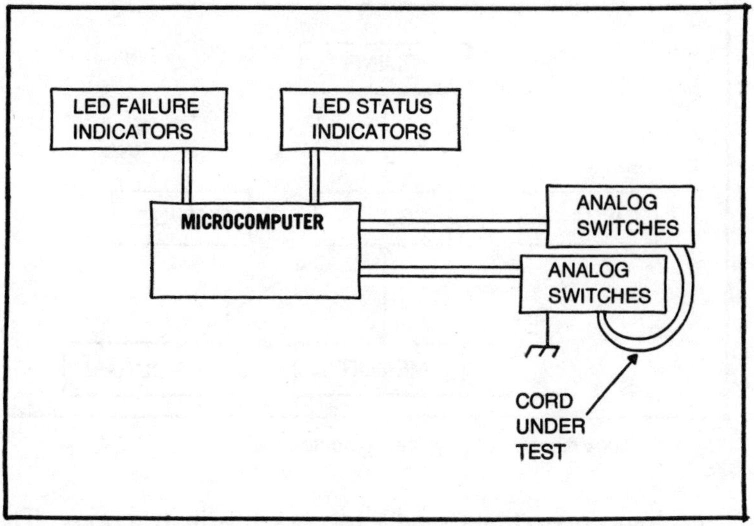

Fig. 1-2. Block diagram for a microcomputer-controlled test set that tests four-conductor cords.

its hardware operation and programming must be known and understood. The instruction set is present along with the steps required to write programs. Then come some actual programs for the reader to run in the computer. By that time the reader will have acquired enough knowledge and experience to write programs and program the computer. This step-by-step process allows exploiting the computer's capability as desired. The applications for microcomputers are limited only by the ingenuity of the reader.

COMPUTER BUILDING BLOCKS

Figure 1-3 illustrates a typical computer's simplified block diagram. All computers comprise these basic blocks; the size of the computer is determined by how much is in the basic blocks. Large computers have a larger CCU, larger memory, and more and different input and output devices. The basic blocks include:

Central control unit. The central control unit (CCU), sometimes called the central processor unit (CPU), forms the central part of the computer. It is the brains of the system; it decodes the instructions, performs the arithmetic

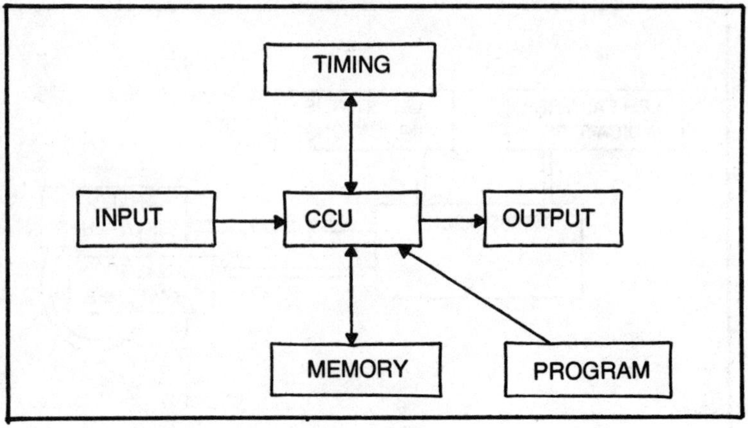

Fig. 1-3. Block diagram of a typical computer.

and logic operations, and executes the instructions. The program counter in the CCU keeps track of the address of the next instruction to be executed.

Memory. The memory stores programs, data, and program variables. The memory used by microcomputers is usually a semiconductor memory, and comprises both permanent and temporary memory. Random-access memories (RAM) furnish temporary storage. The computer writes into them and reads from them but the information is lost when the computer is powered down, whether intentionally or accidentally.

Erasable Programmable Read-Only Memories (EPROM's). These are permanent semiconductor memories. They can be erased with an ultraviolet lamp, and programmed using a programming circuit (PROM programmer). Their contents can't be altered under program control during normal computer operation, and are not lost when the computer is powered down.

Some computers, microcomputers included, use some type of mass storage to store data, programs, and information. This mass storage device may be a cassette recorder, special tape units, or disk units. These store large amounts of data, and many programs, which can be read into the computer one section at a time.

Input/output. The input and output devices allow communication between the computer and the outside world. For a general-purpose computer, the input may be a keyboard, terminal, or tape unit. The output may be a printer, display, or graphics plotter. For specialized machines, the input may be a position code, flow meter, cash register keys, or another computer. The output device may be a stepping motor, gas pump display, printer, or other control device (Figs. 1-4 and 1-5).

Timing. Ensuring that the total computer operates with everything in step requires timing circuitry. This timing circuitry provides the timing and control signals required for the computer to operate and execute instructions.

Program. The program (software) is just as important as the computer's hardware. The program comprises a series of instructions which the computer hardware executes to accomplish a desired task. Programs come in all shapes and sizes, and each programmer programs in a slightly different manner.

For a program to operate the hardware, the CPU reads the program one instruction at a time. Each instruction consists of a unique set of ONEs and ZEROs, which, when read into the computer at the proper time, decode as the commands that enable specific logic circuits within the mi-

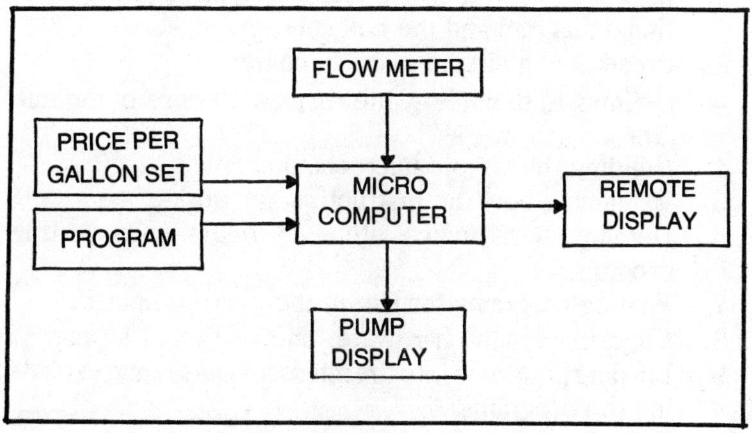

Fig. 1-4. Block diagram of a microcomputer-controlled gasoline pump.

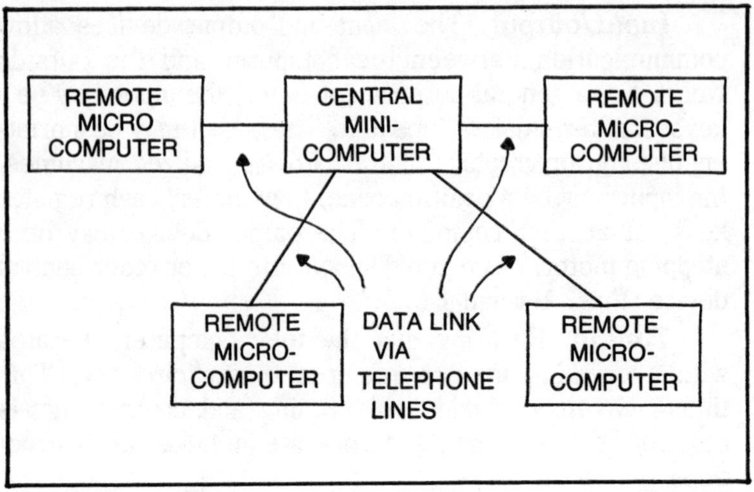

Fig. 1-5. Block diagram of a computerized test network using a centralized minicomputer connected to microcomputer-controlled test sets via a data link.

croprocessor to execute the instruction. In another time frame the same set of ONEs and ZEROs might be decoded as data.

As previously alluded to, the objective of this book is to introduce the reader to a microcomputer, to present and discuss the hardware, build a microcomputer, learn the instruction set, and program the computer. This is done in the following steps:

1. Introduction to the microcomputer through the functional diagram and the bus concept.
2. Presenting a simple microcomputer.
3. Defining in detail how the various sections of the microcomputer works.
4. Building the simple microcomputer.
5. Explaining how the instruction set works.
6. Defining some logical steps to follow when writing programs.
7. Writing programs for use in the microcomputer.
8. Checking out the hardware, one section at a time.
9. Loading programs into the microcomputer, and executing the programs.
10. Expanding the capabilities of the microcomputer.

The computer presented in this book is only the starting point for a larger, expanded microcomputer with many capabilities.

It is advised that the reader read the book completely before starting to build the system. Study the chapters describing the system and learn how the various components work. Also study the chapters on instructions and programming. Make sure that you understand what you are getting into, because it is no simple task to build and program the computer. Several hours will be spent wiring the system, and a few more getting it running. But the accomplishment is worth the effort, for it a rewarding effort to see the computer running, and knowing you did it. And you can be the computer's master—make it do what you want to.

You don't need to be an electronics expert to build the computer. An exposure to electronics, along with the desire to learn microcomputers, are the prerequisites.

Chapter 2
Microcomputer Basics

A microcomputer is a complex system, with most of the complexity incorporated into its individual chips. A functional diagram serves to simplify the drawing and understanding of this complex system. This diagram is a shorthand method of presenting complex functions with a series of blocks and lines. The first part of this chapter deals with the functional diagram; the second part deals with 8080 microprocessor itself and how it operates. Several new terms arise throughout this book, and these terms are defined in the appendix.

THE FUNCTIONAL DIAGRAM

The functional diagram is a shorthand method of presenting a complex system with a series of blocks and lines. It is a type of block diagram, but is based on functions and functional definitions. Typically each chip comprises one functional block; the function of the input and output lines are shown.

Thus, the functional diagram gives the functions of the interconnecting lines, and possibly the block's overall function. The detailed chip descriptions gives additional information used to determine how the signals interact. Appendix B provides the chip descriptions for processors used in this book.

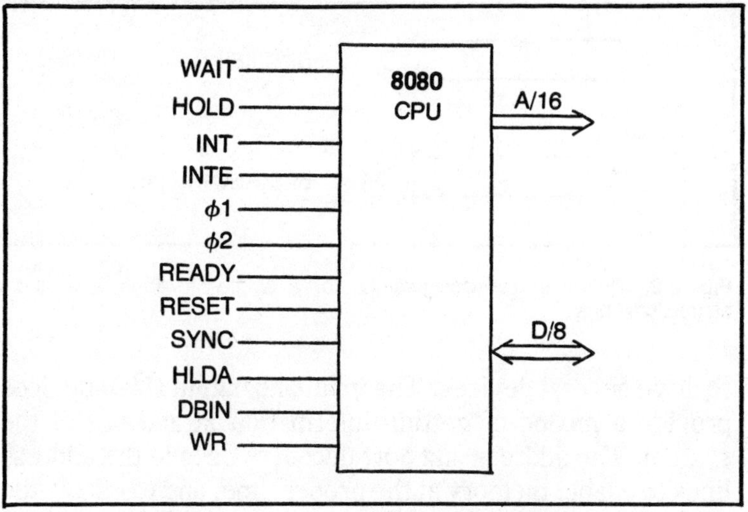

Fig. 2-1. A functional diagram for the 8080 microprocessor.

Figure 2-1 shows a functional diagram for the 8080 microprocessor. Notice that it is simple and straightforward. Compare this to the block diagram of the 8080 given later in this chapter and notice the considerable difference. Project this complexity upward to include even six large chips, and the schematic becomes a nightmare. The functional concept's desirability readily apparent.

The standard blocks that make up a system are:

- Microprocessor
- Clock generator
- System controller
- Memory
- Bus drivers
- Input and output devices
- Address and port decoders.

These parts make up every computer. The microprocessor is the central control unit, controlling the total system. It forms the computer's heart. The clock generator provides the timing required for the computer. The system controller generates the control signals required. Memory provides storage areas for the processor's instructions and data. The bus drivers drive the buses, giving them the ability

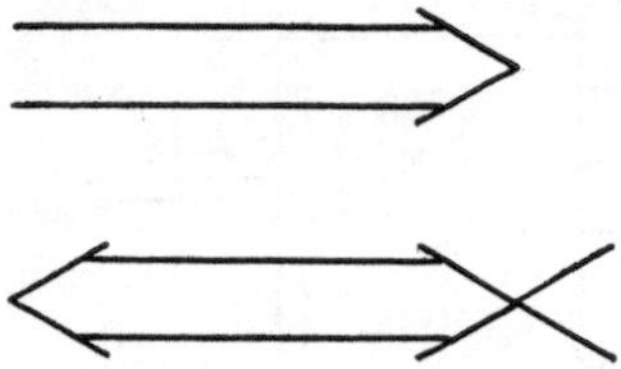

Fig. 2-2. Illustrating the designations for a single-directional bus and a bidirectional bus.

to drive several devices. The input and output (I/O) devices provide a means of getting information in and out of the system. The address and port decoders decode the address lines to enable memory at the proper time, and to enable the port when the port is called for.

Some system chips perform more than one function and for small simple systems, some functions might not be needed. A small system that doesn't have many devices connected to its address bus, for example, might not need address-bus drivers—the microprocessor has all the drive capability necessary. Some of the microprocessor families incorporate more than one function into each chips, so fewer chips may be required.

MICRO BUS STRUCTURES

Microprocessor systems (microcomputers) use the concept of buses quite extensively. A bus is a series of lines with similar functions—such as address—that transfers information around the system. The bus may contain many lines or a few; it can be single directional (undirectional) or bidirectional. Figure 2-2 shows these buses and their representation. Also shown is the breaking out of one of the bus lines.

Single-direction buses, such as the address bus and the control bus, have only one source, and can have many destinations. A bidirectional bus, such as the data bus, can have more than one source and several destinations. Only one source must enabled at a time, however. If several devices

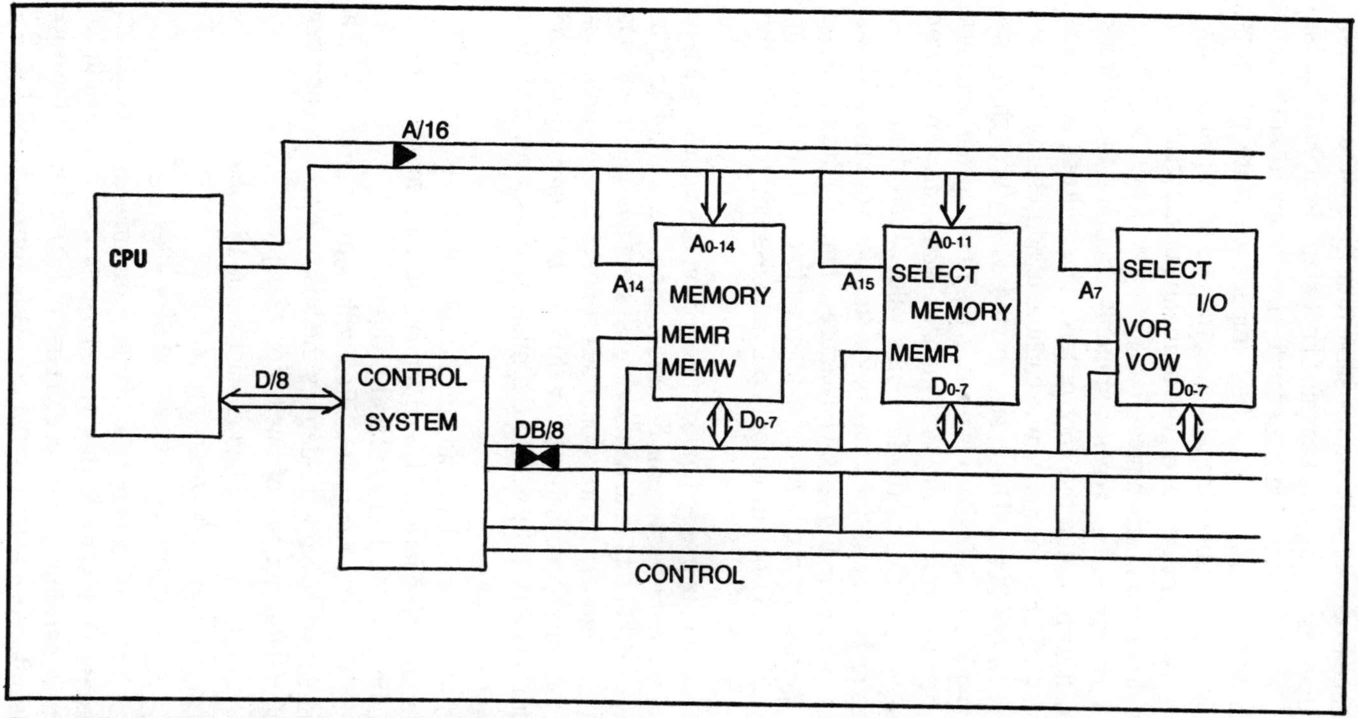

Fig. 2-3. Functional diagram of a typical microcomputer.

manage to drive the bus at the same time the system will fail. All devices driving any bus must be 3-state devices. That is, they must have a high-impedance state in addition to their high and low state. This high-impedence state prevents devices not enabled from loading the bus and causing problems. Also, any device driven from the bus must have a very low drive requirements.

The three bus types commonly used are the address bus, data bus, and the control bus. The address bus comprises 16 lines for a machine capable of addressing 16 lines such as the 8080. These are notated as A_0 through A_{15} as shown in Fig. 2-1. Zero is used as the first address and data bit because zero is the first number—2 to the zero power equals 1 and this is the first bit's value. Individual address lines or groups of lines may be broken out from the address bus as shown in Fig. 2-3. Only address lines A_0 through A_8 go to the memory; a high-order address line selects the memory. The I/O port uses only one address line to define the port number.

The data bus is a bidirectional 8-bit bus which transfers data around the system. For the system shown in Fig. 2-3, the external bus is driven by the system controller and bus driver. Another bidirectional bus connects the external bus to the microprocessor. Over this bus the instructions read from memory returned to the microprocessor for decoding and execution.

The control bus contains the control signals required to operate the system. These signals include memory read, memory write, I/O read and I/O write.

When the bus is identified with both a character and a number, the character defines the bus type and the number defines the number of lines. For example:

A/16—Address bus consisting of 16 lines

D_8—Data bus consisting of 8 lines

C_4—Control bus consisting of 4 lines

The bus concept is simple, and makes schematics cleaner. You can see this by comparing Fig. 2-4 (a detailed functional diagram that doesn't use buses) to Fig. 2-3. Notice the difference in the complexity of the drawings. Yet Fig. 2-3

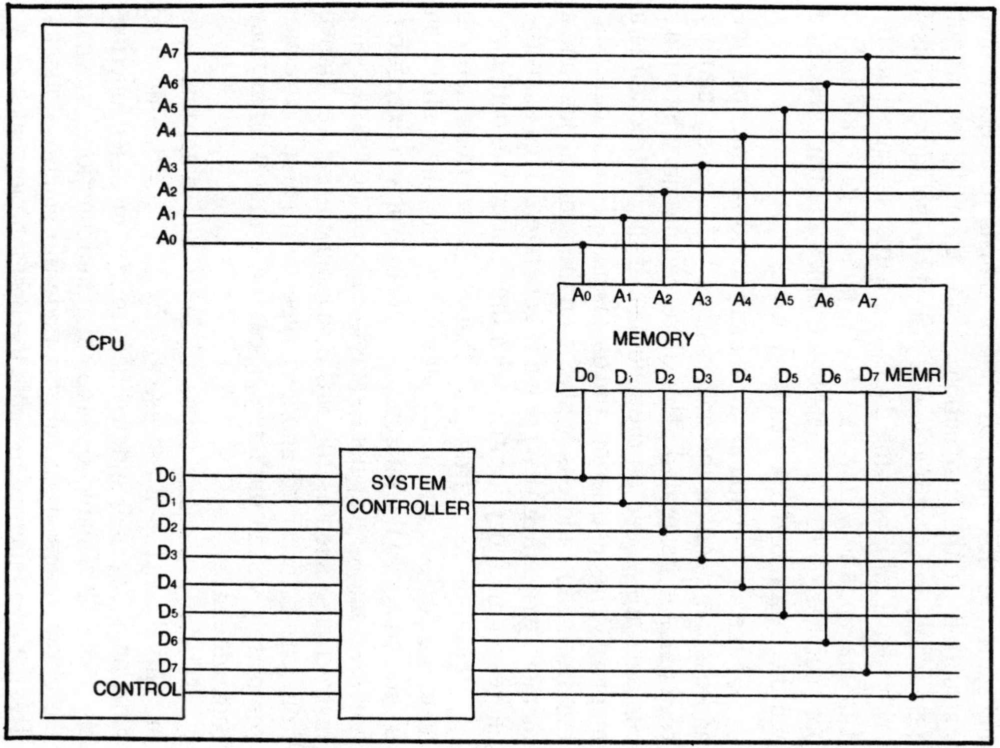

Fig. 2-4. A functional diagram that doesn't use the bus concept.

conveys more information and includes more circuitry than Fig. 2-4. Thus, it's apparent that bus concept is a requirement when dealing with complex systems.

The system shown in Fig. 2-3 illustrates how the system and its buses work together. At the start of an instruction cycle, the CPU places program instruction address on the address bus and generates a memory read (MEMR) pulse. This reads the specified memory location and places the contents of that location on the data bus. This information is read by the microprocessor and decoded to set up the logic and generate the required control signals to execute that instruction. If the instruction is, for example, an output instruction, the port number is placed on the address bus's low-order 8 bits, bus, the data to be output is placed on the data bus, and the I/O write (I/O W) pulse is generated. The port number on the address bus enables the port specified and the data transferred to the port.

If the instruction is a memory read instruction, the address is placed on the address bus and another memory read pulse is generated. The addressed memory location's contents are placed on the data bus. If the instruction is a memory write instruction, the data is placed on the data bus, the destination address is placed on the address bus, and a memory write (MEM W) pulse is generated. This loads the addressed memory location with the data on the data bus.

It can be seen from this that all instructions use the address, control, and data buses to transfer the instruction from memory to the microprocessor. Instruction execution, however, may or may not require the use of the buses. Some instructions, such as the MOV register-to-register (move from one register to another) type instructions, execute completely within the microprocessor, eliminating any bus requirement.

There are many types of functional diagrams: the simplified functional represented by Fig. 2-3; the detailed functional (Fig. 2-4) and two more termed modified functionals. Figure 2-5 shows one type modified functional in which the pin numbers are notated outside the functional blocks. The upper number represents the first function, such as A_0

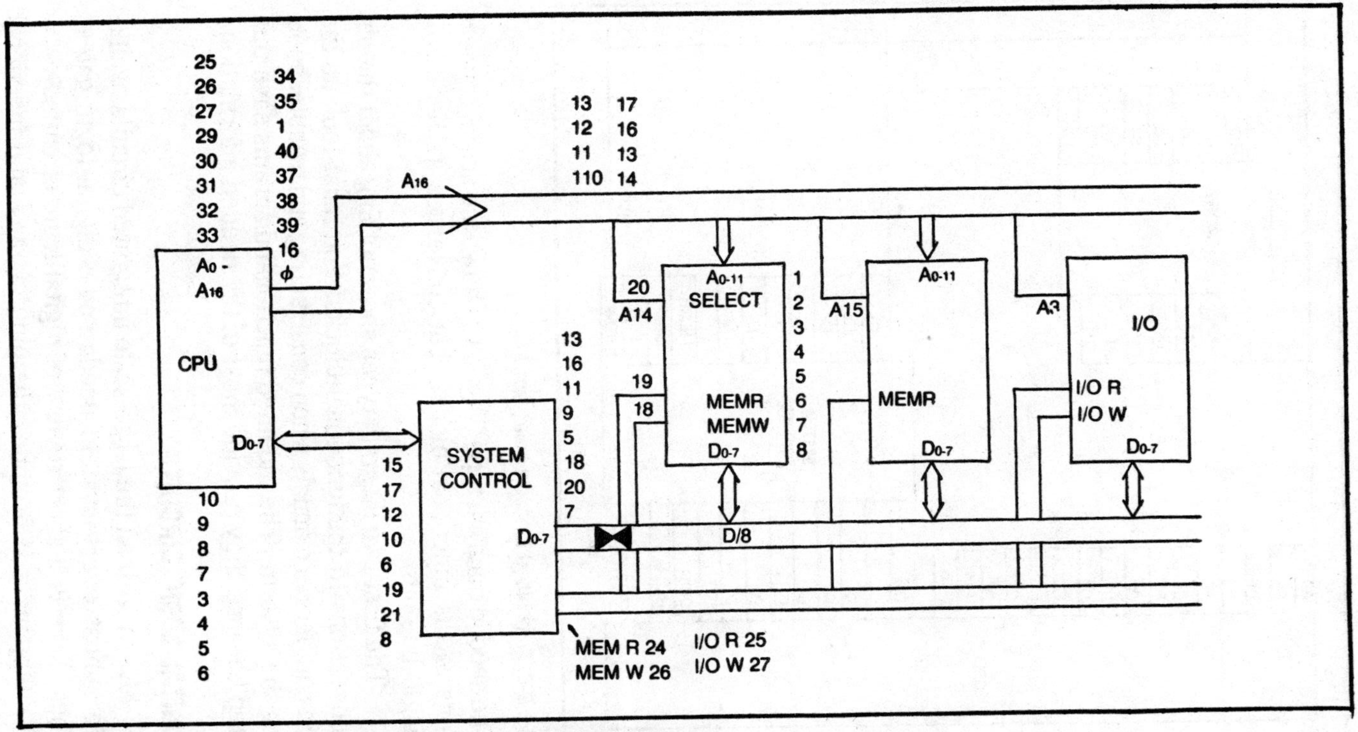

Fig. 2-5. One method of showing pin numbers on a functional diagram.

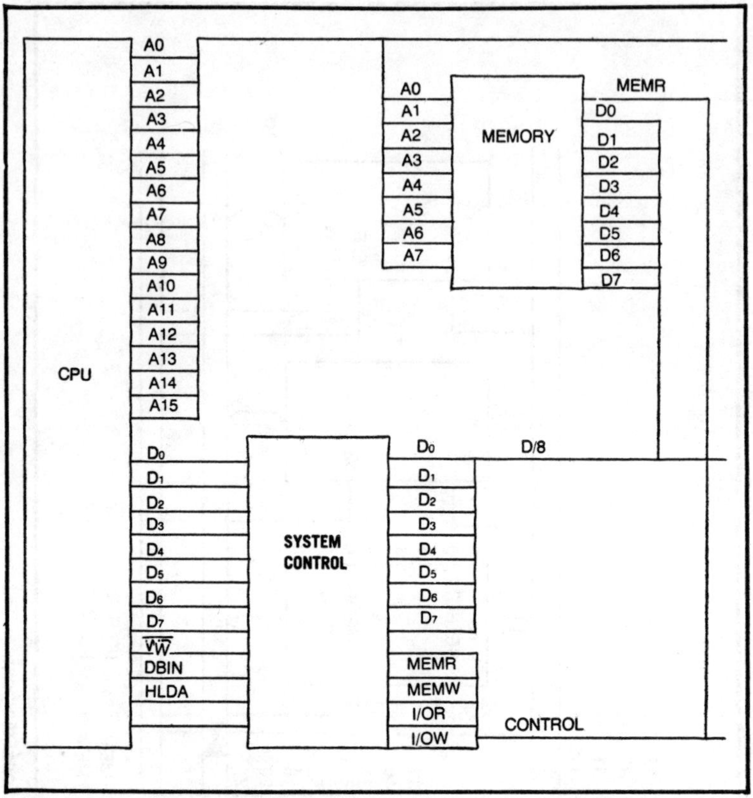

Fig. 2-6. A modified functional diagram.

The second diagram type (Fig. 2-6) shows the actual connections to the functional blocks, but converges its lines into single-line buses.

The first two diagram types show nothing about the pin connections to the functional blocks. You must look up the pin numbers in manuals when constructing and troubleshooting the system. The modified functional diagrams save this step because they provide most of the needed information.

DIGITAL-LOGIC CIRCUITS

Even with all the large-scale integrated circuits available almost every system needs some digital-logic gates. Thus, here is a short review of digital-logic circuits.

Appendix B provides the pin diagrams and functional

descriptions of the chips used in the microcomputer. Here we will delve into what the various circuits do,and some of the logical functions available. Figure 2-7 shows the standard logic diagrams for some of the common logic circuits.

The buffer, or driver, increases the drive current that the circuit can supply. The output has the same polarity as the input— that is, a HIGH input results in a HIGH output. The gates buffer has an enable input which, when disabled, places the output in its high impedance mode. Otherwise this circuit operates in a similar manner to the buffer. The inverter inverts the input signal—a HIGH input results in a LOW output. Diagrams portray the inverter with a small circle attached to the output of a standard buffer. This circle designates an active LOW output for a HIGH input.

The AND gate has a HIGH output when all its inputs are HIGH. That is, for a 2 input AND, when input A and input B are both HIGH, the output goes HIGH. When either input is LOW, the output is LOW. You can consider the NAND gate as and AND gate with an inverter connected to its output. Its output will be LOW when all its inputs are HIGH. If any input is LOW, the output will be HIGH. The OR gate has a HIGH output when one or more of its inputs are HIGH. The only condition that will produce a LOW output is all inputs LOW. The NOR gate acts as an OR gate with its output inverted— any HIGH input produces a LOW ouput.

The latch circuit comprises two NAND gates tied in parallel. When power is first applied, the latch assumes some state, unless it is forced into a reset state. The latch remembers the last LOW input until it receives another LOW on the other input. For example, if input 1 is initially LOW and input 2 is HIGH, output A will be HIGH because any LOW into a NAND gate will cause a high output. As long as input 2 is HIGH output B will be LOW. This low feeds to the upper NAND gate to latch it when input 1 goes HIGH. So as long as both inputs remain HIGH, the latch will stay in this condition. Applying a LOW to input 2 causes output B to go HIGH, changing the state of the latch by forcing output A LOW. It will remain in this condition as long as both inputs are HIGH.

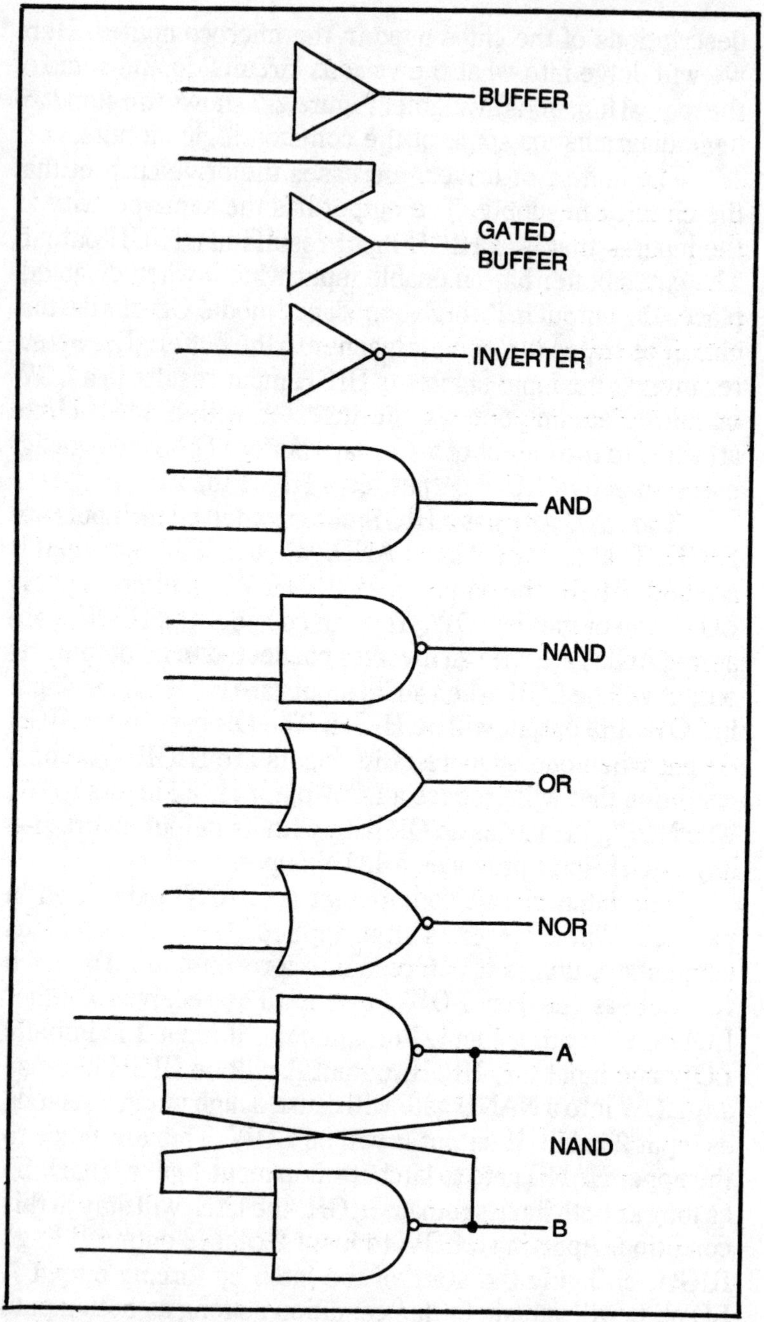

Fig. 2-7. Some basic digital-logic gates.

Some signals convey information in their HIGH state, while others convey information in their LOW state. Those which use the high state are called active-HIGH signals. They are the normal signals whose static condition is LOW, with their pulse going HIGH. Those signals which use the LOW state are called active-LOW signals, and are normally HIGH. An example of an active-HIGH signal is the reset pulse, which resets the system by pulsing the line HIGH. An example of a typical active-LOW pulse is the memory read pulse, which commands a memory read when the pulse goes LOW.

Figure 2-8 illustrates the difference between active-HIGH and active-LOW signals. The term simply refers to whether a HIGH or a LOW state commands the action. Active-LOW signals are overlined to indicate that they go negative. For example $\overline{\text{MEM R}}$ is the active-LOW memory read pulse.

The logic function of a gate changes for active-LOW states, because the standard definition is given for active-HIGH logic. For active-LOW logic an OR gate has a LOW output when all the inputs are LOW; the OR gate becomes and AND gate for active-LOW signals. The same reasoning applies to all other logic gates.

The computer transmits information in a series of pulses. These can be active LOW, active HIGH, or a com-

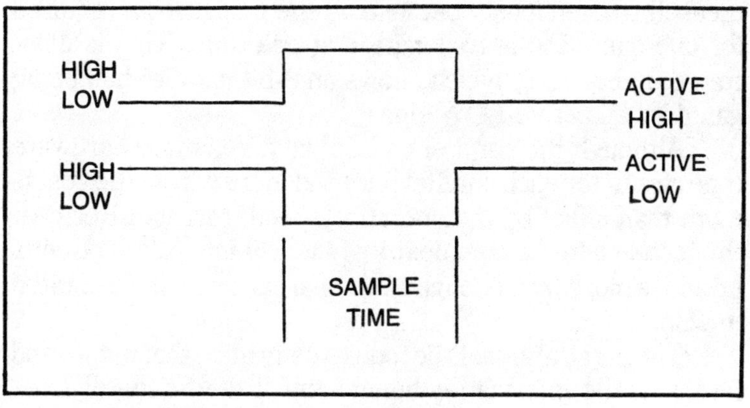

Fig. 2-8. Active-HIGH and active-LOW signals.

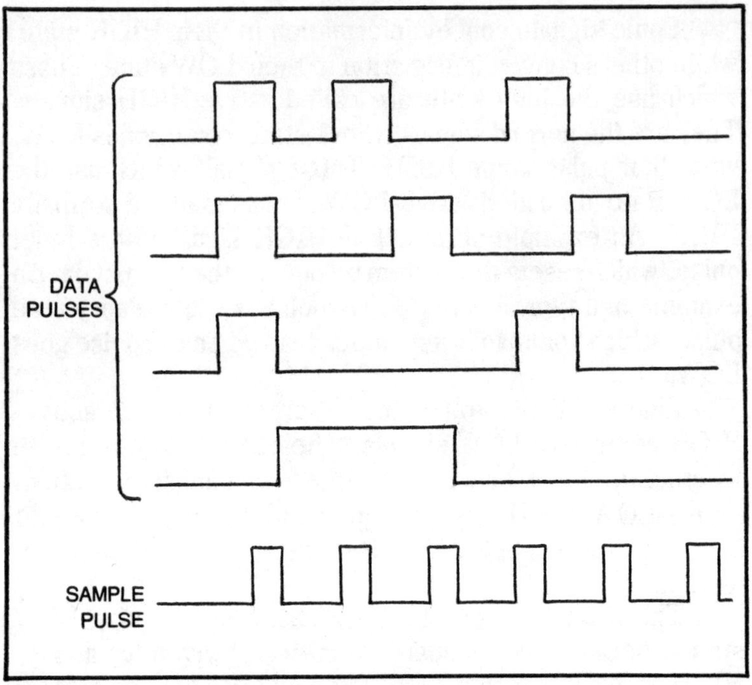

Fig. 2-9. A parallel-pulse train with a sample pulse identifiying data-valid sample time.

bination of both. The early computers were serial devices—information was transmitted one bit at a time. Although this minimized the hardware and wiring needed it was slow. With the advent of parallel computers, computation speed increased tremendously because all the information required for one operation is transmitted at one time. This is illustrated by Fig. 2-9, which shows an 8-bit parallel bus being gated by an active-LOW signal.

Although the parallel concept requires more hardware (one circuit for each parallel line) and more wires, the cost is more than offset by the operating speed increase. Besides, the increase in the complexity of the LSI integrated circuits provides more than enough additional hardware incorporated in chip.

The parallel signals decode to determine that nature and format of the information being sent. If the timing dictates that the signal is an instruction signal, for example, the computer decodes the instruction to determine which logic circuits must be enabled in order to execute that instruction. If the signal is an address, the signals are gated to the address bus by a previously decoded instruction.

NUMBERING SYSTEMS

Logic circuits and signals have only two states: HIGH and LOW. The binary number system, also called the base-2 system, uses only 2 numbers—1 and 0. A number is defined as each digit times the base of the number to the power of the place. For example, in the decimal numbering system (base 10) the number 53926 is actually:

$$\begin{aligned} 53926 &= (5\times10^4)+(3\times10^3)+(9\times10^2) \\ &+ (2\times10^1)+(6\times10^0) \\ &= 50000+3000+900+20+6 \\ &= 53926 \end{aligned}$$

Remember that any number to the first power is that number, and any number to the zero power is one. Thus $10^1=10$ and $10^0=1$.

The same procedure works for binary numbers except that the base is two instead of 10. To convert a number from

BINARY	PLACE VALUE	DECIMAL EQUIVALENT	BIT POSITION
1	2^0	1	0
10	2^1	2	1
100	2^2	4	2
1000	2^3	8	3
10000	2^4	16	4
100000	2^5	32	5
1000000	2^6	64	6
10000000	2^7	128	7
100000000	2^8	256	8
1000000000	2^9	512	9
10000000000	2^{10}	1024	10

Fig. 2-10. The binary numbering system.

binary to decimal, set up the equation in binary, and carry out the multiplication in decimal. For example:

$$\begin{aligned} 110111 &= (1\times 2^5)+(1\times 2^4)+(0\times 2^3) \\ &\quad + (1\times 2^2)+(1\times 2^1)+(1\times 2^0) \\ &= (1\times 32)+(1\times 16) + (0\times 8) + (1\times 4) \\ &\quad + (1\times 2) + (1\times 1) \\ &= 32+16+0+4+2+1 \\ &= 55 \end{aligned}$$

From the above example, it is apparent that to convert from binary to decimal you must determine the decimal equivalent for each bit position containing a 1. For example, to convert 1011011:

Bit position	Decimal equivalent
0	1
1	2
3	8
4	16
6	64
	91

From Fig. 2-10, notice that the decimal equivalent of each bit position doubles for the next higher bit position. This is because the binary number system is to the base 2.

Binary addition is carried out in the same manner as decimal addition, except that there are only two numbers allowable, zero and one. The following are the basic rules for binary addition.

0 + 0 = 0
0 + 1 = 1
1 + 0 = 1
1 + 1 = 0 carry 1
0 + 0 + carry 1 = 1
0 + 1 + carry 1 = 0 carry 1
1 + 0 carry 1 = 0 carry 1
1 + 1 + carry 1 = 1 carry 1

To add two binary numbers, add the individual bits one digit at a time starting from the least significant bit. Carry forward any carry bits generated. The rules for binary subtraction are:

0 – 0 = 0
1 – 0 = 1
0 – 1 = 1 borrow 1
1 – 1 = 0
0 – 0 borrow 1 = 1 borrow 1
1 – 0 borrow 1 = 0
0 – 1 borrow 1 = 0 borrow 1
1 – 1 borrow 1 = 1 borrow 1

To subtract two binary numbers, subtract the bits one digit at a time starting from the least significant bit. Carry forward any borrow bits generated.

Logical operations (AND and OR operations) can be performed on binary numbers because they have only two states. The rules for the basic logic operations are:

0 AND 0 = 0
0 AND 1 = 0
1 AND 0 = 0
1 AND 1 = 1
0 OR 0 = 0
1 OR 0 = 1
0 OR 1 = 1
1 OR 1 = 1

When using the NAND and NOR operations, invert the results of each operation.

Binary numbers can grow quite unwieldy. Most microprocessors have an 8-bit data bus that represents each word with 8 binary bits. For the address bus, 16 binary bits are usually required. These numbers can grow quite large making them difficult to handle and comprehend. The hexadecimal numbering system is used as a form of shorthand. This number system uses the base 16: each digit can be 16 different numbers. Since there are only 10 standard numbers, 0 through 9, the remaining numbers are represented by the alphabetic characters A through F.

The hexadecimal characters are created from binary numbers by taking 4 binary bits at a time and determining their hexadecimal equivalent. For example, to convert 110101110001 1001 to hex:

Binary	Hexadecimal
0000	0
0001	1
0010	2
0011	3
0100	4
0101	5
0110	6
0111	7
1000	8
1001	9
1010	A
1011	B
1100	C
1101	D
1110	E
1111	F

Fig. 2-11. Binary-to-hexadecimal conversion.

$$\begin{aligned} 1101011100011001 &= 1101\ 0111\ 0001\ 1001 \\ &= \text{D} \quad\ 7 \quad\ 1 \quad\ 9 \\ &= \text{D719} \end{aligned}$$

Figure 2-11 provides a binary-to-hex conversion table, and the hex numbering system. When converting numbers always remember to start with the least significant bit and work toward the most significant bit.

Hexadecimal numbers are used extensively in microcomputer literature. All machine-language programs and instruction codes are shown in hexadecimal. Sometimes hex notations are labeled with the subscript 16, or with the word hex following the number. When handling hexadecimal numbers realize that there are 16 numbers for each digit, and when adding and subtracting them the extra numbers must be taken into account. For example, 8 + 7 = F in the hex number system.

To convert from hexadecimal to decimal, take the decimal equivalent of each digit, times 16 to the power of the bit position. For example:

$$B709_{16} = 11 \times 16^3 + 7 \times 16^2 + 9 \times 16^0$$
$$= 45056 + 1792 + 9 = 46857$$

Figure 2-12 shows the hex-to-decimal conversion for one hex digit and for several of the powers of 16.

THE 8080 MICROPROCESSOR ARCHITECTURE

The term "architecture" refers to the microprocessor's organization and how the internal blocks work together. Since the microprocessor is the central control unit, or the brains, of the computer, it is very complex internally. Control signals regulate all the operations within the computer, including addressing, instruction decoding, and control-signal generation.

Hexadecimal Number	Decimal Number	Power of 16	Multiplier
0	0	0	1
1	1	1	16
2	2	2	256
3	3	3	4096
4	4	4	65536
5	5	5	1048576
6	6	6	16777216
7	7		
8	8		
9	9		
A	19		
B	11		
C	12		
D	13		
E	14		
F	15		

Fig. 2-12. Hexadecimal-to-decimal conversion.

Figure 2-13 shows the block diagram for an 8080 microprocessor. The 8080 consists of the following basic functional units:

- Register array and address logic
- Arithmetic and logic unit
- Instruction decoder and control section
- Bus buffers

The arithmetic unit contains the ALU, the accumulator, status flags, and associated circuits. This section performs many of the arithmetic and logic instructions, with the results of its computations usually ending up in the accumulator. The status flags indicate the results of most of the instructions executed by this section. The accumulator is an 8 bit register where most of the results and information from the execution of the instructions is routed to. This accumulator is the main entry and exit point for data.

The register array contains used by the instructions and those used by the hardware. The W and Z registers are available only to the hardware, and are not addressable. The program counter contains the address of the next instruction. When the system is turned on or reset, this counter is set to 0000. To read an instruction, this counter is placed on the address bus, then incremented the proper number of times to set up for the next instruction. Program-transfer instructions change the contents of this register.

The stack pointer is loaded initially by the program, then it is decremented and incremented as required by the hardware. The stack pointer contains the current stack address. When information is loaded onto the stack, this pointer is decremented by two. The stack is an area in memory reserved for use as the stack, and is used as one 16-bit register.

The six general-purpose registers (B, C, D, E, H, and L) are for use by the program, and may be used as single 8-bit registers or 16-bit register pairs. When using these registers you must be careful not to destroy a register's contents. One of the major uses of the H and L register pair is to provide memory address for several of the instructions which affect memory.

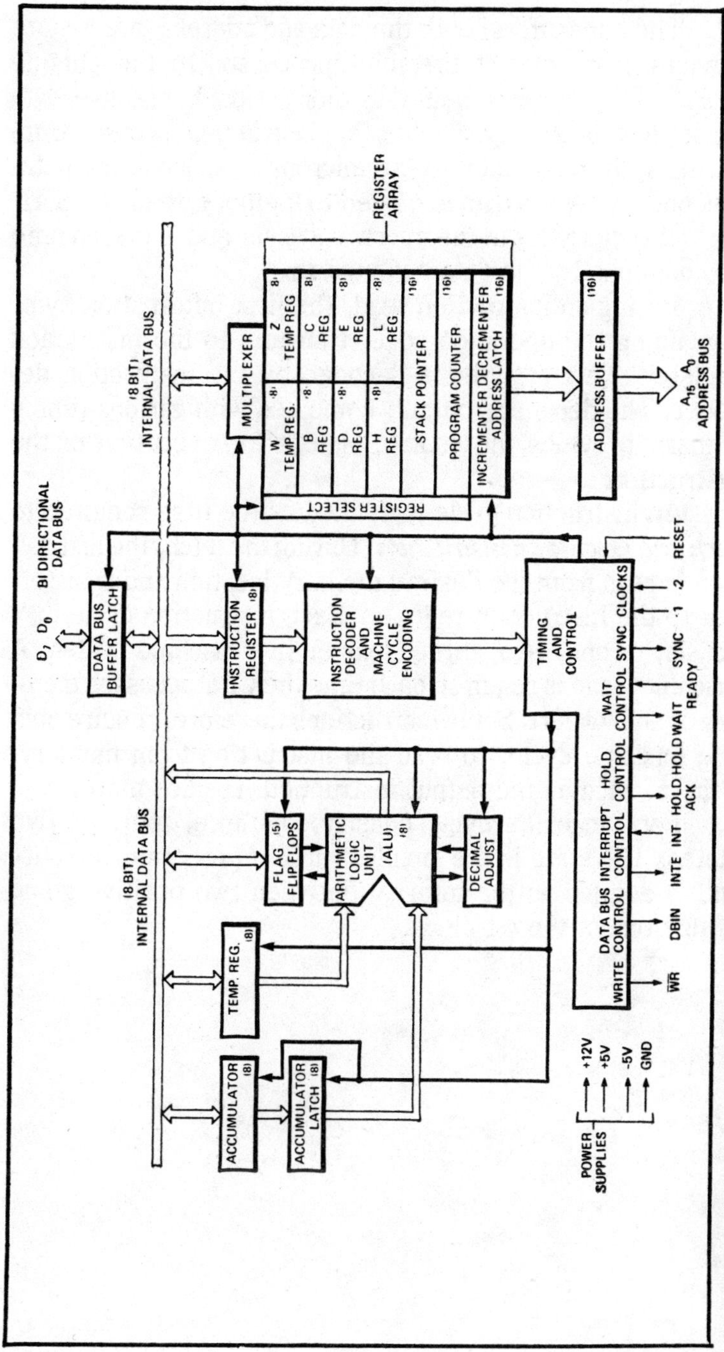

Fig. 2-13. Block diagram for the 8080 microprocessor.

The bus buffers, both the data and address, are 3-state devices that connect the microprocessor to the outside world. The data-bus buffer is bidirectional, because data must flow both ways. When an instruction is read from memory, it is routed into the microprocessor via the data-bus buffers. When data is moved to memory or an I/O port, the data originates in the microprocessor and is loaded onto the data bus by the data-bus buffers.

During an instruction read, the first information byte, containing the operation code, transfers to the instruction register. This register is decoded by the instruction decoder. The decoder's output, combined with various timing signals, provides the control signals for execution of the instruction.

An instruction cycle is defined as the time required to *fetch and execute an instruction*. During the fetch, the instruction is read from the desired memory location and transferred to the instruction register. Each instruction cycle may consist of one, two, three, four or five machine cycles. A machine cycle is required each time the CPU accesses memory or an I/O port. Some instructions therefore, require only one machine cycle, to read the instruction from memory. Others, such as the output instruction, require more.

Each machine cycle consists of three, four, or five states. The state is the smallest unit of processing activity and is defined as the interval between two positive-going transitions of the $\phi 1$ clock.

Chapter 3
The Basic Microcomputer

One of the objectives of this book is to take the reader through the construction and use of a simple microcomputer. Building and using this computer will provide an understanding of how a computer works. The computer serves both as a self-teaching aid and as a starting point for investigating the interesting world of microcomputers. It allows the user to write simple programs, program EPROMs, and even expand its capabilties—to the point where it is no longer recognizable as the simple starting computer.

The basic computer consists of the computer, control circuitry, switch inputs, LED indicators, an EPROM programmer, keyboard input, hex readout, control-switch inputs, and programmable-LED indicators. The switch inputs and the LED indicators allow the user to load the computer from the switches. The computer can be single-stepped through memory to aid in program debugging. The hardware-load capability allows the user to bring up the computer cold; it doesn't requiring a program generated by another computer. Once the initial control program is loaded, the system can be controlled using the keyboard and hex readout.

This chapter presents the basic computer, and describes the integrated circuits it uses. Then the hardware

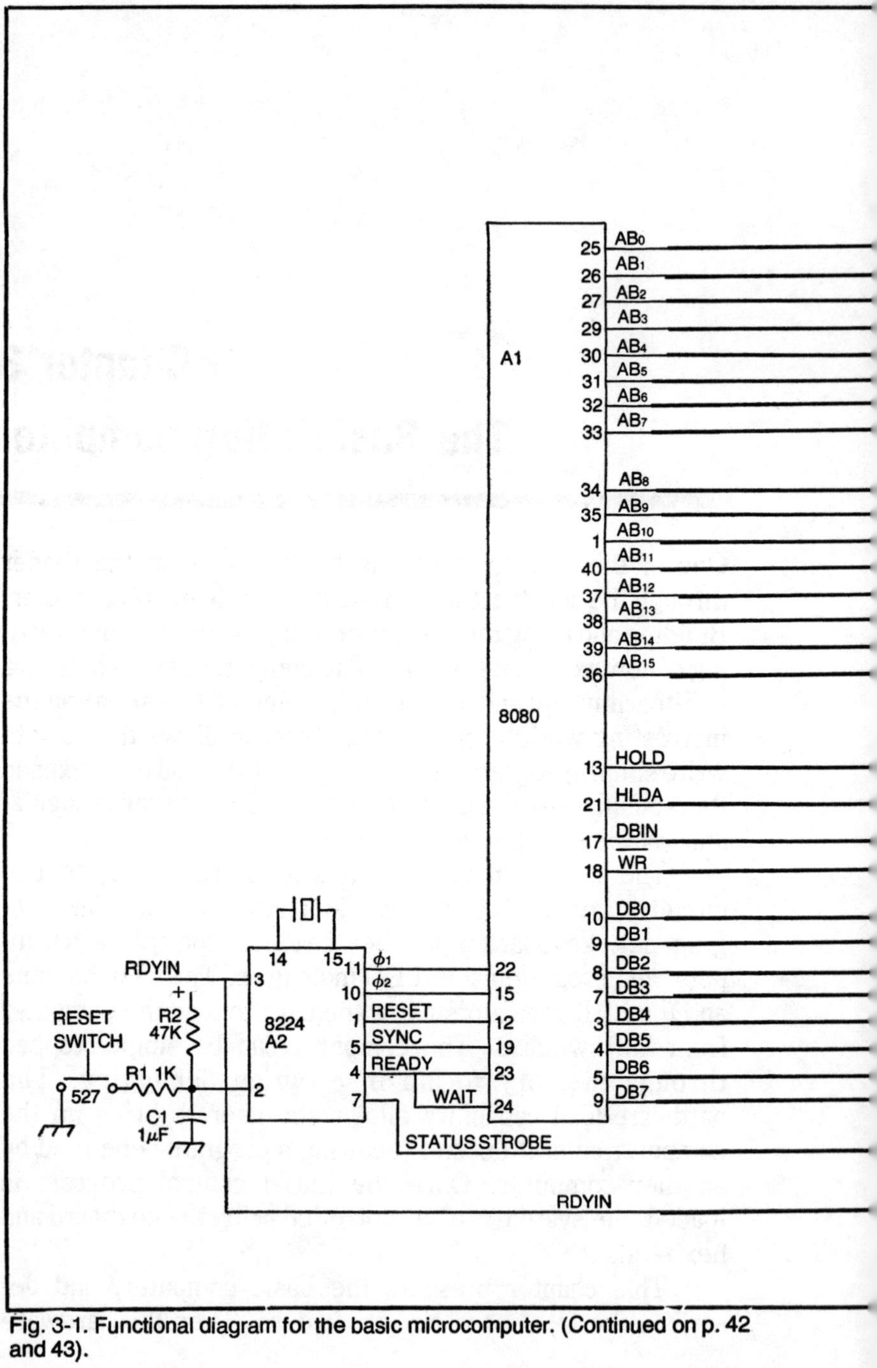

Fig. 3-1. Functional diagram for the basic microcomputer. (Continued on p. 42 and 43).

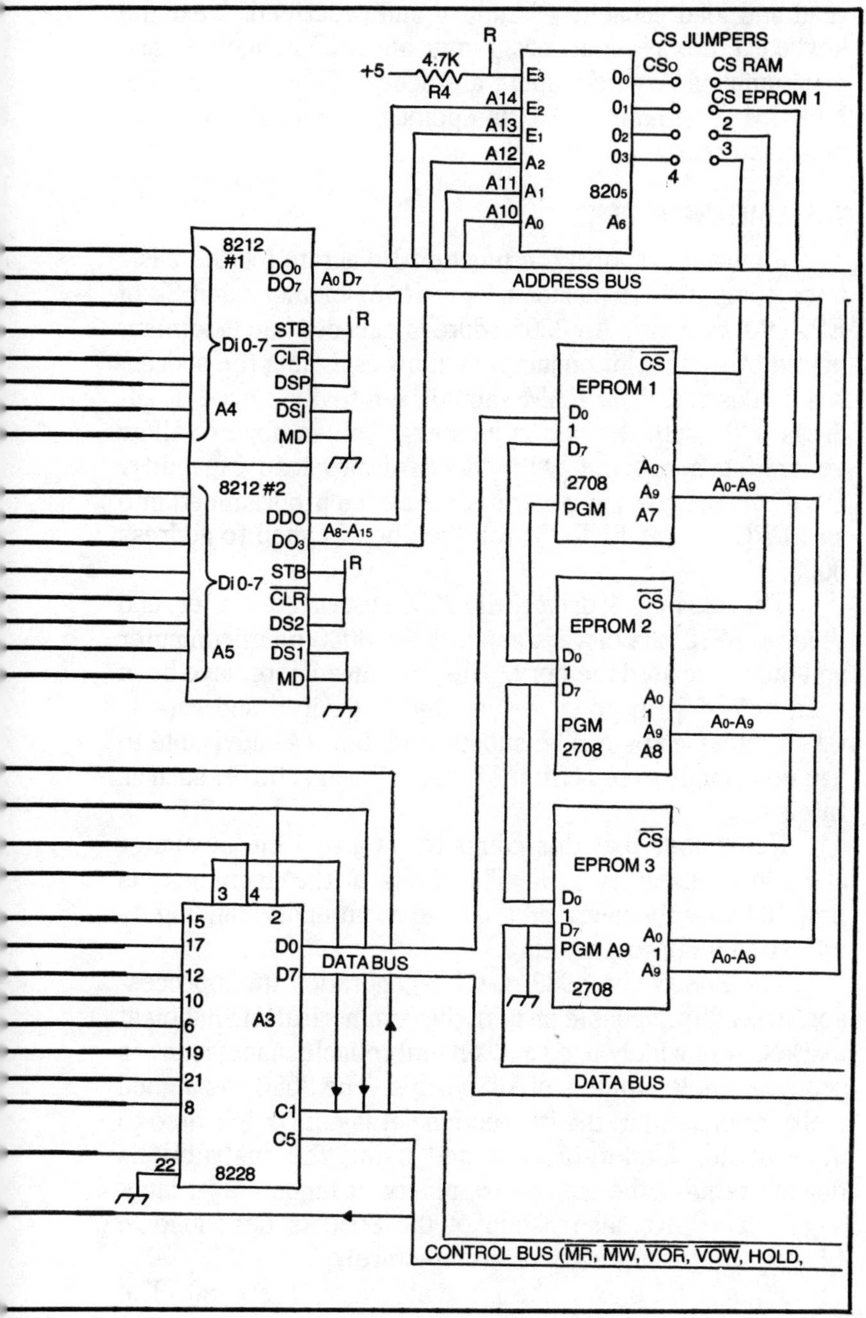

R
CS JUMPERS
+5
4.7K
R4
E3
CSo
CS RAM
A14
E2
CS EPROM 1
A13
E1
2
A12
A2
3
A11
A1
8205
A10
A0
A6
4
8212 #1
DO0
DO7
A0 D7
ADDRESS BUS
STB
CLR
DSP
DSI
MD
Di 0-7
A4
CS
EPROM 1
D0
D7
A0
2708
A9
PGM
A7
A0-A9
8212 #2
DDO
DO3
A8-A15
STB
CLR
DS2
DS1
MD
Di 0-7
A5
CS
EPROM 2
D0
D7
A0
A9
PGM
2708
A8
A0-A9
CS
EPROM 3
D0
D7
PGM A9
A0
A9
2708
A0-A9
3
4
2
15
17
12
10
6
19
21
8
22
D0
D7
DATA BUS
A3
C1
C5
8228
DATA BUS
CONTROL BUS (MR, MW, VOR, VOW, HOLD,

read and load capability is added and described. Next the keyboard, hex readout, programmable LED indicators, and programmable switch inputs are added. Finally comes the EPROM programmer. At this point the computer is complete and ready to use.

THE BUILDING BLOCKS

Figure 3-1 shows the functional diagram for the basic microcomputer. It includes 1k of RAM memory and 3k of EPROM memory. An 8205 address decoder handles memory addressing. Option jumpers allow assigning the addresses as desired. The RAM should be initially placed at address 0000 with the option jumpers. This is done to allow generating a program with the hardware load capability. Once this program is generated, it can be programmed into an EPROM; that EPROM can then be assigned to address 0000.

The 8224 clock driver, the 8228 system controller, and the two 8212 bus drivers support the 8080 microcomputer and the associated memory. The chips used here have been used before with good results, but if desired and care is taken, other chips can be substituted, but it is advisable to use good quality chips from a reliable manufacturer, such as Intel.

Remember that this computer is a real-life computer and can be used as such. The limits of the usefulness is limited by by the user and the time spent understanding its operation and programming.

The 8080: The 8080, a third-generation microprocessor, is readily available on both the commerical and hobbiest market. It is widely used and several reliable manufacturers produce whole families of 8080 chips. The 8080 has a good instruction set, but the instruction set is not complicated to understand. Understanding and using the instructions doesn't require the aid of assemblers or higher level languages. The internal makeup of the 8080 is described in Chapter 2 (microprocessor architecture).

Figure 3-2 shows the pin diagram for the 8080. The functional pin definition is given below:

IC #	TYPE	+5	+ 12	−5	GND	# PINS
1	8080	20	28	11	2	40
2	8224	16	9		8	16
3	8228	28			14	28
4-5	8212	24			12	24
6	8205	16			8	16
7-9	2708	24	19	21	12	24
10-17	2102	10			9	16

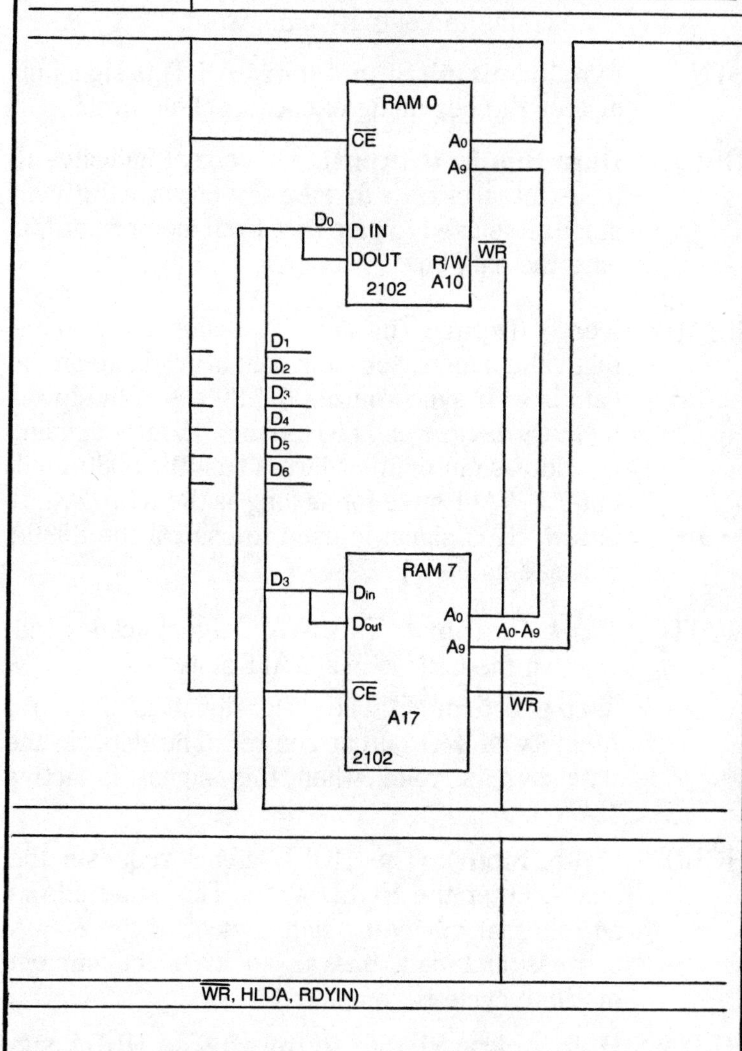

Fig. 3-1. Continued from page 42.

A_{15}-A_0 **Address Bus:** The address bus provides the address to memory, and the port number for I/O devices. It is 3-state, and A_0 is the least significant address bit.

D_7-D_0 **Data Bus:** The data bus provides bidirectional communication between the microprocessor and the external circuits and components. In addition, it transmits the output-status word.

SYNC **Synchronizing Signal (output):** This signal indicates the beginning of each machine cycle.

DBIN **Data Bus In (Output):** This signal indicates to the external circuits that the data bus is in the input mode. It is used to gate data from memory or I/O onto the data bus.

READY **Ready (Input):** This signal indicates to the 8080A that valid memory or input data is available on the data bus. It synchronizes the 8080A with slower memory devices and I/O circuits. If, after sending an address out on the address bus, the 8080A will enter a WAIT state for as long as the READY line is low. This signal is used to control the 8080A during single step.

WAIT **Wait (output):** The WAIT signal acknowledges that the CPU is in a WAIT state.

$\overline{WR}$ **Write (output):** The WR signal is used for memory or I/O output control. The data on the data bus is valid when this signal is active (LOW).

HOLD **Hold (input):** The HOLD signal requests the 8080A enter the HOLD state. This state allows an external device to gain control of the 8080A address and data bus as soon as the current machine cycle is completed.

HLDA **Hold Acknowledge (output):** The HLDA signal indicates that the HOLD input has been

Signal	Pin	Pin	Signal
A_{10}	1	40	A_{11}
GND	2	39	A_{14}
D_4	3	38	A_{13}
D_5	4	37	A_{12}
D_6	5	36	A_{15}
D_7	6	35	A_9
D_3	7	34	A_8
D_2	8	33	A_7
D_1	9	32	A_6
D_0	10	31	A_5
−5V	11	30	A_4
RESET	12	29	A_3
HOLD	13	28	+12V
INT	14	27	A_2
ϕ_2	15	26	A_1
INTE	16	25	A_0
DBIN	17	24	WAIT
$\overline{WR}$	18	23	READU
SYNC	19	22	ϕ_1
+5V	20	21	HLDA

Fig. 3-2. The 8080 pin configuration and definition.

acknowledged and that the data and address busses will go to the 3-state condition.

INTE **Interrupt Enable (output):** This signal indicates that the CPU is capable of accepting interrupts. They are enabled by the enable interrupt instruction, and disabled by the disable interrupt instruction or reset or by accepting an interrupt.

INT **Interrupt Request (input):** This signal requests that the 8080A look for interrupts, if so enabled.

RESET **Reset (input):** While the reset signal is active, the content of the program counter is cleared. After RESET, the program will start at address 0000. The INTE and HLDA are reset.

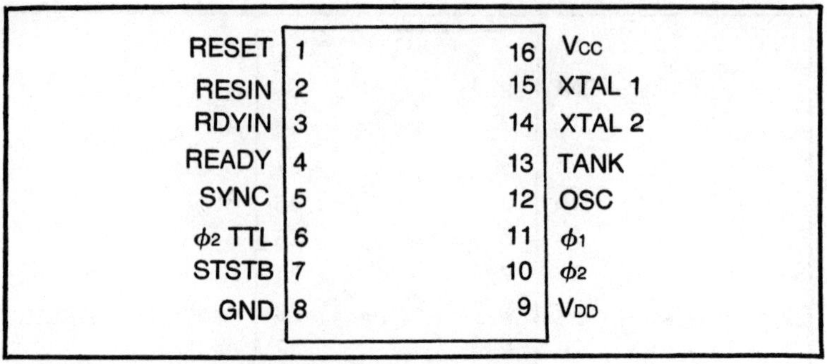

Fig. 3-3. The 8224 clock generator pin configuration.

V_{SS} Ground reference
V_{DD} +12 ± 5% Volts
V_{cc} +5 ± 5% Volts
V_{BB} −5 ± 5% Volts
ϕ_1,ϕ_2 Externally supplied clock pulses

The 8224: The 8224 is a single chip clock generator/driver for use with the 8080A microprocessor. It is crystal controlled, includes circuits to provide power-up reset, advance status strobe, and synchronization of the ready signal.

Figure 3-3 shows the pin connections for the 8224. The functional pin definition is as below:

$\overline{\text{RESIN}}$ **Reset input:** This input is connected to the reset switch as shown in Fig. 3-4. As shown, an external RC network is connected to this pin. This slows the transition of the power supply during power up. This slow transition is sensed by a schmitt trigger, which fires, setting the power on flip/flop, after the power supplies are up to voltage.

RESET **Reset output:** This is the system reset, derived from the power/on reset flip/flop. This pulse is generated at power on and when the reset switch is depressed and released.

RDYIN **Ready input:** The ready input to the 8080A has timing specifications, thus an external synchronizing flip/flop is required. This input is internally clocked to control the ready flip/flop.

READY **Ready output:** This is the ready signal which drives the ready input to the 8080A.

SYNC **Sync input:** This input, from the 8080A syncs the clock generator and the microprocessor.

ϕ_2(TTL) **Phase 2, TTL compatible:** This timing signal is brought out for external timing purposes.

$\overline{\text{STSTB}}$ **Status strobe:** This active LOW strobe occurs at the start of each machine cycle at the earliest possible moment that status data is stable on the data bus. This resets and strobes the control signal decoder part of the 8228 system controller.

ϕ_1,ϕ_2 **Phase 1 and Phase 2:** These are the system clocks used by the 8080A. Figure 3-5 shows the timing of these signals and their relationship to the crystal frequency.

XTAL 1 **Crystal connections:** The oscillator circuit de-

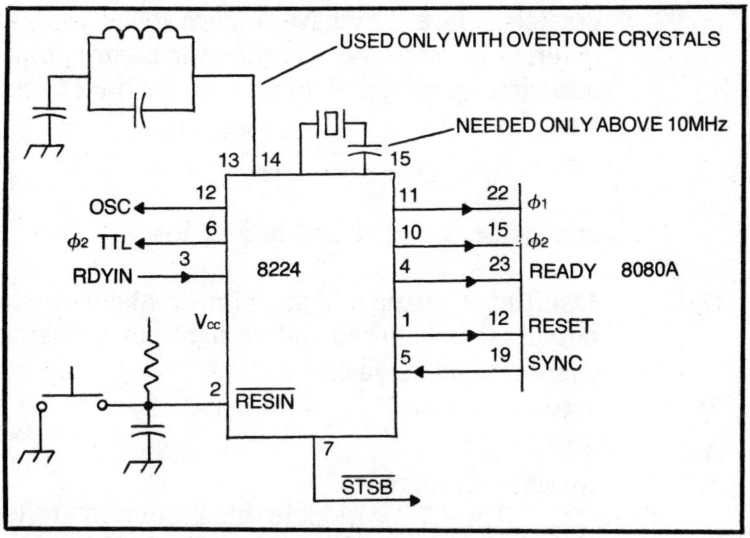

Fig. 3-4. Typical use of the 8224 clock generator.

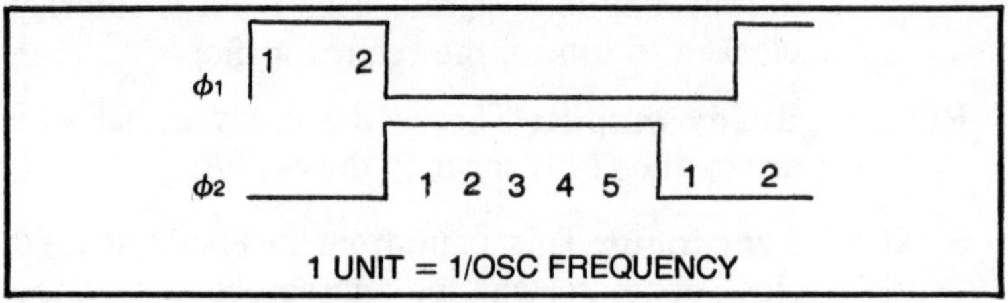

Fig. 3-5. Timing diagrams for $\phi 1$ and $\phi 2$.

XTAL 2 rives its basic operating frequency from an external, series resonant, fundamental mode crystal. The crystal frequency is given by:

$$\text{Crystal frequency} = \frac{1}{T_{cy}}$$

times 9. Where T_{cy} is the basic computer clock period. A 500 ns clock period requires a 18MHZ crystal. This is the maximum speed that the 8080A will operte at. When using crystals above 10mHz, a small capacitor (3-10pf) may be needed in series with the crystal as shown in Fig. 3-4.

TANK **Tank input:** This input allows the use of overtone crystals. Since they have a much lower gain, an external LC network is requires to assure proper oscillator operation. The formula for the LC network is:

$$F = \frac{1}{2 \quad LC}$$

and connected as shown in Fig. 3-4.

OSC **Oscillator output:** This is the crystal oscillator output. It is buffered and brought out for use as system timing signals.

V_{cc} +5V
V_{DD} +12V
GND Ground reference.

The 8228: The 8228 is a single chip system controller and bus driver to work in conjunction with the 8080A microprocessor. It generates all the signals required (except ad-

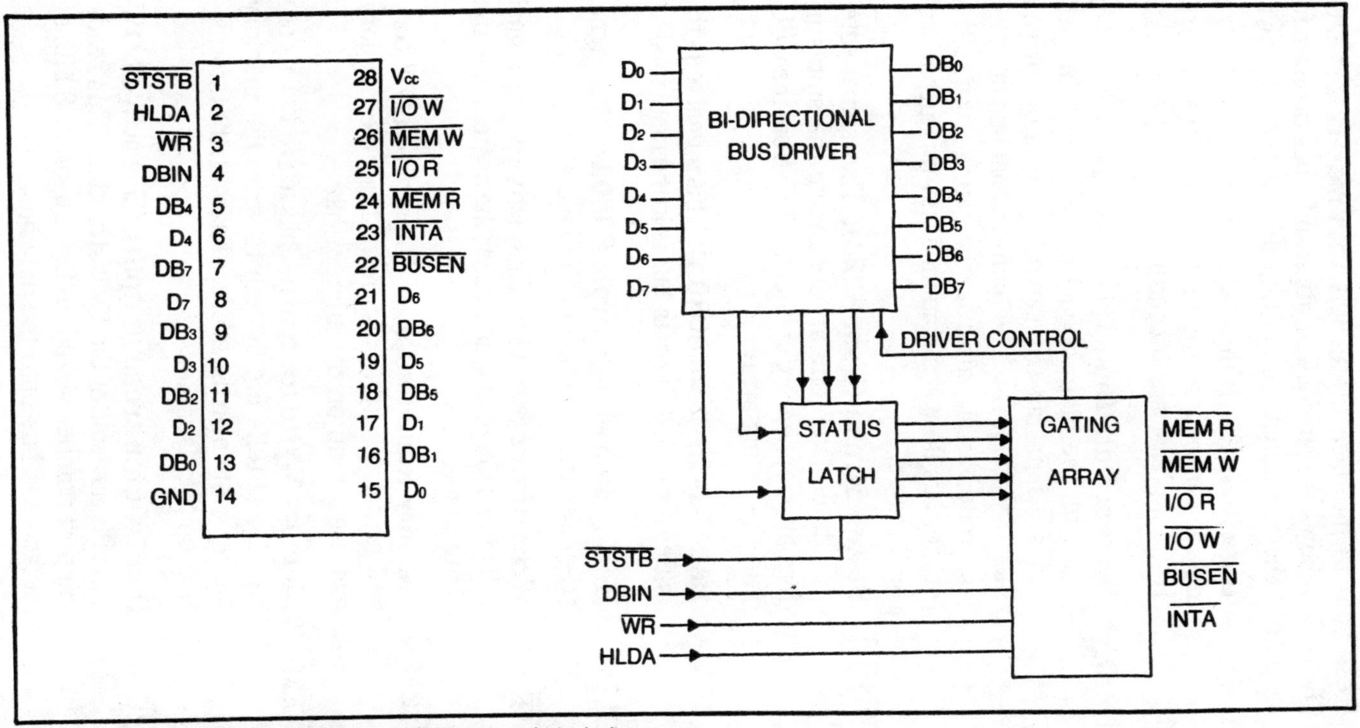

Fig. 3-6. The 8228 system controller pin definition and block diagram.

dress bus) to interface the 8080A with mexory and I/O. Figure 3-6 shows the pin configuration and block diagram for the 8228. The functional pin definition is as given below:

D_7-D_0 **Data Bus:** This is the connection for the CPU data bus. It connects to the bi-directional bus drivers. D_0 is the least significant bit.

D_{B7}-D_{B0} **System Data Bus:** This drives the system data bus with the bidirectional bus drivers. This provides a high fan out capability to allow driving memory and I/Os. The bidirectional bus driver is controlled by signals from the gating array so that proper bus flow is maintained and its outputs can be 3-stated.

$\overline{\text{STSTB}}$ **Status Strobe (from 8224):** This signal gates the status latch output, containing the status information appearing on the data bus from the CPU, into the gating array.

DBIN **Data Bus In (from 8080A):** This signal tells the gating array that the data bus is in the input mode.

HLDA **Hold Acknowledge (from 8080A):** This signal tri-states the data bus in the hold state.

$\overline{\text{WR}}$ **Write (from 8080A):** This active LOW signal tells the 8338 gating array that the system is in the write mode.

$\overline{\text{MEM}}$ $\overline{\text{R}}$ **Memory Read (output):** This active LOW control signal tells the system to read the memory address set up on the address bus.

$\overline{\text{MEM}}$ $\overline{\text{W}}$ **Memory Write (output):** This active LOW control signal tells the system to write the memory address set up on the address bus with the information on the data bus.

$\overline{\text{I/O}}$ $\overline{\text{R}}$ **Input/Output read (output):** This active LOW signal is a result of the IN instruction. This reads the port number set up on the low-order 8 bits of the address bus onto the data bus.

$\overline{I/O\ W}$ **Input/Output write (output):** This active LOW control signal is a result of the OUT instruction. This transfers the data from the data bus to the port number set up on the low- order 8 bits of the address bus.

$\overline{BUSEN}$ **Bus enable (input):** This active LOW signal forces the data bus output buffers and the control signal buffers to their 3-state condition if HIGH. A LOW enables normal opertion.

$\overline{INTA}$ **Interrupt:** This signal is normally used to gate interrupts into the system and onto the data bus. An added feature is that if only one interrupt is required for the system, this line is tied to +12 volts through a 1k resistor. When an interrupt request is given, this will automatically put RST 7 on the bus at the proper time, and the program will jump to the appropriate address for RST 7.

The 1708 EPROM: The 1708 is equivalent to the 8708, and is organized as 1k× 8 bits. The three in this system allows programming of up to 3k of permanent program. The EPROMs can be programmed on the programmer built into the system with a short program. That is covered later in this book.

Figure 3-7 shows the pin diagram for the 1708, and the pin definition is as given below.

A_0-A_9 **Address bus:** These are the address inputs for this chip. One chip has addresses 0000 thru 03FF (hex). So the three included into the system will be capable of 03FF addresses. These can be assigned to almost any starting address.

0_0–0_8 **Data outputs:** These are the data-bus outputs, and place the data stored in the addressed memory location, when the chip is enabled.

$\overline{CS}$/WE **Chip Select/write enable input:** When this input is LOW, the chip is selected, or enabled. When this is at +12 volts, the programming capability is enabled. When it is floated (or the driver

A_7	1	24	V_{CC}
A_6	2	23	A_8
A_5	3	22	A_9
A_4	4	21	V_{BB}
A_3	5	20	$\overline{CS}$/WE
A_2	6	19	V_{DD}
A_1	7	18	PROGRAM
A_0	8	17	O_7
O_0	9	16	O_6
O_1	10	15	O_5
O_2	11	14	O_4
V_{SS}	12	13	O_3

Fig. 3-7. The EPROM pin definition.

3-stated) there is no action from the chip. This input is normally driven by some type of address decoder.

PROGRAM

Program pulse: The program pulse (26 volt 1 millisecond pulse) is applied to this pin. This is the pulse that gates the information in as permanent memory.

V_{DD} +12 volts
V_{CC} +5 volts
V_{BB} −5 volts
V_{SS} Ground reference.

One of the advantages of using EPROM memory is that the program can be written into the permanent memory by the user. This can be done using the programmer described later in this book, with the program given.

When an EPROM is completely erased, all locations are ones or in the HIGH state. Information is introduced by selectively programming zeros into the desired bit locations. This is done by using the following procedure. The programming waveshapes are given in Fig. 3-8.

- Raise $\overline{CS}$/WE to +12 volts.
- Set up the address on the address inputs.

● Set up the data to be programmed into the selected address on the data output lines.

● Apply the +26 volt 1 millisecond programming pulse to the program pin.

One pass through all the addresses to be programmed is defined as a program loop. The number of passes through the program loop must be such that the program pulse width times the number of passes is equal to or greater than 100 msec. So, using a 1-millisecond pulse width, at least 100 passes are required to assure reliable writing of the EPROM. Due to heating of the chip, the same address should not be written 100 times consectively. If this is done, that one bit or word may burn out.

The information in the EPROM is erased using an traviolet light of the wavelength of 2537 A. Typically, 20 to 30 minutes is required to erase the 1708s. When using UV lamps, the short wave filters should be removed and the chips placed about 1 inch from the lamp. Do not look into the UV lamp when it is turned on, eye damage may result.

The 2102: The 2102 (or 8102) RAM is organized as a 1k×1 bit RAM. This means that 8 chips are required for an 8-bit computer. This is a static random access memory in which data is read out nondestructively. The various dash numbers refer to different access times. The 2102A has access time of 450 nsec, which is fast enough to operate directly off the address bus on a 500 nsec system—the cycle time of this system. Figure 3-9 shows the pin configuration for the 2102. The definition of the pins are as follows:

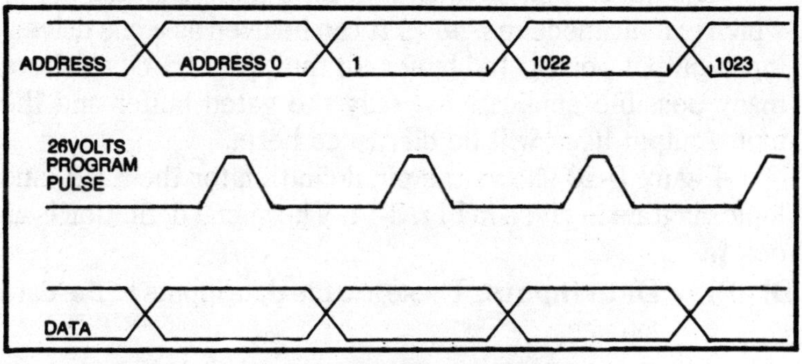

Fig. 3-8. Waveshapes required to program the EPROM.

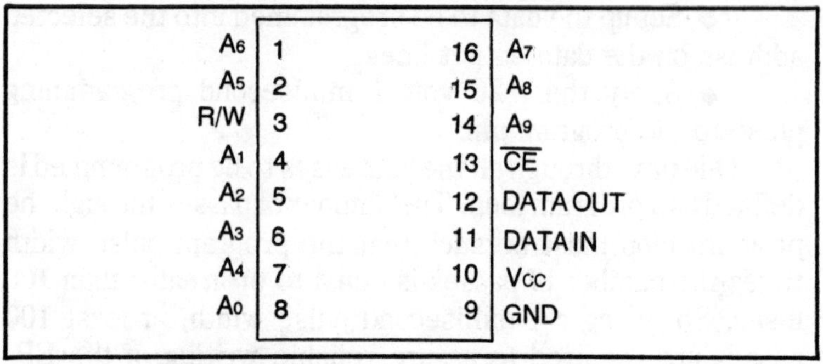

Fig. 3-9. The RAM pin definition.

D_{in} **Data input:** This is the input-data line, which is connected to the bit line of the data bus. It is connected to the bit line for the bit that the chip is connected to and defined as.

D_{out} **Data output:** This is the output-data line, and is normally connected to the data-input line.

A_0-A_9 **Address inputs:** These comprise the address-bus connections for the individual addresses within the chip.

R/W **Read/write input:** A LOW commands a write to the chip, and a HIGH commands a read.

$\overline{CE}$ **Chip enable:** This is the active LOW signal which enables the chip. It is normally connected to the address decoder output.

V_{cc} +5 Volts

GNR Ground reference.

The 8212: The 8212 is an 8-bit 3-state latching buffer which is multimode in nature. It can be used as a bus driver, input/output port, gated buffer, or multiplexer. Of all these many possible applications, only the gated buffer and the input/output uses will be discussed here.

Figure 3-10 shows the pin definition for the 8212, and logic diagram is given in Fig. 3-11. The signal definition is as below:

DI_0-DI_7 **Data inputs:** These are the data inputs to the data latches.

DO_0-DO_7 **Data outputs:** This is the output of the gated-data

	buffers. These 3-state outputs are connected to the load (data bus, address bus, output device, etc).
$\overline{DS_1}$-DS_2	**Device select:** These 2 inputs are used for device selection. When active ($\overline{DS_1}$ LOW and DS_2 HIGH) the chip is selected. The output buffer is enabled and the servie-reset flip/flop is set.
MD	**Mode:** This input controls the state of the output buffer and determines the source of the clock input to the data latch. When MD is HIGH the output buffers are enabled and the clock is from the device selection logic. When MD is LOW, the output buffer state is determined by the device-selection logic; the source of the clock is the STB input.
STB	**Strobe:** This input is used as the clock to the data latch for the input mode (MD=0) and to reset the service-request flip/flop.
$\overline{INT}$	**Interrupt:** This active LOW output is generated by the service-request flip/flop and gated by the device-selection logic.
$\overline{CLR}$	**Clear:** This active LOW input resets the data latch and sets the SR flip/flop.
V_{cc}	+ 5 volts
GND	Ground reference.

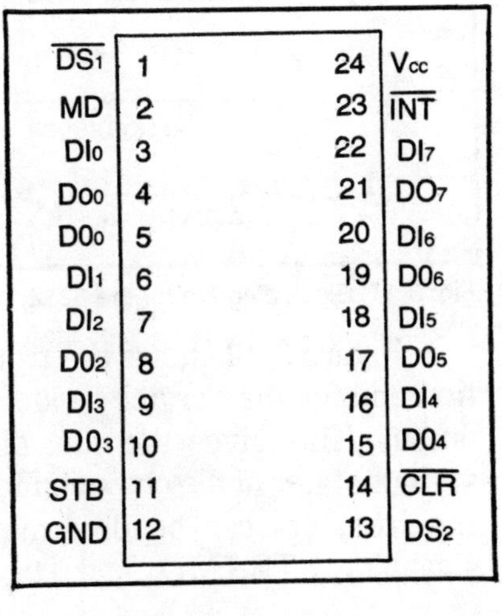

Fig. 3-10. The 8212 Pin Definition.

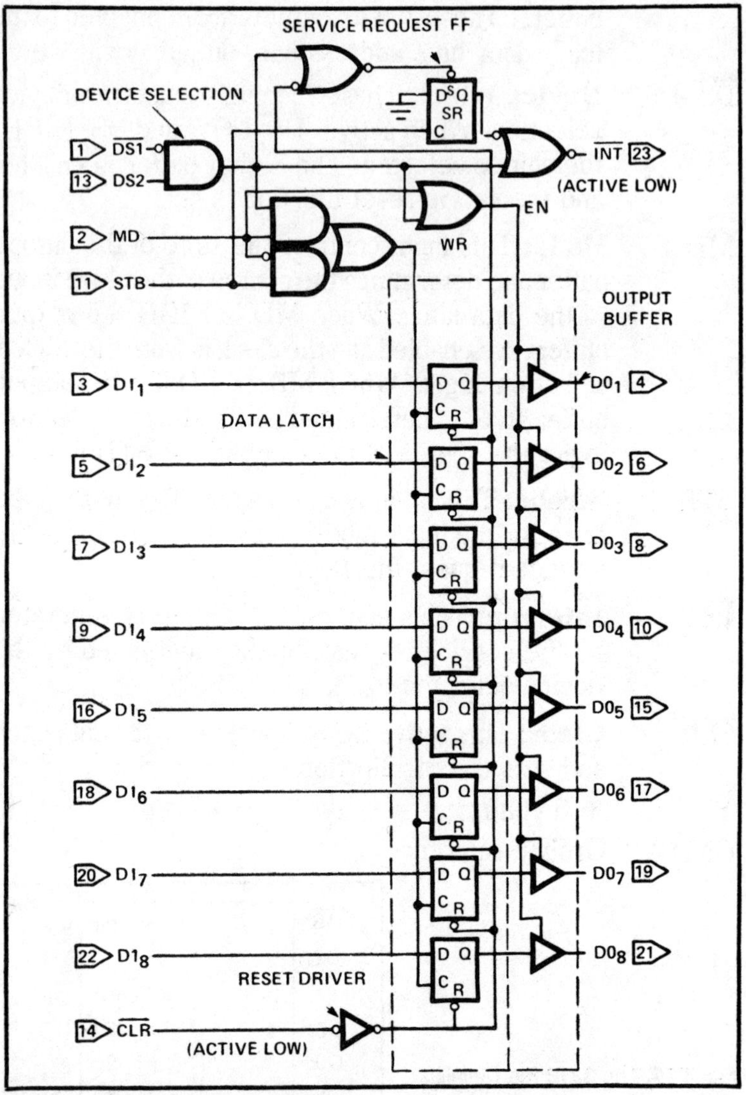

Fig. 3-11. Block diagram for the 8212.

Figure 3-12 shows the truth table for the device selection and for the service request (SR) flip/flop and the INT output. This gives the control-input requirements for the various states of the output buffer. From this table, the signal requirements can be determined for the application. By strapping STB, MD, and DS_2 HIGH, and $\overline{DS_1}$ LOW the device acts as a buffer. If the device select inputs are connected to gating signals, this device can operate as a gated buffer. This application is shown in Fig. 3-13. Either $\overline{DS}_1$, and DS_2 or both, can act as the gating control. If only one is used, the other must be connected to its active state

Figure 3-14 illustrates how to use the 8212 as an input and output device for a microcomputer system. The circuit connects the data bus to external circuits. When the device is selected ($\overline{DS}_1$ and DS_2 both active) and the I/O read pulse (active LOW) is present, the output will be the same as the input. When the I/O read pulse goes high, data latches for as long as the device is selected. This can be seen from Fig. 3-12.

Selecting an I/O device is similiar to selecting memory, and both will be discussed in detail later in this chapter.

The 8205: The 8205, or the equivalent 3205, is a high-speed one-of-eight binary-decoder chip. This chip decodes address lines for address and I/O selection. The circuit can be expanded and cascaded to decode as many address lines as required. Figure 3-15 shows the pin

STB	MD	$\overline{DS}_1 \cdot DS_2$	Data out equals
0	0	0	TRI-STATE
1	0	0	TRI-STATE
0	1	0	DATA LATCH
1	1	0	DATA LATCH
0	0	1	DATA LATCH
1	0	1	DATA IN
0	1	1	DATA IN
1	1	1	DATA IN

CLR	$\overline{DS}_1 \cdot DS_2$	STB	SR	INT
0	0	0	1	1
0	1	0	1	0
1	1		0	0
1	1	0	1	0
1	0	0	1	1
1	1		1	0

Fig. 3-12. Selection tables for the 8212.

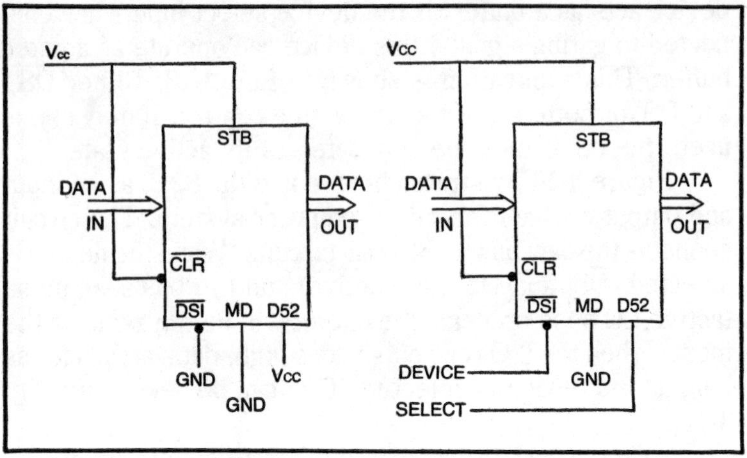

Fig. 3-13. Using the 8212 as a gated buffer.

configuration and the selection table. The definition of the signals is as given below:

O_0-O_7 **Decoded outputs:** These are the active LOW outputs which are a result of decoding the inputs.

A_0-A_2 **Address inputs:** These are the address inputs that are decoded for the select signals.

E_1-E_3 **Enable inputs:** These enable the chip. E_1 and E_2 are active LOW and E_3 is active HIGH.

V_{CC} + Volts

GND Ground reference

From the selection table in Fig. 3-15, the addresses required for the desired outputs can be determined. For example, if A_0, A_1, and A_2 are connected to the address bus lines A_8, A_9, and A_{10}, and the chip is enabled, 0_0 will be active for addresses 0000 thru 00FF(hex), and 0_1 will be active for addresses 0100 thru 01FF.

MEMORY AND INPUT/OUTPUT ADDRESSING

Memory chips come in several sizes, such as 256 bytes, 512 bytes, 1k, etc. If more than one memory chip is used, some type of addressing decoding is needed to select the proper memory chip. A 1k memory has addresses 0000 thru

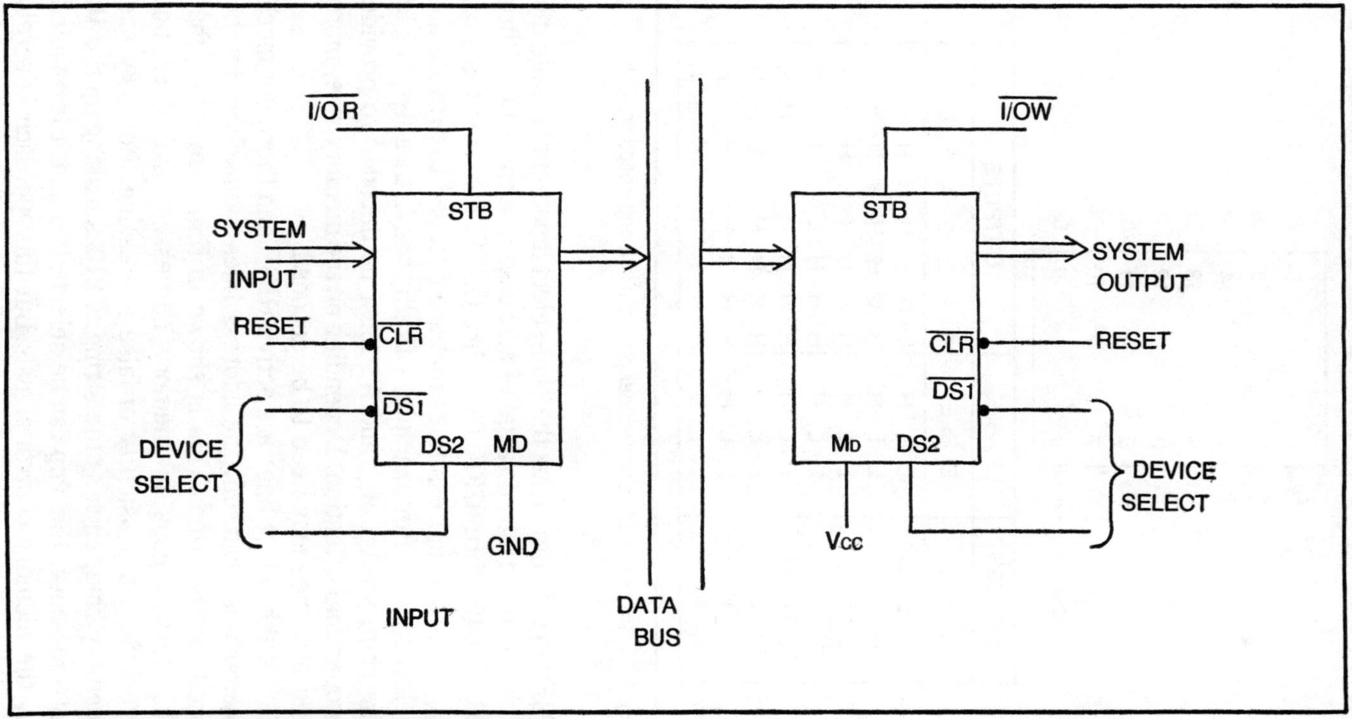

Fig. 3-14. Using the 8212 as an input and output device.

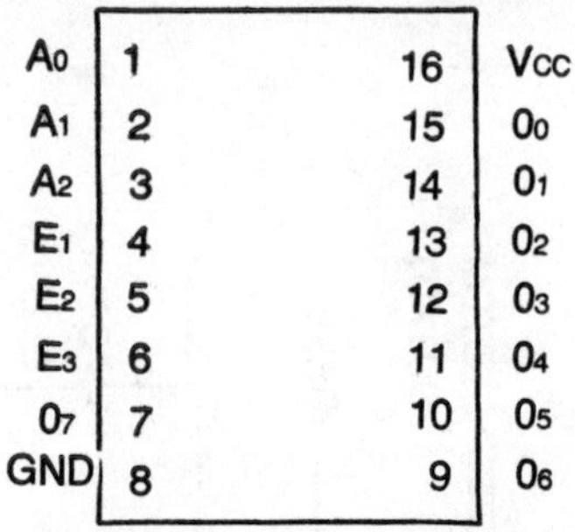

ADDRESS	ENABLE	OUTPUTS
A_0 A_1 A_2	E_1 E_2 E_3	0 1 2 3 4 5 6 7
L L L	L L H	L H H H H H H H
H L L	L L H	H L H H H H H H
L H L	L L H	H H L H H H H H
H H L	L L H	H H H L H H H H
L L H	L L H	H H H H L H H H
H L H	L L H	H H H H H L H H
L H H	L L H	H H H H H H L H
H H H	L L H	H H H H H H H L

Fig. 3-15. The 8205 address decoder pin definition and decoding table.

03FF in the chip. Thus the chip-select input must enable the chip for the desired range of addresses, such as 0000 thru 03FF, 0400 thru 07FF, 0800 thru OBFF, etc. It is the next higher-order address lines that are decoded to provide the select signals. For example, a 1k chip has A_0 thru A_9 going to the chip, so A_{10}, A_{11}, and A_{12} must be decoded to provide proper chip selection. Depending on the memory size, more address lines may need to be decoded.

If the select lines are active HIGH and there not much memory is required, the address lines themselves can be used for selection. This is shown in Fig. 3-16. Note that this leaves gaps in memory addresses, and does not preclude the possibility of false addressing. For only one memory chip, such as the string of 2102s making up the 1k by 8 memory, the chip can be selected so that it is enabled by the memory control signals. But this approach severely limits the size and usefulness of the memory. It is advisable, therefore, to use a memory address decoder.

Figure 3-17 shows the memory address decoder used in the microcomputer shown in Fig. 3-1. Also given is the selection table showing the active outputs for the various inputs. Address bus lines A_{10}, A_{11}, and A_{12} drive the decoding inputs. A_{13} and A_{14} connect to the active LOW enable inputs, and the active HIGH enable input is connected to a HIGH. This decoder can drive up to 8 blocks of memory, each containing 1k bytes. Four of these lines are used by the system, so the other 4 select lines are available for memory expansion. The low-order 4 select lines are connected to

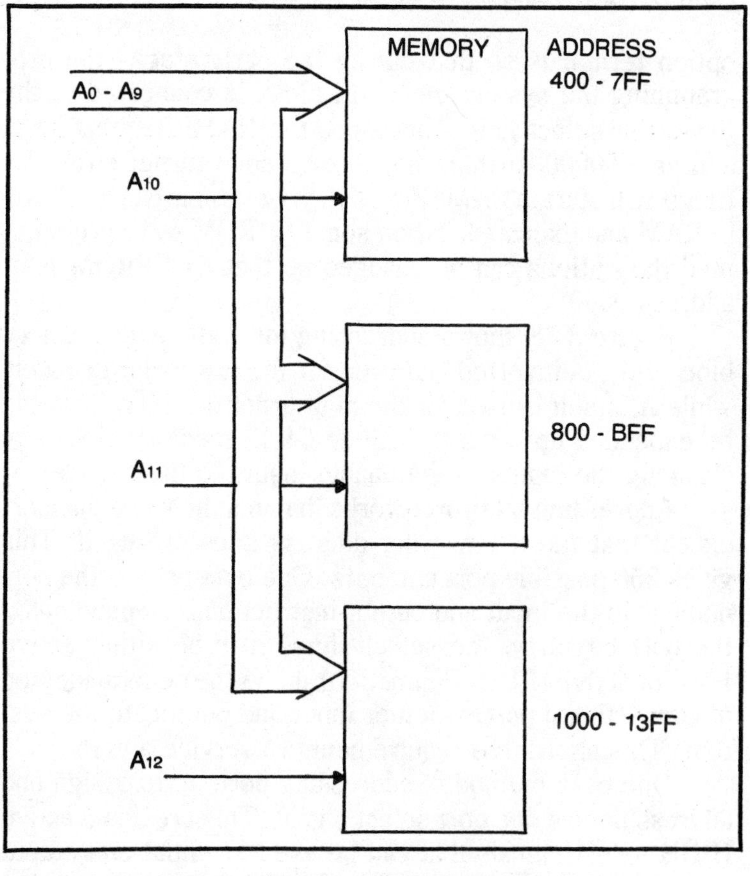

Fig. 3-16. Using address lines as memory enable signals.

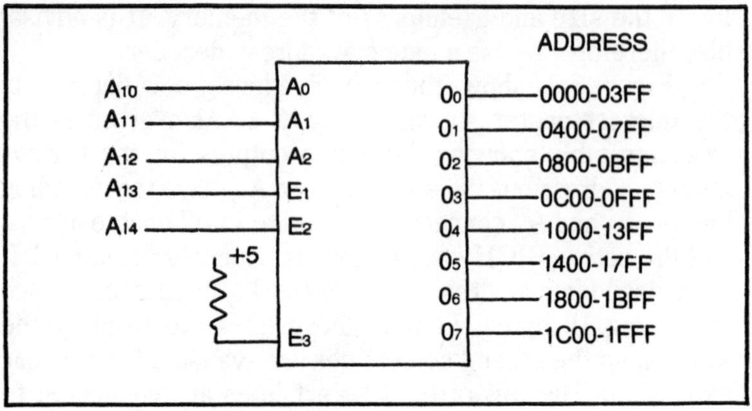

Fig. 3-17. Address decoding for the microcomputer.

option terminals so that during the early stages the programming the system the RAM block is connected to the low-order select line. This gives the RAM the starting at address of 0000, so that when the system is turned on and let run, it will start in RAM. In this way, programs can be placed in RAM and executed. When some EPROM's are programmed the options can be changed so that an EPROM is at address 0000.

Figure 3-18 shows addressing for sixteen 1k memory blocks. A_{15} is inverted and used for the low-order decoder, while A_{15} itself is used for the high-order decoder. This can be expanded upwards to include 64 1k memory blocks by changing the inputs to the enable inputs to the decoder.

Addressing I/O ports works in much the same manner, except that the 8 low-order address lines are used. This gives 256 possible port numbers. One byte acts as the port number in the input and output instructions. Depending on the port circuitry, the select signal may be either active LOW or active HIGH. Figure 3-19 shows the general method of connecting a port, whether input and output, to the system. This shows the requirements to service a port.

One easy method of addressing ports is to assign one address line as one port select signal. This creates 8 active HIGH select signals that can be used for input and output ports. Realize that the same port number can be assigned to

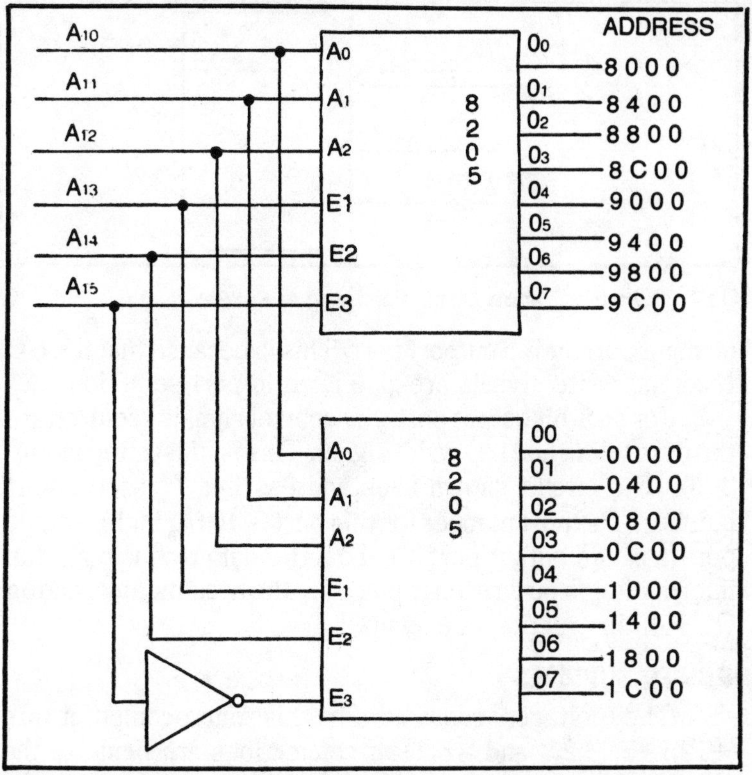

Fig. 3-18. Address decoders for addressing 16 1K blocks of memory.

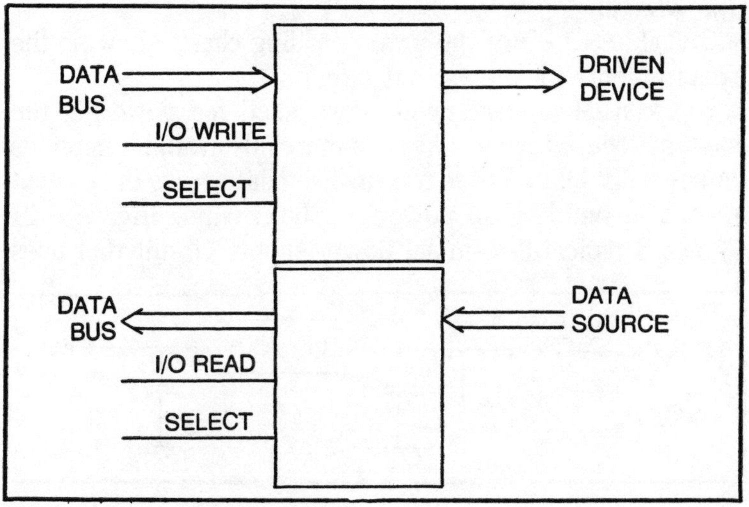

Fig. 3-19. General Input/Output ports.

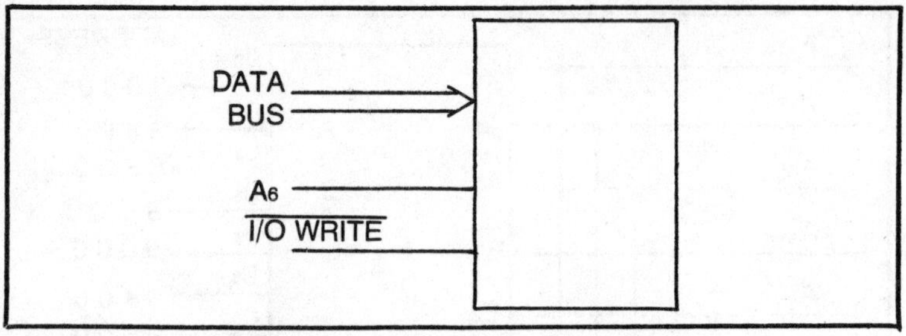

Fig. 3-20. An 8-bit Parallel Output Port Using A6 For Select.

an input port and an outport port. This is because that the I/O read and write signals are also used in port selection.

For an 8-bit output port, the control signals required are the port select and $\overline{\text{I/O}}$ write signal. This is illustrated in Fig. 3-20. The circuit shown uses address line A_6 as the port number. The port number for this port is 40 (A_6 high), so this port is called output-port 40. To write data to this port, the information to be written is placed in the accumulator, and an OUT 40 instruction is executed.

POWER SUPPLIES

The voltages required for this microcomputer are +12, +5, +27, and −5. The connections are made to the top of the microcomputer board, with several inputs for the +5 volts.

Table 3-1 gives the power-loading chart, showing the requirements for the various circuits.

External power supplies are used for powering the system. These can be either commercially available supplies or specially-built. Three terminal regulators are the easiest to use in building up power-supply circuits. Figure 3-21 shows a typical 3-terminal power-supply circuit that uses

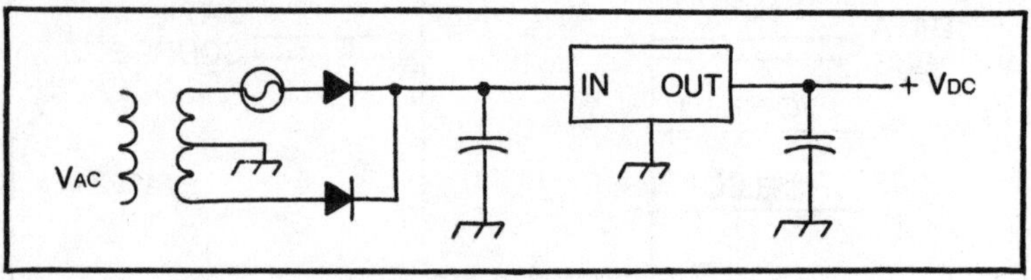

Fig. 3-21. Typical 3-terminal power supply.

Table 3-1. Power-Loading Chart for the Microcomputer.

Circuit & Figures	+5V (Ma)	−5V (Ma)	+12 (Ma)	+27 (Ma)
Microcomputer 3-1	850	90	200	
Hardware read/Load & single step 3-28 & 3-29	560			
Keyboard Display 3-31	185			
Eprom Programmer 3-35 & 3-36	150	30	50	20

only 7 components. A fuse is shown in the secondary side of the transformer. Sometimes this is placed in the output side of the regulator, but if this is done, there will be a variable voltage drop across it which reduces the output voltage level. This fuse can also be placed on the input side of the transformer.

Table 3-2 gives the characteristics of several common 3-terminal regulators, along with the pin assignments. Also see Fig. 3-22.

Table 3-2. Several Common 3-Terminal Regulators.

Number	Voltage	Current (amps)	Pin Configuration 1	2	3
LM 341−5	+5	.5	in	gnd	out
LM 341−12	+12	.5	in	gnd	out
LM 342−5	±5	.25	in	gnd	out
LM342−12	+12	.25	in	gnd	out
LM7805C	+5	1	Gnd	in	out (c)
LM7812C	±12	1	gnd	in	out (c)
LM7905C	−5	1.5	gnd	in	out
LM140/240/340 −5	−5	1	in	gnd	out (c)
LM123/223/323	+5	3	in	out	gnd (b)
LM120/220/320−5	−5	1.5	gnd	in	out (a)
MC7805	−5	1.5	in	gnd	out (c)
MC7812	+12	1.5	in	gnd	out (c)
MC7912	−12	1	gnd	in	out (a)

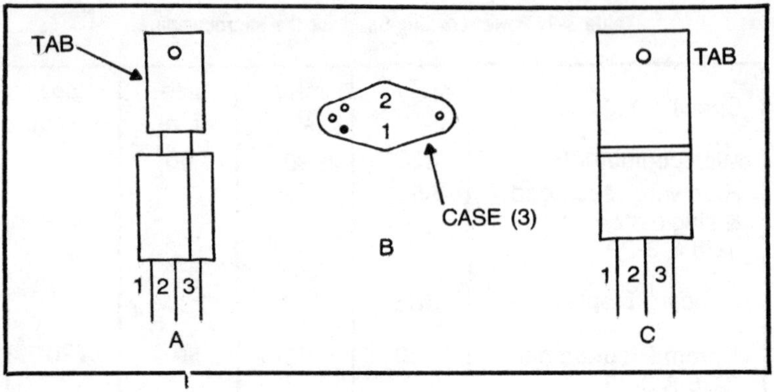

Fig. 3-22. 3-terminal pin definitions.

The three basic rectifier circuits are half wave, full-wave center tapped, and full-wave bridge. Of these, the half wave bridge is the most inefficient and should be used only when nothing else can be. Figure 3-23 shows the diagrams for the full wave center tapped and the full wave bridge circuits. Table 3-3 compares these two rectifier circuits. Figure 3-24 shows the diagram for a full-wave bridge-complementary circuit. This rectifier generates two complementary voltages, such as +5 volts and −5 volts.

The rectifier-output capacitor (C) filters the ripple from the rectifier circuit. The capacitor selection is relatively straightforward. The size of the capacitor is given by the equation:

$$C = \frac{I_L}{V} \times 6 \times 10^{-3}$$

Where V is the allowable ripple into the regulator, and I_L is the maximum-load current. The ripple voltage for 3-terminal

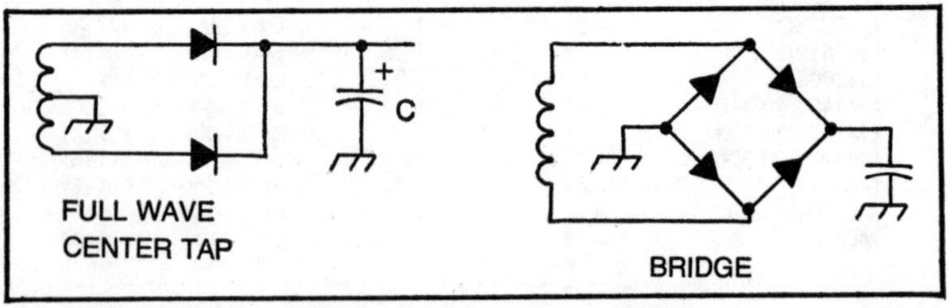

Fig. 3-23. Full-wave center tapped and bridge rectfiers.

Table 3-3. Comparison of Full-Wave Center Tapped and Bridge Rectifiers.

Full-wave Center Tapped	Full-wave Bridge
Uses ½ of secondary winding at a time Requires center tap Uses 2 diodes Secondary current = 1.2 x DC current	Uses full secondary winding continuously No center tap required Uses 4 diodes Secondary current = 1.8 X DC current

regulators should be 3 volts or less. The higher the allowable ripple voltage the smaller the capacitor. For 1 amp and 3 volt ripple, the capacitor works out to 2000 μF. For 3 amp and 4 volts ripple, it works out to be 4500 μF. The larger the capacitor the lower the ripple to the regulator.

Figure 3-25 illustrates a power supply capable of delivering all the voltages required for the microcomputer. It uses a 16-V AC center-tapped transformer, and grounds one end. Voltage-doubler circuits generate the +27 and −5 volts. The −5 voltage doubler references the 8 VAC and provides a −8 to −9 volts on C_6. This doubler consists of CR_1, CR_2, C_1, and C_6. The +27 voltage doubler consists of CR_3, CR_4, C_2, and C_3.

VR_1 is a +15-volt regulator which is referenced to the +12 volts to generate the +27. Since the +5 volts has the highest current requirement, a full-wave bridge is used. The +12V, therefore, must use a half-wave rectifier since a bridge would short the 5-volt bridge.

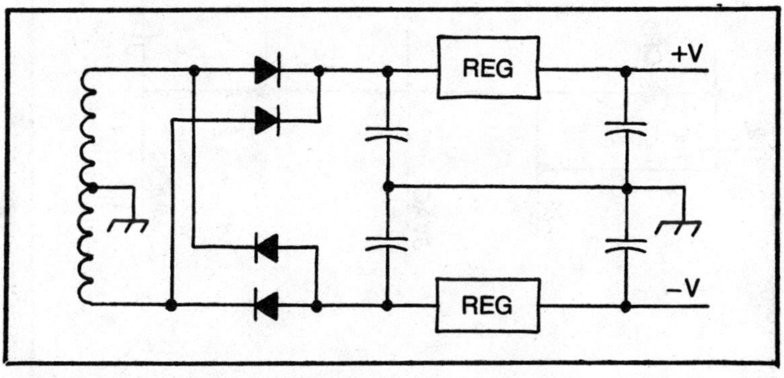

Fig. 3-24. Dual-output power supply.

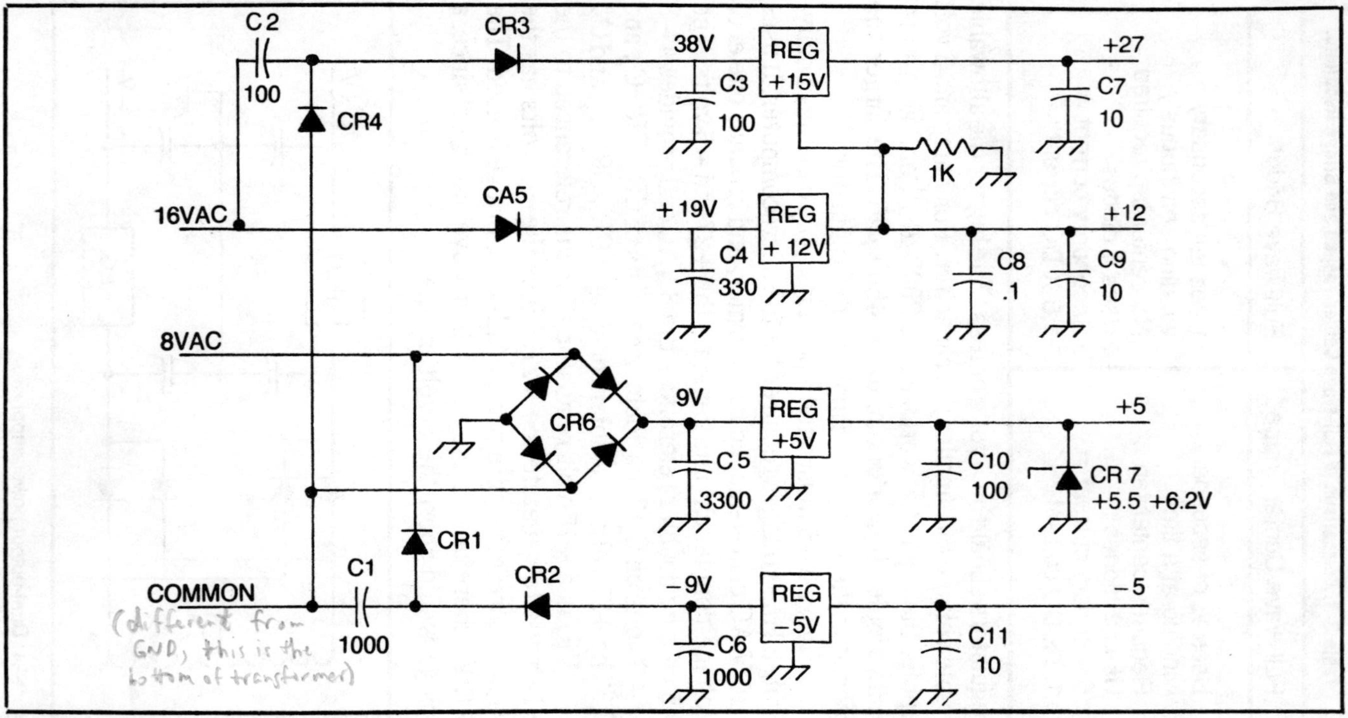

Fig. 3-25. Quad-output power supply.

Increasing the value of C_4, C_5, and C_6 increases the current capability. But care should be taken not to overload the diodes or transformer.

Additional +5-volt outputs can be achieved by adding three terminal regulators in parallel with the existing regulator, as shown in Fig. 3-26. One bridge drives several regulators, and there is more than one 5 volt bridge. It is advisable to use one bridge with diodes large enough to carry all the current required (Fig. 3-27).

The zener diode is present to prevent overvoltage on the +5-volt line. This prevents voltage spikes from getting on the logic line; spikes can cause problems in the logic and the microcomputer.

All voltage regulators should be tied to a heat sink. This dissipates the heat generated and prevents overheating. The heat is generated by the voltage drop across the regulator. For example, if the input voltage is 9 volts, the output voltage is 5 volts, and the current is 2 amps, the power dissipated is (9 volts - 5 volts) × 2 amps which is 8 watts. This must be dissipated by a heat sink, otherwise the regulator will heat up and eventually shut off.

HARDWARE READ AND LOAD CIRCUITRY

The hardware read and load capability provides a means of loading and reading selected memory locations with a

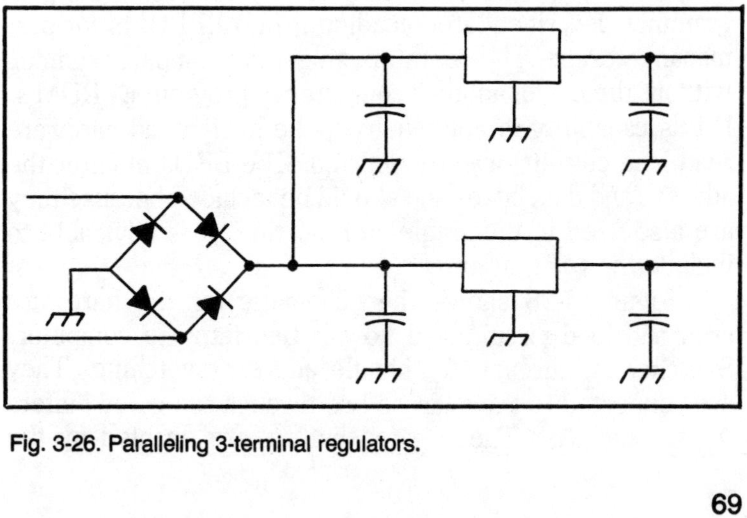

Fig. 3-26. Paralleling 3-terminal regulators.

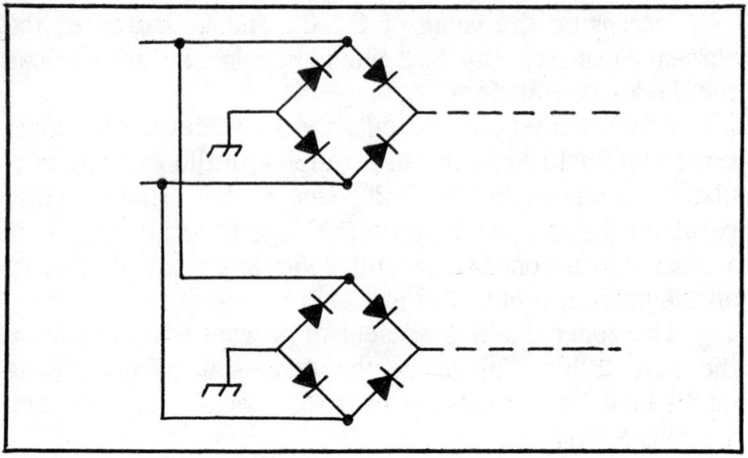

Fig. 3-27. Paralleling bridge rectifiers.

series of switches and discrete LEDs. Setting the address switches to the desired address and setting the control switch to read displays the contents of the desired memory location on the data LEDs. Setting the control switch to load and the desired data to be loaded into that address on the data switches, and depressing the load switch, loads the desired data into the selected-memory location. This provides the capability to load or read any memory location without a computer program.

Switch control gives the operator the capability of generating a program, checking it out, and (using the programmer described later) loading it into EPROMs for permanant storage. The operator can get the computer running without the use of another computer to program EPROM's. If this capability is not required, the switch and hardware read load circuitry can be omitted. The LEDs monitor the address and data buses and should be included because they are also used in the single-step portion. It is advisable to include the total circuitry.

Figure 3-28 shows the schematic for the hardware read and load circuit, and how it ties into the computer. Switches A_0 through A_{15} handle address switching. They are connected to the address bus through the gated buffers A_{18} through A_{21}. These gated buffers are enabled by the active LOW signal from IC A_{25} pin 1. This signal is generated when the read/load switch is in either the read or load position. The data switches D_0 through D_7 are connected to the data bus through the gated buffers A_{22} through A_{23}. The active LOW signal from IC A_{26} pin 2 enables the data switches only in the load position. This is because the switches are used only in the load function. During read, the data is read from the memory location.

The steps required to read a memory location for the type of RAM chips used are:

- Put the computer in the hold condition.
- Set up the address to be read on the address bus.
- Place the read/load switch in the read position.
- Read the data on the data LEDs.

The steps required to load a memory location are:

- Put the computer in the hold condition.
- Set up the address to be loaded on the address bus.
- Set up the data to be loaded into the address on the data switches.
- Place the read/load switch in the load position.
- Apply the memory write pulse.
- Read the memory location to verify the data is properly loaded.

The hold/run switch places the computer in the hold condition by applying a high on the processor's hold input pin. The HLDA signal is the response from the 8080 indicating that the computer is in the hold condition. This signal turns on the hold LED and enables the read/load circuitry.

The AND gate (A_{24}) has a LOW output when either input is LOW. To get the desired HIGH output, the HLDA signal must be HIGH, and the read/load switch must be in the proper position. The HIGH output gives a LOW output from the NOR gate A_{25}. This LOW output enables the desired buffers.

To load data into the RAM, the RW pulse must be LOW. This is generated by the one-shot A_{27}. This is gated onto the RW control line when the gated buffer A_{28} is enabled by an active LOW signal on the control pin (pin 1). Normally this

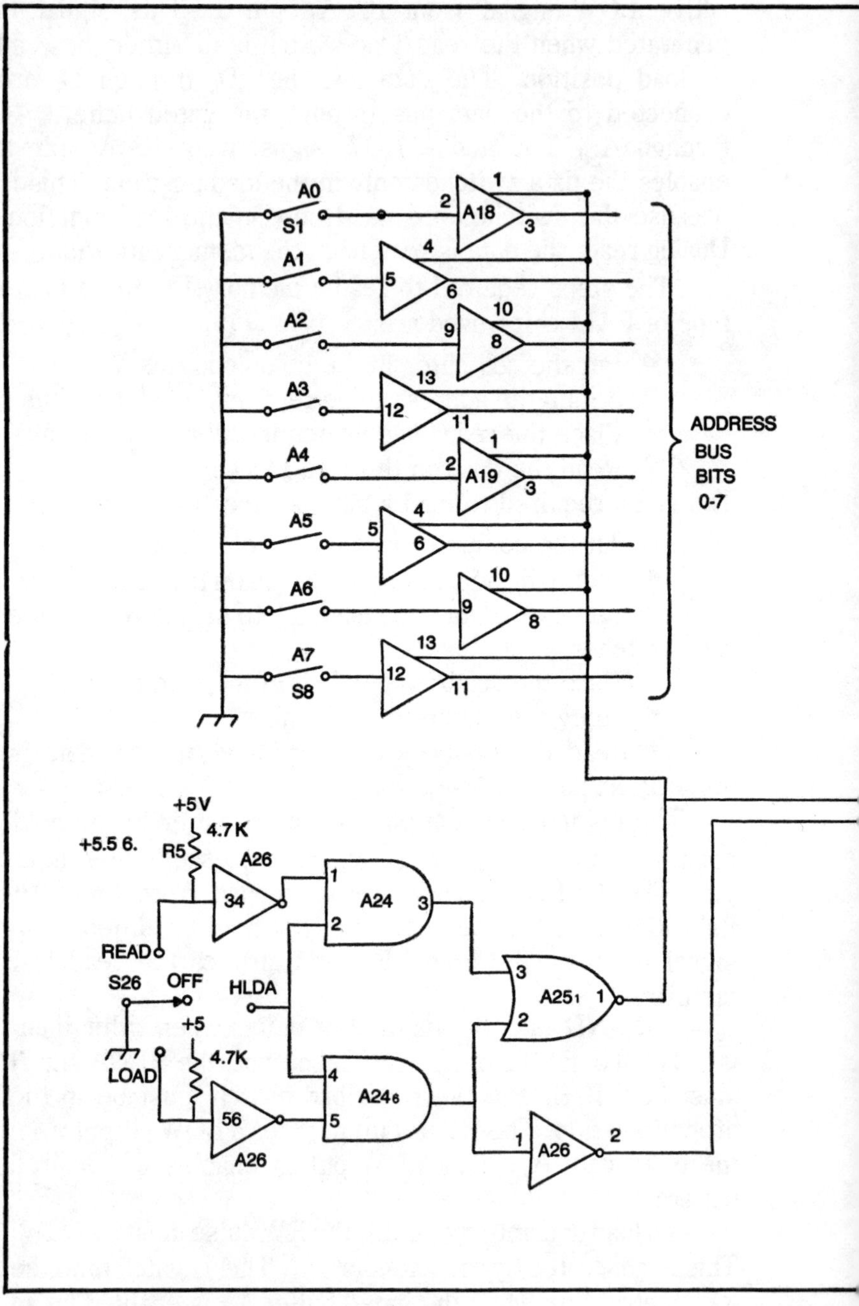

Fig. 3-28. Hardware read and load circuit.

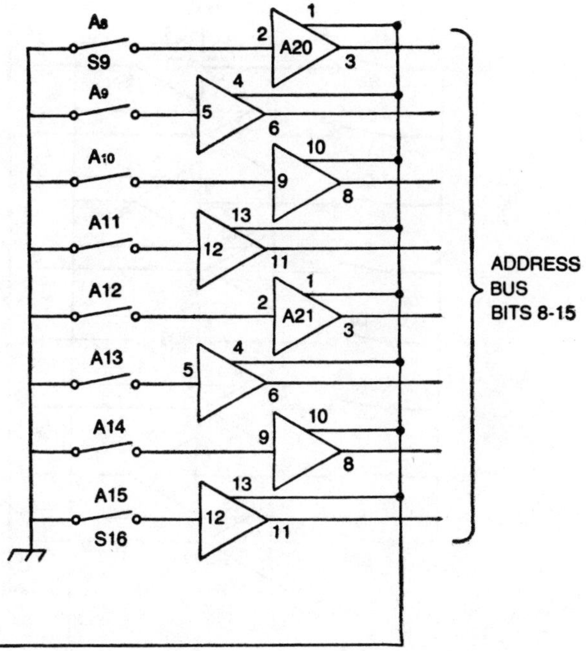
A8
S9
A9
A10
A11
A12
A13
A14
A15
S16
A20
A21
ADDRESS
BUS
BITS 8-15

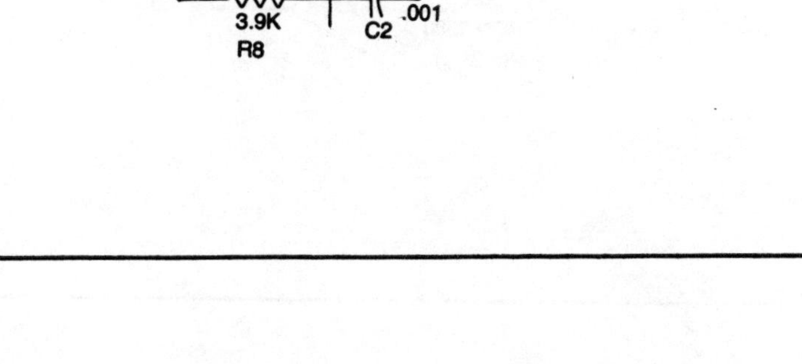
4.7K
1+5V
R7
A32
L1 TO A25/1
A27
RW
(CONTROL BUS)
WRITE
S27
3.9K
R8
C2
.001

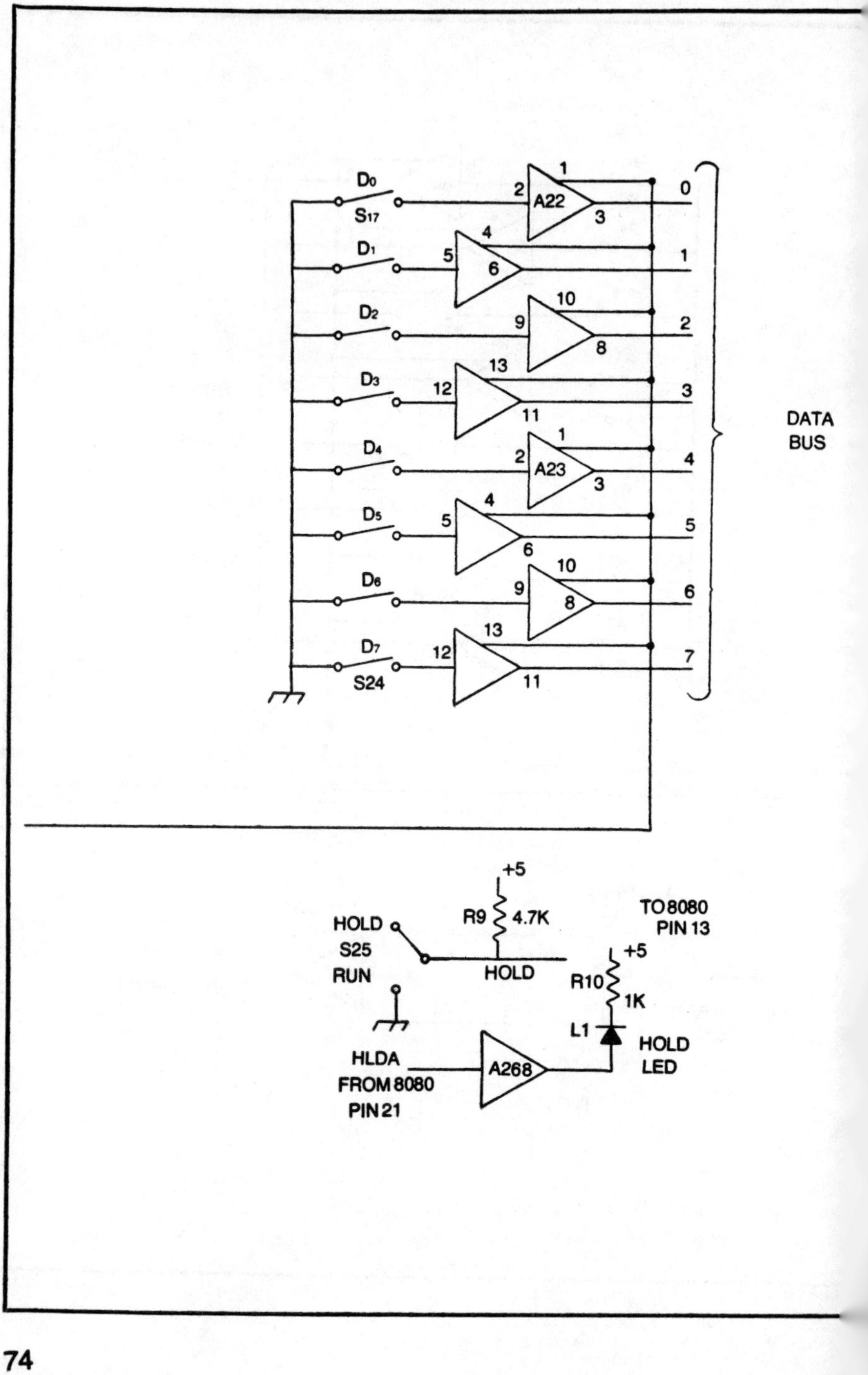

D0
S17
A22
D1
D2
D3
D4
A23
D5
D6
D7
S24
DATA BUS
+5
R9
4.7K
HOLD
S25
RUN
HOLD
TO 8080 PIN 13
R10
1K
L1
HOLD LED
HLDA FROM 8080 PIN 21
A268

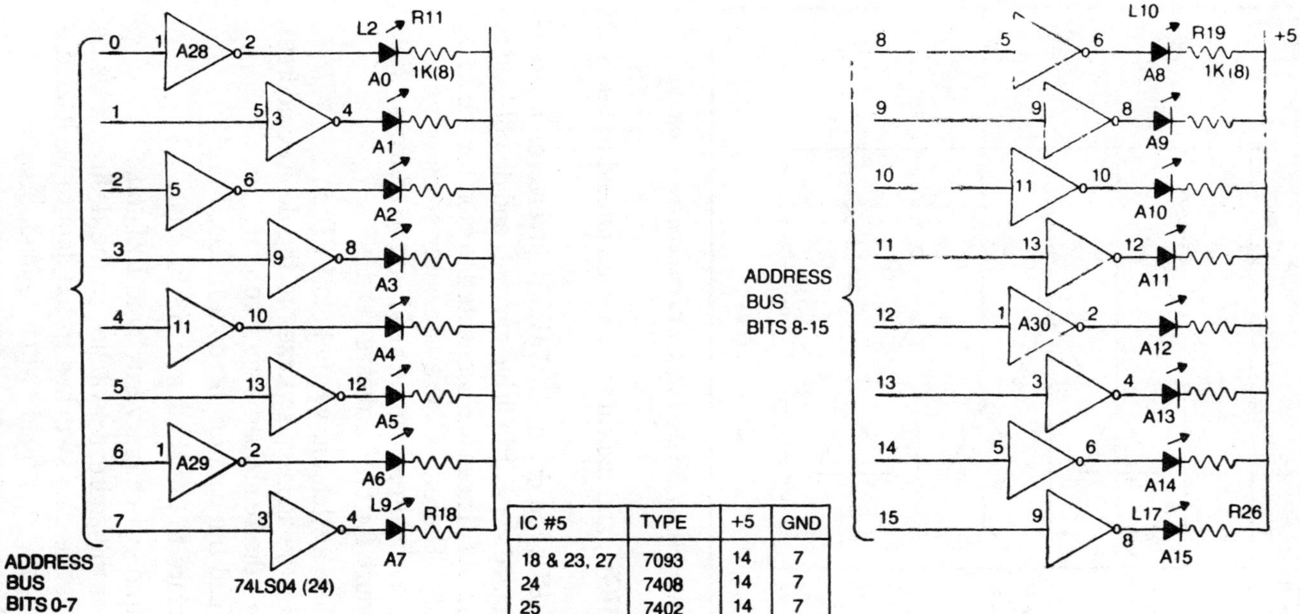

IC #5	TYPE	+5	GND
18 & 23, 27	7093	14	7
24	7408	14	7
25	7402	14	7
26	7404	14	7
32	74123	16	8
28-31	74LS04	14	7

Fig. 3-28. Hardware read and load circuit. (Continued from page 73).

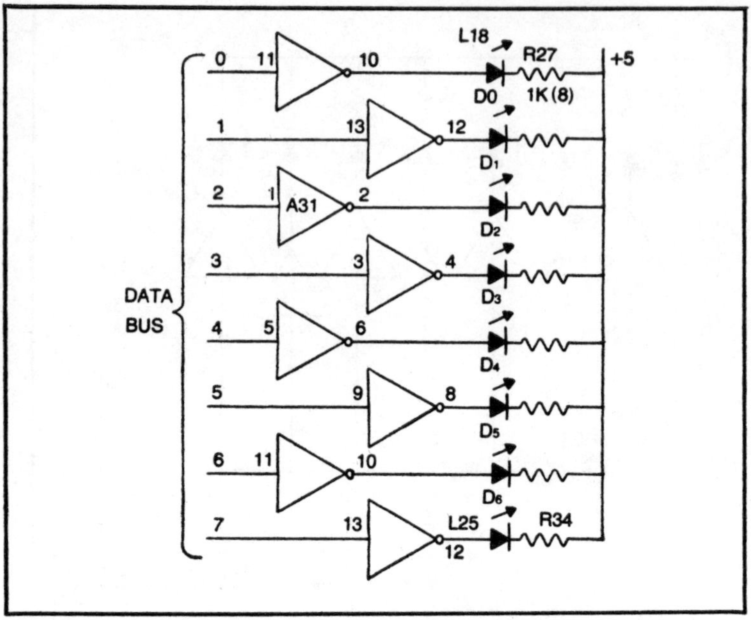

Fig. 3-28. Hardware Read and Load Circuit. (Continued from page 75).

signal is HIGH, and indicates a read command to the RAM memory.

The LEDs are driven by 74LS04 inverters. These inverters require very little drive current, and do not load the bus excessively. These are connected to monitor the busses continuously. Therefore if the computer stops or gets in a tight loop, the address can be read on the address LEDs. The procedure for the hardware read is:

- Hold switch on, verify hold LED on.
- Set the address switches to the desired address.
- Set the read/load switch to read.
- Read the data on the data LEDs.

The procedure to use the hardware load is:

- Hold switch on, verify hold LED on.
- Set the address switches to the desired address.
- Set the data switches to the data to be loaded.
- Set the read/load switch to load.
- Depress the memory write switch.

For normal operation always set the hold switch off and the read/load switch to the center off position. This allows the computer to run.

SINGLE STEP

The single-step capability allows the user to execute one instruction at a time and read the address and data lines. This is an aid in troubleshooting hardware and programs.

The CPU's ready input is active HIGH, so it must be HIGH for the system to run. When the ready line is pulled LOW, the computer enters the wait state, which stops the computer after time T_2. The operation is stopped in the active condition so that the data bus and address bus can be read.

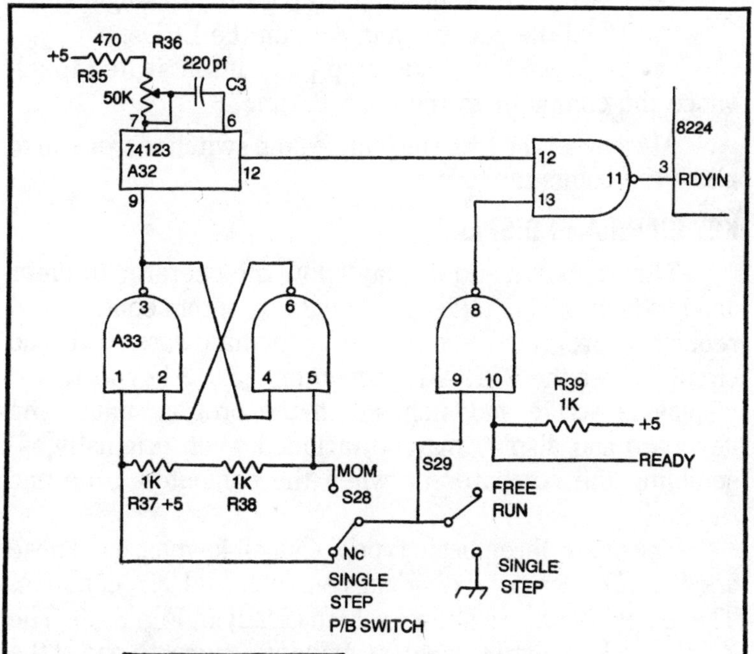

IC#	TYPE	+5	G
A32	74123	16	8
A33	7400	14	7

Fig. 3-29. Single-step circuit.

Because the operation is stopped after time T_2 during the machine cycle, it will stop on every byte for two and three byte instructions.

Figure 3-29 shows a schematic for the single-step circuit, and its connection to the microcomputer. The free/run single-step switch applies a LOW to the RDYIN (ready input) to the system. The pushbutton switch triggers the one-shot to apply a pulse to the RDYIN line. This allows the computer to execute to the next T_2 time. This pulse must be less than one machine cycle, otherwise the operation will be erratic. The adjustable resistor allows adjustment of the pulse width of the ready pulse. It should be adjusted for reliable single step operation. During single step, the address and data are read on the address and data LEDs.

To operate single step:

- Set the free run/single step switch to single step.
- Read the address and data on the LEDs.
- Depress the single step pushbutton switch to advance the computer to the next T_2 time.

Always set the free run/single step switch to free run to allow the computer to run.

KEYBOARD AND DISPLAY

The keyboard and display allow the operator to enter and read data. This takes place under program control, and requires a program to be loaded by the hardware read/load circuit. When the EPROM is programmed, the keyboard and display is active and included in the programming. The keyboard and display may be included when originally assembling the computer or when the computer is up and running.

There are three basic types of small keyboards. These are the XY matrix, individual contacts, and XY common. These keyboards are shown schematically in Fig. 3-30. The XY matrix keyboard is used by applying a signal to one of the horizontal inputs and scanning the vertical outputs. Realize that either the horizontal or vertical can be the input, and the other the output. This requires sequencing the inputs though all the horizontal inputs.

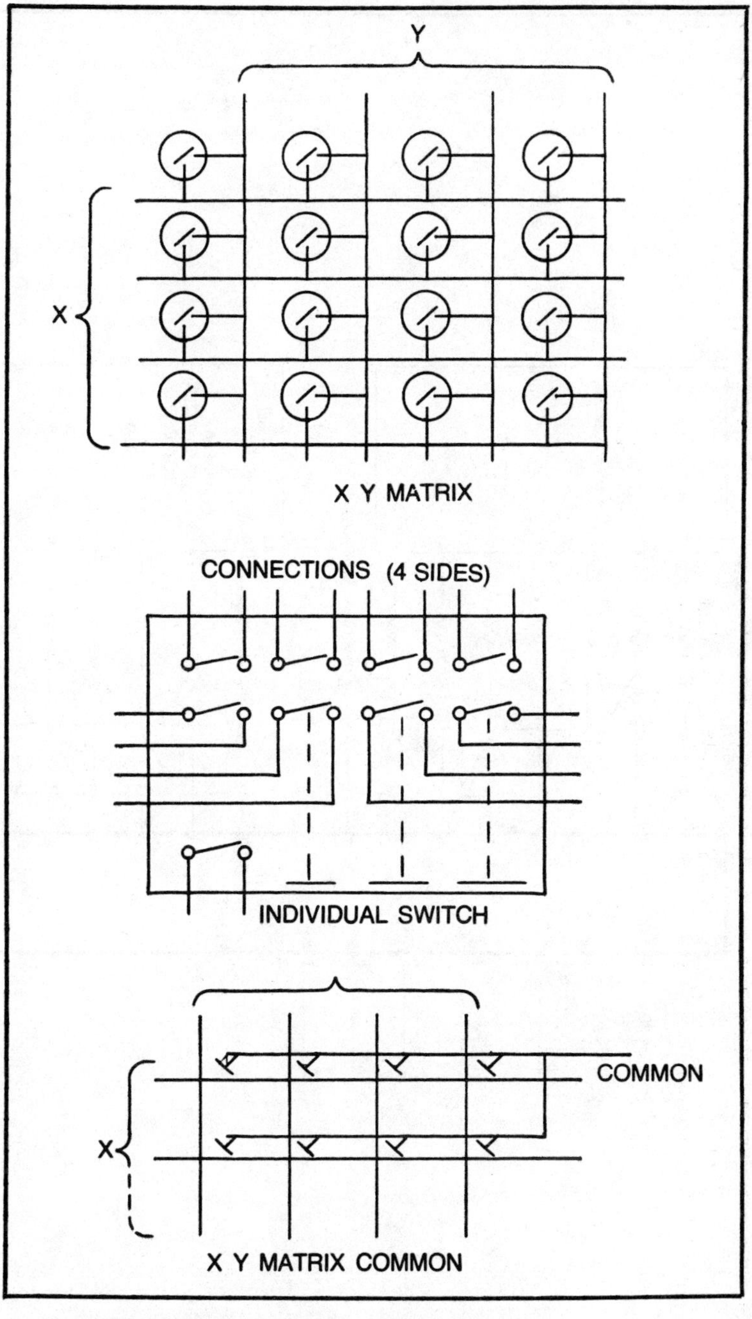

Fig. 3-30. Schematics for three basic keyboard types.

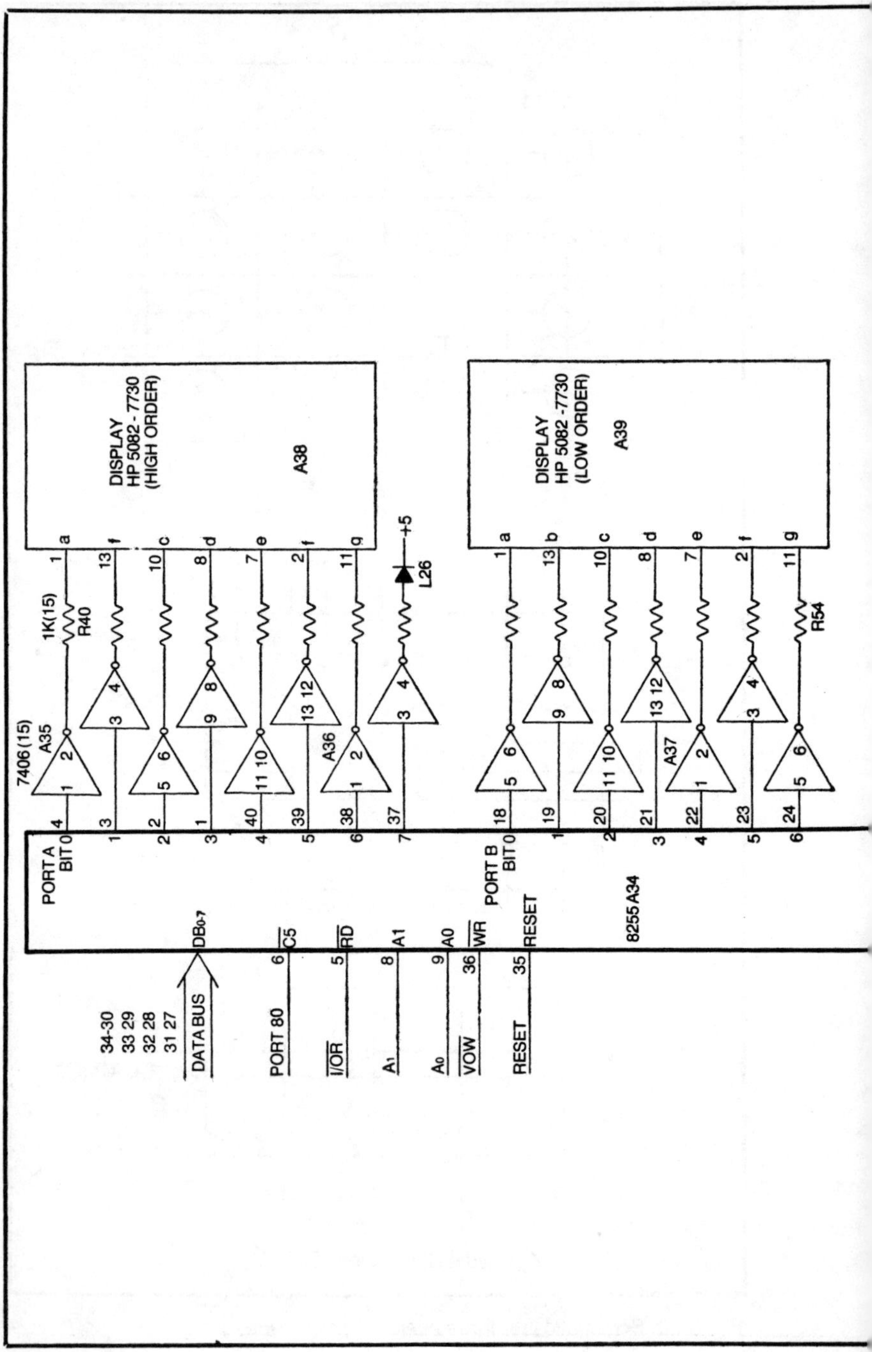
DISPLAY
HP 5082 - 7730
(HIGH ORDER)
A38
DISPLAY
HP 5082 -7730
(LOW ORDER)
A39
7406 (15)
A35
A36
A37
1K(15)
R40
R54
L26
+5
PORT A
BIT 0
PORT B
BIT 0
8255 A34
DB0-7
C5
RD
A1
A0
WR
RESET
34-30
33 29
32 28
31 27
DATA BUS
PORT 80
I/OR
A1
A0
VOW
RESET

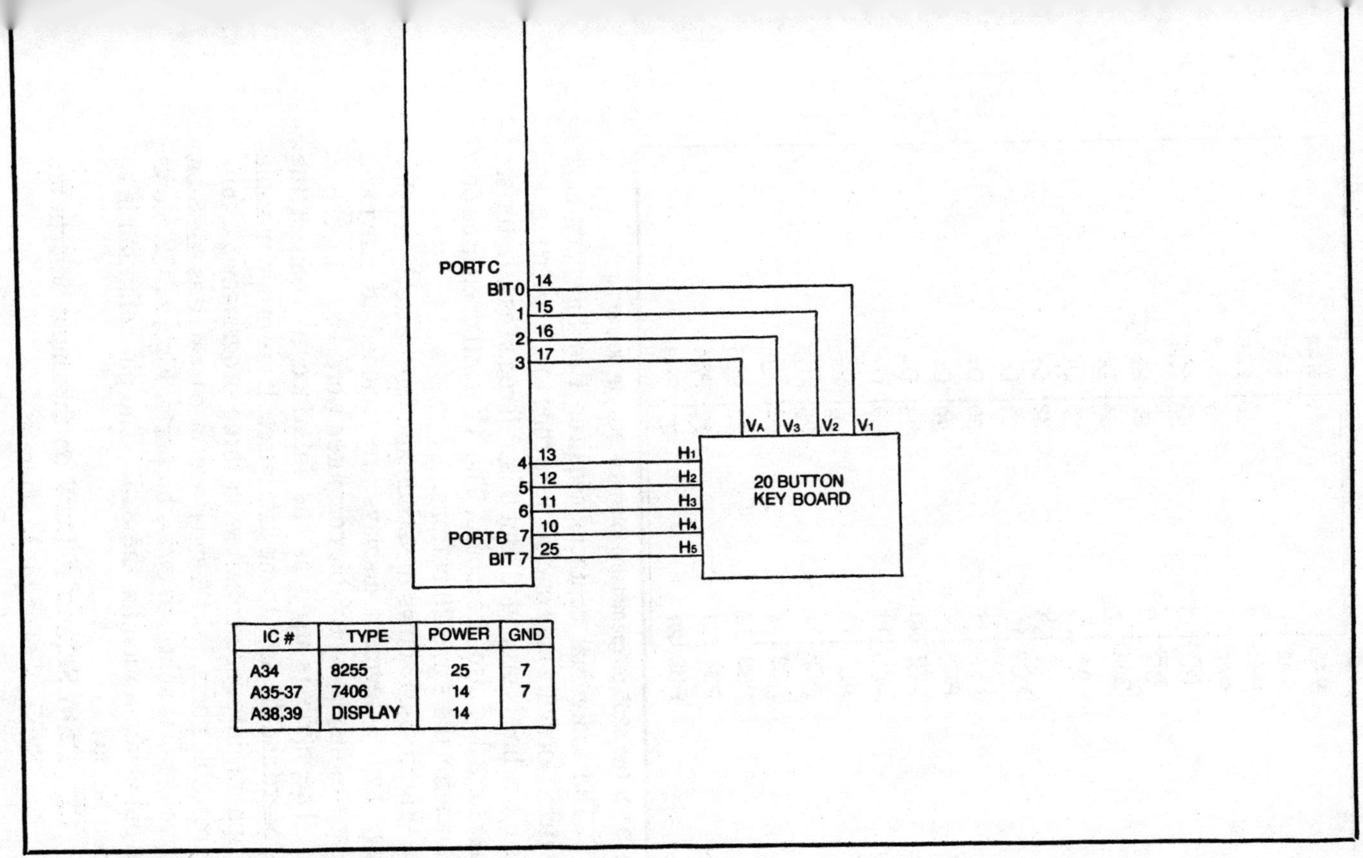

IC #	TYPE	POWER	GND
A34	8255	25	7
A35-37	7406	14	7
A38,39	DISPLAY	14	

Fig. 3-31. The keyboard and display circuitry.

Signal	Pin	Pin	Signal
PA3	1	40	PA4
PA2		39	PA5
PA1	3	38	PA6
PA0	4	37	PA7
$\overline{RD}$	5	36	$\overline{WR}$
$\overline{CS}$	6	35	RESET
GND	7	34	D_0
A1	8	33	D_1
A0	9	32	D_2
PC7	10	31	D_3
PC6	11	30	D_4
PC5	12	29	D_5
PC4	13	28	D_6
PC0	14	27	D_7
PC1	15	26	V_{cc}
PC2	16	25	PB7
PC3	17	24	PB6
PB0	18	23	PB5
PB1	19	22	PB4
PB2	20	21	PB3

Fig. 3-32. The 8255 programmable interface chip pin definition.

The individual contacts requires two lines for each switch. Normally only one of these runs to the interface, and the other line is grounded. But this still requires 20 interface lines for a 20-button keyboard. The XY matrix requires only 9 lines for the same 20 buttons.

Figure 3-31 shows the schematic for the keyboard display. Two 7-segment displays are included to provide a means to display one 8-bit computer word.

The 8255 is used as the interface to connect the keyboard and displays to the data buses. It is a programmable peripheral interface circuit with three programmable fully addressable ports. Port A and B are each treated as one 8-bit port. Port C is split into two 4-bit ports. Figure 3-32 shows the pin configuration for the 8255. The pin definition is as given below.

$\overline{CS}$ **Chip Select:** A LOW on this input selects the 8255, allowing it to operate.

$\overline{RD}$ **Read:** A LOW on this input enables the data to be read from the selected port to the data bus.

$\overline{WR}$ **Write:** A LOW on this input pin enables data to be transferred from the databus to the selected port.

A_0, A_1 **Port select 0 and 1:** These input signals control the port-selection logic. They are normally connected to the address bus, bits 0 and 1.

RESET **Chip reset:** A HIGH on this input clears the 8255 and sets all ports to the input mode.

D_7-D_0 **Data Bus:** This is the data bus connection to the chip.

PA_7-PA_0 **Port A:** Connections to the port A.

PB_7-PB_0 **Port B:** Connections for port B.

PB_7-PB_0 **Port C:** Connections for port C.

V_{cc},GND +5 volt and ground

Table 3-4 gives the program-addressing requirements for the 8255. Table 3-5 defines the control word for the various chip configurations. To use the chip, write the control word into the chip using the addressing requirements for the control word as given in Table 3-4. The desired port is read from or written to using the appropriate input or output instruction with the port number from Table 3-4.

A simple, common-anode 7-segment display is used. This type display is readily available, and is easy to drive. Its

Table 3-4. Addressing the 8255 Chip.

A_1	A_0	$\overline{RD}$	$\overline{WR}$	$\overline{CS}$	Input Operation (read)
0	0	0	1	0	Port A to data bus
0	1	0	1	0	Port B to data bus
1	0	0	1	0	Port C to data bus
					Output Operation (write)
0	0	1	0	0	Data bus to port A
0	1	1	0	0	Data bus to port B
1	0	1	0	0	Data bus to port C
1	1	1	0	0	Data bus to control

Table 3-5. Control Words for the 8255.

Port A	Port B	Port C Bits 0-3	Port C Bits 4-7	Control Word
Output	Output	Output	Output	80
Output	Output	Output	Input	88
Output	Output	Input	Output	81
Output	Output	Input	Input	89
Output	Input	Output	Output	82
Output	Input	Output	Input	8A
Output	Input	Input	Output	83
Output	Input	Input	Input	8B
Input	Output	Output	Output	90
Input	Output	Output	Input	98
Input	Output	Input	Output	91
Input	Output	Input	Input	99
Input	Input	Output	Output	92
Input	Input	Output	Input	9A
Input	Input	Input	Output	93
Input	Input	Input	Input	9B

basic requirements are the selection of the proper segments to display the desired character; they are grounded through a resistor. Figure 3-33 shows the schematic for a typical display, of the common-anode type. Figure 3-34 shows the segments and the segments required for the hex characters. The current must be limited to between 5 and 16 mA to prevent damage to the device. The higher the current, however, the brighter the display.

EPROM PROGRAMMER

The EPROM programmer is designed to program the 1708 EPROMS to provide a permanant storage for computer programs. Figure 3-35 shows the schematic for the programmer. It connects to the system through an 8255 interface chip. All of ports A and B and 4 bits of port C are used. This leaves 4 bits available for use at a later time.

The requirements to program the EPROM are:

- Raise the $\overline{CS}/\overline{WE}$ input to the EPROM to +12 volts.
- Enable the address inputs for the address to be programmed.
- Apply the data to be programmed into the address to the data inputs.

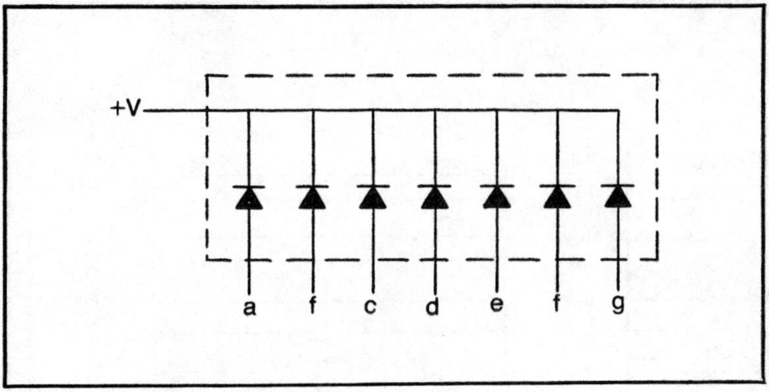

Fig. 3-33. Common-anode display schematic.

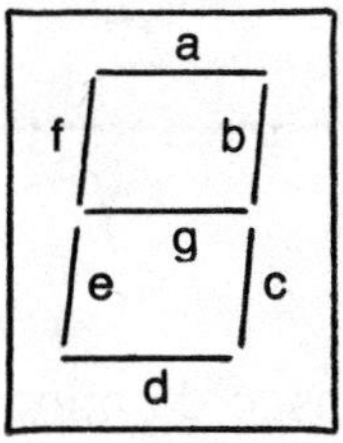

Character	Segments
0	abcdef
1	bc
2	abdeg
3	abcdg
4	bcfg
5	acdfg
6	acdefg
7	abc
8	abcdefg
9	abcfg
A	abcefg
B	cedfg
C	adef
D	bcdeg
E	adefg
F	aefg

Fig. 3-34. Segment definition.

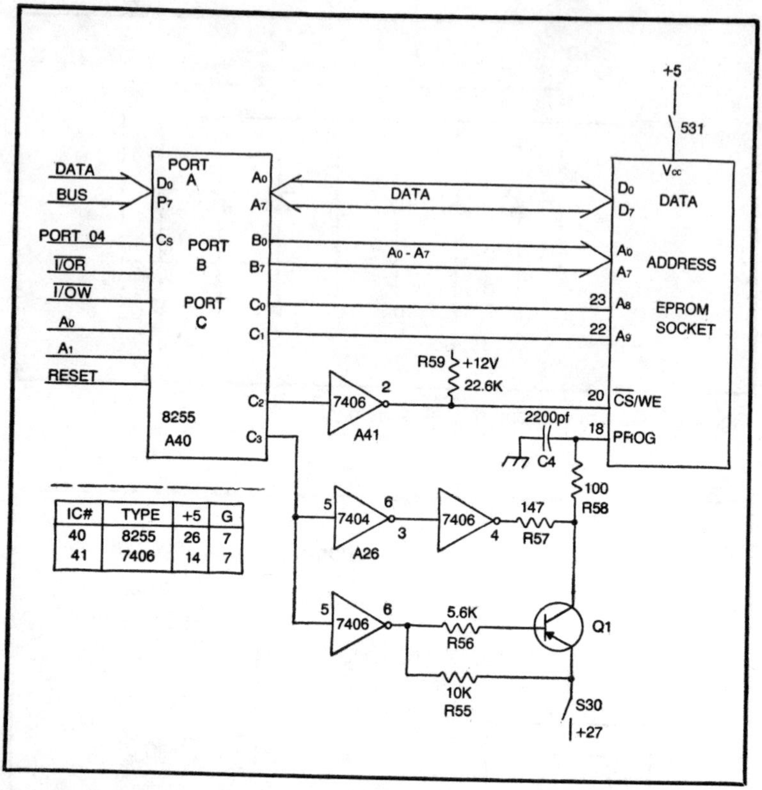

Fig. 3-35. The EPROM programmer schematic.

- Apply a 27 volt pulse of 1 msec duration to the program pin. The rise and fall time of this pulse should be about 1 μsec.
- Sequence to the next address to be programmed and repeat the above sequence.
- When all the addresses are programmed, repeat until each address has been programmed 100 times.

The program generates the program pulses, and controls the address and data lines to the chip. The 2200 pf capacitor and the 100-ohm and 147-ohm resistors generate the 1 μsec rise and fall times for the program pulse.

Use a zero insertion force socket for the EPROM to avoid bending the EPROM's with repeated insertions.

After programming the EPROM it can be read and verified by bringing the $\overline{CW}$/WE input low and setting up the address on the address inputs.

I/O PORT DECODER

To select the keyboard display port or the programmer port, you need an active LOW chip select signal. The simplest method is to use a decoder chip, such as the 8205. This is connected to the address bus as shown in Fig. 3-36, with the port numbers given alongside the outputs.

Since only two select signals are presently required, the remaining 6 remain available for future expansion. The port number assigned to the keyboard display is port 80. The port number for the programmer is 84.

OTHER INPUT/OUTPUT DEVICES

You can use other I/O devices in place of the 8255 chip. But the 8255 is convenient and easy to use. One chip provides three 8-bit ports and has its control and select logic included. The only select signal required is an active LOW select which defines the addresses of the chip. In addition,

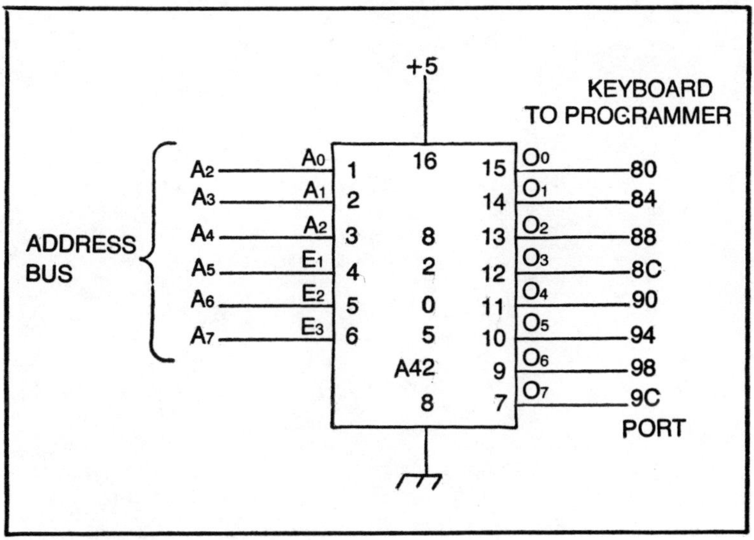

Fig. 3-36. The I/O port decoder.

the chip can be used either for input ports or output ports, or some of the ports each.

Any device that is driven by the bus must not load the bus, so its drive requirements must be low. The 74LS series and the CMOS family both have low drive requirements. Either can be used providing the signals are compatible.

Any device that drives the bus, such as an input port, must not load the bus. The 3-state families provide 3 output levels—HIGH, LOW, and high impedance. The high impedance state occurs when the chip is not enabled.

Chapter 4
Assembling The System

Assembling the system is the most time consuming and tedious part of learning about microcomputers. Certainly you can purchase a simple computer but that bypasses the hardware part of the learning. By the time the computer is constructed and checked out and running, you'll have learned much about the computer's hardware.

Use care and patience in the assembly process because it is easy to make errors. But don't worry, either. If errors are made they can be found and corrected. The result will be a computer that is useful for many applications.

This chapter starts off with construction hints, to help the builder get off on the right foot. Next comes the parts list, broken down into sections, with the totals given. All parts have numbers corresponding to the numbers on the schematics. The wire list is also broken up into sections, with correlation from one section to the next. The master layout provides the layout for the sections. Then the actual assembly is covered in general. The total schematic isn't given; it consists of Figs. 3-1, 3-28, 3-31, 3-33, and 3-34 of chapter 3.

CONSTRUCTION HINTS

Always use the correct tools for building the system. The pins on the IC sockets are on 0.1-inch centers—small cutters, pliers, and low-power soldering irons must be used. A list of the tools required is given below:

- Small dikes
- Small long-nose pliers.
- Wire strippers
- Hand drill
- Misc. drill bits
- Wooden soldering aid
- Small soldering iron
- Small solder
- Small crescent
- Screwdrivers
- Ruler

The computer is mounted on one piece of vectorboard measuring 8 inches by 16 inches. A base made of ½ inch by 2 inch wood serves to enclose the area under the board and act as a support for the vectorboard. Use a good quality vectorboard, because some crack and chip easily. When drilling the vectorboard, use a hand drill with care, and support the board.

When wiring the computer, use solid hook-up wire of 24 gauge or smaller. Use wire with good insulation, and use good wire strippers when stripping insulation. Using dikes to strip the insulation is a bad practice because it is easy to nick the wire. Once the wire is nicked, it is prone to breakage. This can cause a running computer to quit.

Strip only enough insulation from the wire to make a good connection. Wrap the wire around the pin or connection and clinch it with long nose pliers. Excess stripped and bare wire is a potential problem and must be avoided. Do not run the wire tight against pins or corners. Run the wire so that it is up against the circuit board, and is not a rats' nest.

Soldering is the most critical assembly operation. It must be done correctly, and carefully, because several failures may result from one faulty solder connection. The three most common solder failures are shorts between wires, solder shorts, and solder opens. A short between wires usually results from overheating the solder connection or burning the insulation. Solder shorts result from using too much solder, or creating solder tails. Solder opens results from cold-solder connections, or not flowing the flux from the connection.

Always use a small wattage soldering iron (about 22½ watts) with a small tip. Be careful what the soldering element touches. It is hot and will burn insulation. Use good quality small solder. Have a soldering holder handy and use it. If necessary, mount a piece of copper tubing inside the holder to hold the tip and dissipate some of the heat. Keep a damp rag or sponge handy to clean the tip on.

The soldering-iron tip must always be well tinned. That is, it must be coated with a layer of molten solder. If the tip will not tin properly, wipe it on the rag, and melt some solder on it. Keep wiping it and applying solder until the tip is well tinned. If the tip turns a dark color, cool it down by wiping it on the rag. If the iron is too hot it will not tin properly and will not make good solder connections. Also, it can burn the flux preventing it from flowing out of the connection.

A good solder connection takes only a couple seconds to make, while a bad one takes much longer. One thing that helps is to tin the wire before wrapping it around the pin. This reduces the amount of time the iron must be on the connection, and improves the connection. If the solder does not wick, or flow into the connection, the iron may be too hot, or the connection may be dirty. Excess solder can cause solder shorts and globules, which must be removed.

Inspect each solder connection with a good magnifying glass under a good light. Look for good connections, with a shiny appearance. If a dark line appears between the wire and the pin, reflow the solder. Move the wire and make sure the connection is secure. Look for shorts, excess solder, burned insulation, and solder tails.

LEDs are mounted into the circuit board either by using their mounting rings or by glue. The mounting rings are the best, and if used properly they secure the LED. Drill holes the proper size and insert the inner part of the ring with the fingers. Push the LED into the fingers, spreading them slightly, so that the top of the LED projects slightly above the board. The outer ring slips over the LED leads and

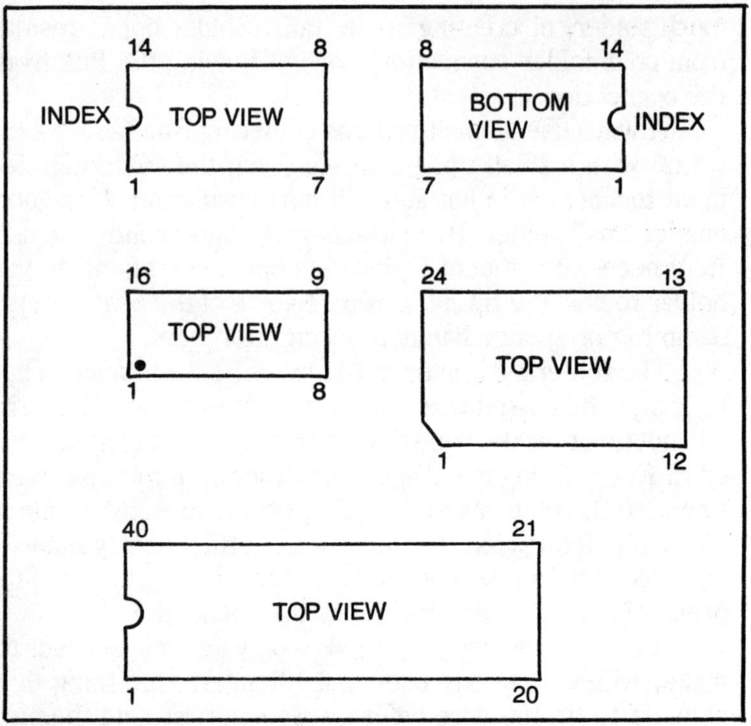

Fig. 4-1. IC pin numbering and index identification.

clamps the fingers on the other piece. Use two nut drivers to push the ring up against the circuit board while holding the top piece.

When soldering to the LED leads, use small pliers as a heat sink between the solder connection and the body of the LED. Apply the soldering iron only long enough to make the connection. It is better to reflow the solder than leave the iron on for more than a couple seconds. The excess heat generated by the iron may damage the LED, yet it might not go bad until later.

When mounting the IC sockets, remember that the pins are numbered (from the top) counterclockwise from the index mark. The index mark can be any mark which makes one corner different from any others. From the bottom, or wiring side, the pins are numbered clockwise. This is illustrated in Fig. 4-1.

Table 4-1. General Parts List.

Size of quan	Description
1—17″ × 8½″	Vectorboard, .042″ holes on 0.1″ grid
100	Vector T42-1 terminals
51 inches	¾ × 2 inch wood for edging under vector board
As Req'd	Wire: Recommend #30 such as GC 41-632
25	Small screws to attach wood to vectorboard

IC sockets should be glued to the board to aid in soldering the first few wires. A small amount of glue at each end of the socket will suffice.

When mounting switches, position the switch and run the mounting nut snug, but not overly tight. It should be tight enough to prevent the switch from turning, but not enough to crack the board. Remember that most vectorboard is somewhat brittle.

PARTS LIST

Tables 4-1 through 4-5 show the parts needed to build the system. Table 4-1 is the composite list and includes the miscellaneous parts. Tables 4-2 through 4-5 give the parts

Table 4-2. Microcomputer Section Parts List.

ID Number	Quan	Part
A1	1	8080A
A2	1	8224
A3	1	8228
A4,5	2	8212
A6	1	8205 (3205)
A7-9	3	2708 or equiv
A10-17	8	2102 or equiv
R1	1	1K
R2	1	47K
R3		Not used
R4	1	4.7 K
C1	1	luf
	1	18 MHZ computer crystal
	1	NO Pushbutton (Reset switch)
	5	24 pin sockets
	1	40 pin sockets
	1	28 pin sockets
	10	16 pin sockets

Tabel 4-3. Hardware Read and Load Parts List.

ID Number	Quan	Part
A18-23,27	7	7093
A24	1	7408
A25	1	7402
A26	1	7404
A28-31	4	74LS04
A32	1	74123
A33	1	7400
R11-34	24	1K (470 may be used for more brightness)
R37-39	3	1K
R35	1	470
R36	1	50K trimpot
C3	1	220 pf
R5-7,9	4	4.7K
R8	1	3.9 K
R10	1	10K
C2	1	.001
L1-25	25	General purpose red LED's
1-25	25	SPST Miniature toggle switches
S26,29	2	SPDT Miniature toggle switches
S27	1	NO Pushbutton switch
S28	1	SPDT Pushbutton
	1	16 Pin sockets
	15	14 pin sockets

required for specific sections of the computer. The individual part numbers are listed and these refer to the parts in the schematics.

Always select a good-quality component instead of the cheapest available. Good-quality components will work the way they should, while some of the cut rate components are marginal. It will pay in the long run. IC sockets are used throughout because soldering directly to the IC chips can damage them causing possible problems at a later date. Another potential problem arises with sockets and IC pins that are not gold. Printed circuit board sockets can be used if the pins are long enough to allow soldering to when they are inserted through the board. PC sockets with short pins shouldn't be used. Wire wrap sockets work well—cut the excess pin length off after completing soldering.

The vector push-in solder terminals are used to run the address, control, and data buses. They are also used for the

Table 4-4. Keyboard and Display Parts List.

ID Number	Quan	Part
A34	1	8255
A35-37	3	7406
A38,39	2	HP 5082-7730 or equiv 7 segment common anode display.
R40-54	15	1K (470 may be used)
L26	1	General purpose red LED
	1	20 button keyboard
	1	40 Pin socket
	5	14 pin sockets

address options. This makes it easier to wire, and aids in expanding and troubleshooting the system.

LAYOUT

Figure 4-2 shows the general layout. The computer resides in the center, the hardware read/load is on the right, and the keyboard/display and the programmer is on the left. Figures 4-3 through 4-6 show the layouts for the various sections. Remember that this is a suggested layout only and need not be followed. The vector terminals are shown along with their numbering.

Any layout can be used, but it should be logical and straightforward. It should provide room for expansion, and

Table 4-5. EPROM Programmer Parts List

ID Number	Quan	Part
A40	1	8255
A41	1	7406
A42	1	8205
R55	1	10K
R56	1	5.6K
R57	1	147 Ohms
R58	1	100 Ohms
R59	1	22.6K
C4	1	2200 pf
Q1	1	General purpose PNP Plastic
SW30,31	2	SPST Miniature toggle switches
	1	14 Pin Socket
	1	16 Pin socket
	1	40 Pin socket
	1	24 Pin socket (Zero insertion force)

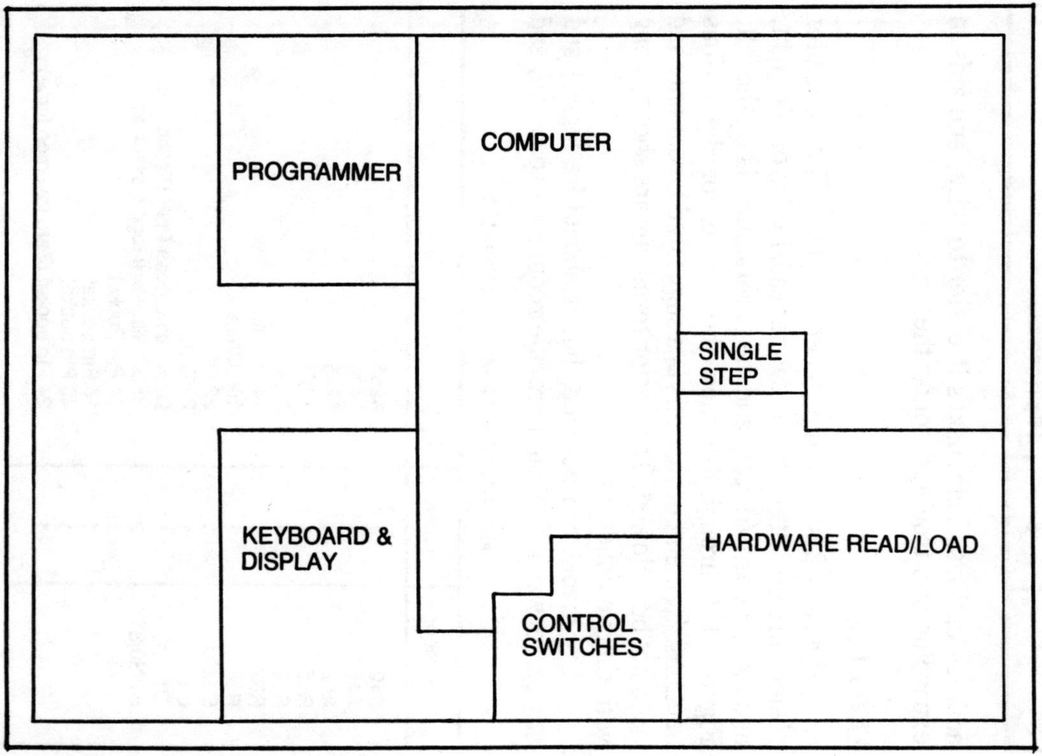

Fig. 4-2. General overall layout.

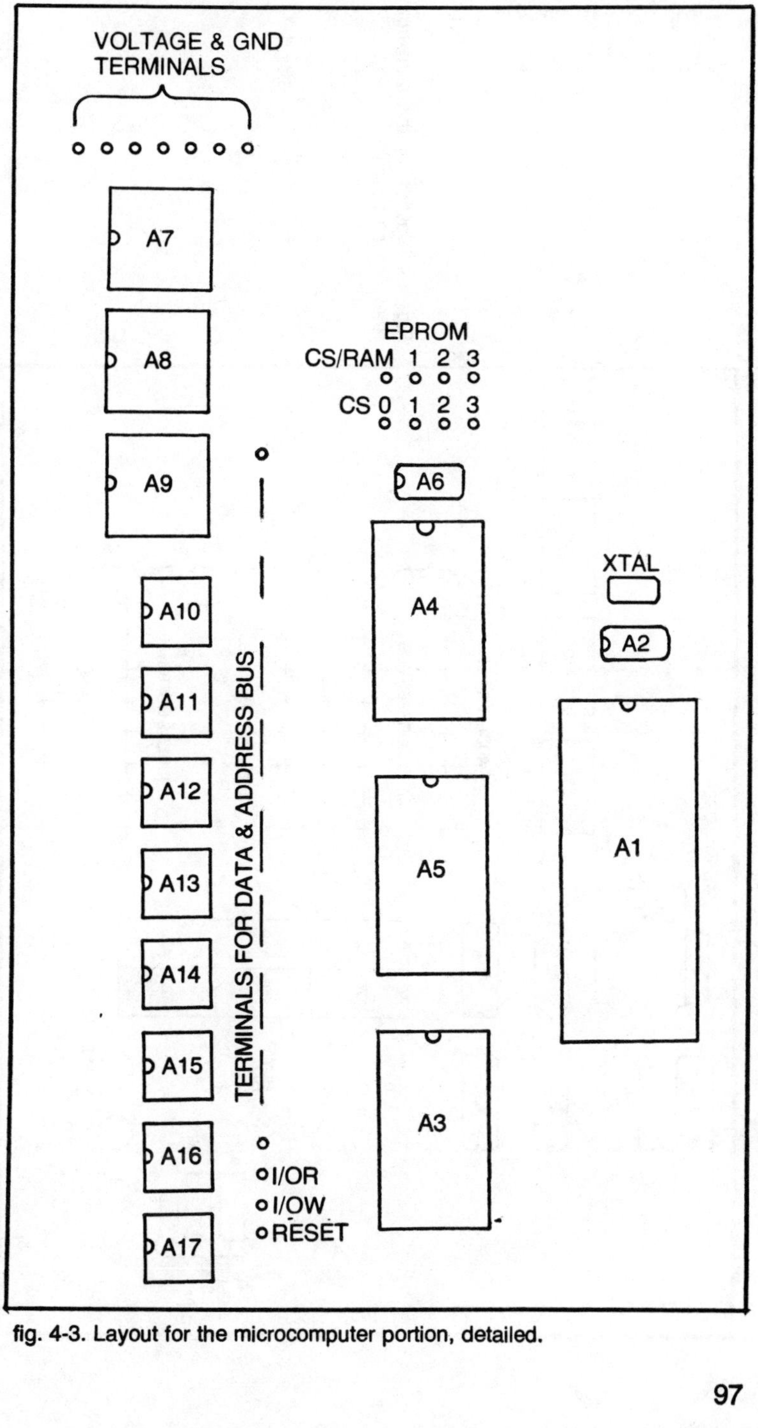

fig. 4-3. Layout for the microcomputer portion, detailed.

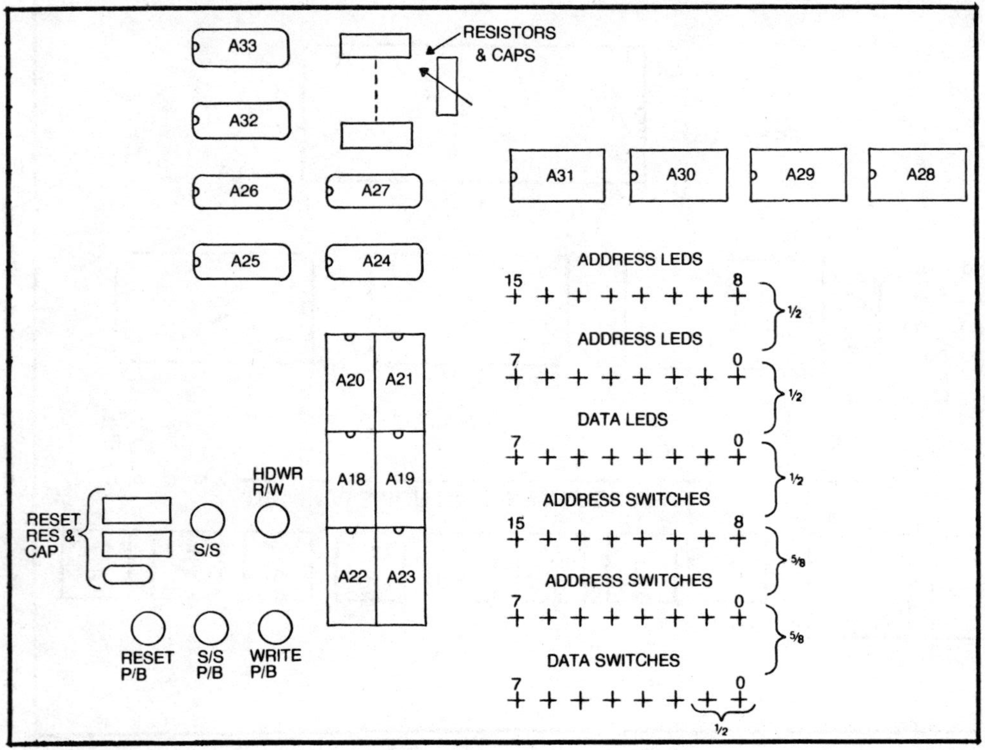

Fig. 4-4. Layout for the hardware read and load circuitry.

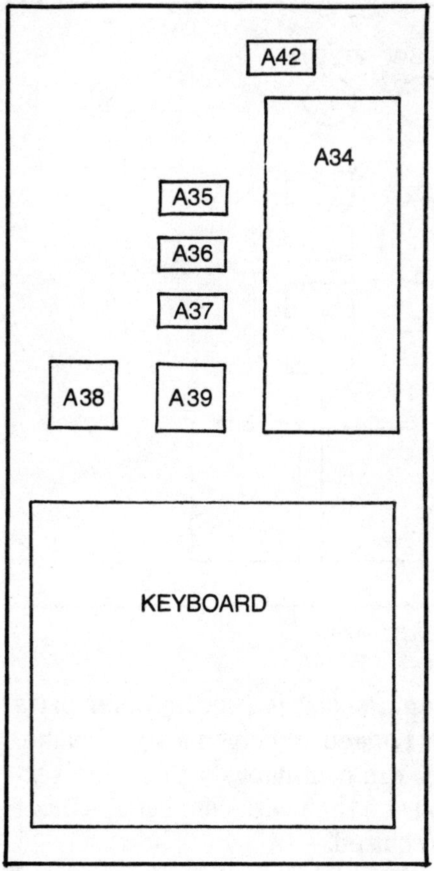

Fig. 4-5. Layout for the keyboard and display.

the operator input devices should be on the lower edge of the board.

Make up a full-scale layout, using the actual parts for sizing. Leave enough room between the sockets for wiring. Mark the hole sizes for the various components requiring mounting. If larger switches are used, clearance must be provided. Leave enough room around the edge for the sides (the ½ by 2-inch pieces of wood).

WIRE LIST

The wire lists shown in Tables 4-6 through 4-9 are broken up into sections. The actual system wiring is done from these lists, one line at a time. Signal names are given

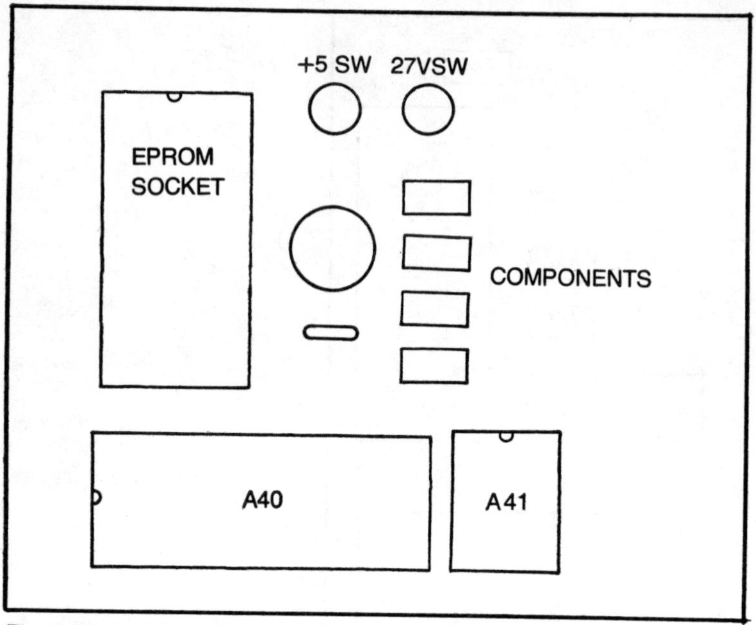

Fig. 4-6. Layout for the EPROM programmer.

when they exist, and when a signal is used in other parts (shown on other lists) it is flagged and given a signal name. These wires can be either run continuously to all the sections, or wired one section at a time with connections made to the other sections as required.

The power and ground run through all the sections. If separate 5-volt power supplies are used for the various sections, run the power line for that section to the corresponding terminal for 5 volts. Run the grounds from the input ground terminals to each section. Do not run the ground in one continuous wire. This can cause excessive voltage drop on the ground line because of the current carried by the ground. Also, do not connect one ground line to the input ground in more than one point; this creates ground loops. Each ground coming off the input ground should be open ended.

Some of the signals are named almost the same, such as AB_0 and A_0, but these are different signals and must be wired as such.

Table 4-6. Microcomputer Section Wire List.

Interface Signal	A1	A2	A3					
	10		15					
	9		17					
	8		12					
	7		10					
	3		6					
	4		19					
	5		21					
	6		8					
	24,23	4						
	19	5						
Reset	12	1						
	15	10						
	22	11						
		7	1					
		14		XTAL 1				
		15		XTAL 2				
		2		R2 L	RI L	CI +		
				R1 H	S 27 1			

Table 4-6. Microcomputer Section Wire List. (Continued from page 101.)

Interface Signal	A1	A2	A3	A4	A5	A6	A7	A8
	25			3				
	26			5				
	27			7				
	29			9				
	30			16				
	31			18				
	32			20				
	33			22				
	34				3			
	35				5			
	1				7			
	40				9			
	37				16			
	38				18			
	39				20			
	36				22			
	17		4					
$\overline{WR}$	18		3					

Table 4-6. Microcomputer Section Wire List. (Continued from page 102.)

Interface Signal	A10	A11	A12	A13	A14	A15	A16	A17
A_0	8	8	8	8	8	8	8	8
A_1	4	4	4	4	4	4	4	4
A_2	5	5	5	5	5	5	5	5
A_3	6	6	6	6	6	6	6	6
A_4	7	7	7	7	7	7	7	7
A_5	2	2	2	2	2	2	2	2
A_6	1	1	1	1	1	1	1	1
A_7	16	16	16	16	16	16	16	16
A_8	15	15	15	15	15	15	15	15
A_9	14	14	14	14	14	14	14	14
D_0	11,12							
D_1		11,12						
D_2			11,12					
D_3				11,12				
D_4					11,12			
D_5						11,12		
D_6							11,12	
D_7								11,12
$\overline{WR}$	3	3	3	3	3	3	3	3

Table 4-6. Microcomputer Section Wire List. (Continued from page 103.)

Interface Signal	A4	A5	A6	A7	A8	A9		
A_0	4			8	8	8		
A_1	6			7	7	7		
A_2	8			6	6	6		
A_3	10			5	5	5		
A_4	15			4	4	4		
A_5	17			3	3	3		
A_6	19			2	2	2		
A_7	21			1	1	1		
A_8		4		23	23	23		
A_9		6		22	22	22		
A_{10}		8	1					
A_{11}		10	2					
A_{12}		15	3					
A_{13}		17	4					
A_{14}		19	5					
A_{15}		21						
	11 13 14	11 13	6					
		14					R4 L	

Table 4-6. Microcomputer Section Wire List. (Continued from page 104.)

Interface Signal	A1	A2	A3	A4,A5	A6	A7,8,9	A10-17	
D_0			13					
D_1			16					
D_2			11					
D_3			9					
D_4			5					
D_5			18					
D_6			20					
D_7			7					
+ 5 Volts	20	16	28	24,	16	24	10	R2 H R2 H
+ 12 Volts	28	9				19		
− 5 Volts	11					21		
Ground	2	8	14,22	12,1,2	8	2	9	C1 - S27 2
HLDA	21		2					
HOLD	13							
RDYIN		3						
$\overline{\text{I/O R}}$			25					
$\overline{\text{I/O W}}$			27					

Table 4-7. Hardware Read and Load Wire List.

Interface Signal	A18	A19	A20	A21	A28	A29	A30	A27	A25
A_0	3				1				
A_1	6				3				
A_2	8				5				
A_3	11				9				
A_4		3			11				
A_5		6			13				
A_6		8				1			
A_7		11				3			
A_8			3			5			
A_9			6			9			
A_{10}			8			11			
A_{11}			11			13			
A_{12}				3			1		
A_{13}				6			3		
A_{14}				8			5		
A_{15}	1,4,10 14	1,4,10 14	1,4,10 14	11			9		
				1,4,10 14				1	1
Ground	7	7	7	7	7	7	7	7	7

Table 4-7. Hardware Read and Load Wire List. (Continued from page 106.)

Interface Signal	A18	A19	A20	A21	A22	A23			
	2						S1 NO		
	5						S2 NO		
	9						S3 NO		
	12						S4 NO		
		2					S5 NO		
		5					S6 NO		
		9					S7 NO		
		12					S8 NO		
			2				S9 NO		
			5				S10 NO		
			9				S11 NO		
			12				S12 NO		
				2			S13 NO		
				5			S14 NO		
				9			S15 NO		
				12			S16 NO		
+5 Volts	14	14	14	14	14	14			

Table 4-7. Hardware Read and Load Wire List. (Continued from page 107.)

Interface Signal	A22	A23	A26				A30	A31
D_0	3						11	
D_1	6						13	
D_2	8							1
D_3	11							3
D_4		3						5
D_5		6						9
D_6		8						11
D_7		11						13
	1,4,10 14	1,4,10 14	2					
	2			S17 NO				
	5			S18 NO				
	9			S19 NO				
	12			S20 NO				
		2		S21 NO				
		5		S22 NO				
		9		S23 NO				
		12		S24 NO				
Ground	7	7	7	S1 through	S26 C	S27 1	7	7

Table 4-7. Hardware Read and Load Wire List. (Continued from page 108.)

Interface Signal	A26	A27	A32			A31	A 24	
	3			R5 L	S26 1			
	5			R6 L	S26 2			
			1	R7 L	S27 2			
			15	R8 L	C2 +			
			14	C2 -				
		2	4					
				L1 -				
	8			L1 +	R10 L			
HOLD				S25 C	R9 L			
+5 Volts		14	16			14		
Ground			8				7	
$\overline{\text{R/W}}$		3						

Table 4-7. Hardware Read and Load Wire List. (Continued from page 109.)

Interface Signal	R28	R29	R30						
	2			L2 -					
	4			L3 -					
	6			L4 -					
	8			L5 -					
	10			L6 -					
	12			L7 -					
		2		L8 -					
		4		L9 -					
		6		L10 -					
		8		L11 -					
		10		L12 -					
		12		L13 -					
			2	L14 -					
			4	L15 -					
			6	L16 -					
			8	L17 -					
			10	L18 -					
			12	L19 -					

Table 4-7. Hardware Read and Load Wire List. (Continued from page 110.)

Interface Signal	A31								
	2	L20 -							
	4	L21 -							
	6	L22 -							
	8	L23 -							
	10	L24 -							
	12	L25 -							
		L2 +	R11 L						
		L3 +	R 12 L						
		L4 +	R 13 L						
		L5 +	R 14 L						
		L6 +	R 15 L						
		L7 +	R 16 L						
		L8 +	R 17 L						
		L9 +	R 18 L						
		L10 +	R 19 L						
		L11 +	R 20 L						
		L12 +	R 21 L						
		L13 +	R 22 L						

Table 4-7. Hardware Read and Load Wire List. (Continued from page 111.)

Interface signal			A24	A25	A26	A28	A29	A30	
	L14 +	R23 L							
	L15 +	R24 L							
	L16 +	R25 L							
	L17 +	R26 L							
	L18 +	R27 L							
	L19 +	R28 L							
	L20 +	R29 L							
	L21 +	R30 L							
	L22 +	R31 L							
	L23 +	R32 L							
	L24 +	R33 L							
	L25 +	R34 L							
+5 Volts	R 5 through	R34 H	14	14	14	14	14	14	
			1		4				
HLDA			2,4		9				
			5		6				
			3	3					
			6	2	1				

Table 4-8. Keyboard and Display Wire List.

Interface Signal	A32	A33						
	9	3,4						
		2,6						
		1	R37 L	S28 NC				
		5	R38 L	S28 MOM				
		9	S28 C	S29 C				
		10	R39 L					
		8,13						
	12	12						
RDYIN		11						
	7		R36	C3 +				
	6		C3 -					
	R36 H		R36 H	R35 L				
+5 Volts		14	R35 H	R37 H	R38 H	R39 H		
Ground		7	S29 NO					

Table 4-8. Keyboard and Display Wire List. **(Continued from page 113.)**

Interface Signal	A34	A35	A36	A37	A38	A39		
D_0	34							
D_1	33							
D_2	32							
D_3	31							
D_4	30							
D_5	29							
D_7	28							
A_0	27							
A_1	9							
$\overline{I/O\ R}$	8							
$\overline{I/O\ W}$	5							
Reset	36							
	35							
	4	1						
	3	3						
	2	5						
	1	9						
	40	11						
Port 80	6							

Table 4-8. Keyboard and Display Wire List. (Continued from page 114.)

Interface Signal	A34	A35	A36	A37	A38	A39	Key board	
	39	13						
	38		1					
	37		3					
	18		5					
	19		9					
	20		11					
	21		13					
	22			1				
	23			3				
	24			5				
	14						V1	
	15						V2	
	16						V3	
	17						V4	
	13						H1	
	12						H2	
	11						H3	
	10						H4	

Table 4-8. Keyboard and Display Wire List. (Continued from page 115.)

Interface Signal	A34	A35	A36	A37	A38	A39	Key board	
	25						H5	
		2						R40 L
		4						R41 L
		6						R42 L
		8						R43 L
		10						R44 L
		12						R45 L
			2					R46 L
			4					R47 L
			6					R48 L
			8					R49 L
			10					R50 L
			12					R51 L
				2				R52 L
				4				R53 L
				6				R54 L
+ 5 Volts	26	14	14	14	14	14		L26 +
Ground	7	7	7	7				

Table 4-8. Keyboard and Display Wire List. (Continued from page 116.)

Interface Signal	Resistor	A38	A39					
	R40 H	1						
	R41 H	13						
	R42 H	10						
	R43 H	8						
	R44 H	7						
	R45 H	2						
	R46 H	11						
	R47 H			L26 -				
	R48 H		1					
	R49 H		13					
	R50 H		10					
	R51 H		8					
	R52 H		7					
	R53 H		2					
	R54 H		11					

Table 4-9. EPROM Programmer Wire List.

Interface Signal	A40	A41	A42	EPROM Socket				
		6						
					R56 L	R55 L		
					R56 H	Q1 B		
+5 Volts	26	14	16		R55 H	Q1 E	S30 C	
+12 Volts					S31 NO			
−5 Volts				19	R59 H			
+27 Volts				21				
					S30 NO			
Ground	7	7	8	12	C4 -			
	6			24	S31 C			
Port 80			14					
			15					
D_0	34							
D_1	33							
D_2	32							
D_3	31							
D_4	30							
D_5	29							
D_6	28							
D_7	27							

Table 4-9. EPROM Programmer Wire List. (Continued from page 118.)

Interface Signal	A40	A41	A26	A42	EPROM Socket			
A_0	9							
A_1	8							
A_2				1				
A_3				2				
A_4				3				
A_5				4				
A_6				5				
A_7				6				
$\overline{I/O\ R}$	5							
$\overline{I/O\ W}$	36							
Reset	35							
	1				13			
	2				11			
	3				10			
	4				9			
	40				14			
	39				15			
	38				16			

Table 4-9. EPROM Programmer Wire List. (Continued from page 119.)

Interface Signal	A40	A41	A26	A42	EPROM Socket			
	37				17			
	25				1			
	24				2			
	23				3			
	22				4			
	21				5			
	20				6			
	19				7			
	18				8			
	17	5	5					
	16	1						
	15				22			
	14				23			
		3	6					
		2			20	R59 L		
		4				R57 L		
						R57 H	R58 L	Q1 C
					18	R58 H	C4 +	

ASSEMBLY

The first step in the assembly is to drill the holes in the vectorboard. Cover the areas to be drilled with masking tape and mark the center of the holes. Drill the holes with a hand drill of the correct size. The hole's center should align with one of the holes in the vectorboard. Drill carefully and secure the board. Do not force the drill because the board may be chipped or broken.

Next, insert the IC sockets and glue them down. The IC socket pins will fit through the holes in the vectorboard, if the type specified is used. Insert the vector terminals from the bottom side for all except the power terminals. Select one section and start wiring. Mounting the external components (with vector terminals) as required.

First wire the power and ground for the individual sections, then do remaining wiring. When ready to wire the hardware read and load section, mount the switches and LEDs. Run all of the common connections first, then mount the resistors on one lead of the LED, with the other end to a vector socket.

When a section is completed, run an ohm-meter check on it. Measure the continuity to every connection along the wire run, and measure for shorts to adjacent pins. ICs should be installed temporarily to allow measuring the continuity to the actual IC pins. It is possible that the socket is bad, especially if a pin is loose. This will help to find those problems.

Mark all the power and ground input connections with a piece of tape or sticker, with the voltage written on it. It is also convenient to mark pin one of each socket from the bottom. This aids in finding the correct pin. Make sure the pins are counted correctly when wiring. There is nothing more frustrating than finding that a socket is wired backwards. So check it often, and do it right the first time.

Chapter 5
Getting The System Running

Now that the hours of assembly work are over, it is time to power up the system. The temptation to plug in the ICs, attach the power supply, and turn on the system must be resisted. Such haste can do a lot of damage to the pride and joy, and the chances are it will not work correctly. It is better to spend a little time checking out the system and powering it up in a logical manner. This will allow the problems to be corrected as they are found, and each section will be checked out before the next section is powered. If this is not done, the system may just sit there and do nothing, and it will be difficult to separate the problems. After spending hours wiring the system, another hour spent in powering up and checking out the sections is well worth it.

COMMON PROBLEMS

There are certain types of problems that might be encountered. The problem that can really burn up chips is wiring errors. Wires going to the wrong place are usually caused by rushing the soldering job. Sometimes the system will appear to almost work with these problems (such as incorrect bus connections). Check the wiring, especially the power and ground wiring, to make sure it is correct. Place one lead of an ohm meter on the ground input, and follow the ground around the system by measuring to each place it is used in the circuit. Also measure to adjacent pins to look for shorts. Do the same for all the power leads.

Another common problem is loose solder connections. These may show up as opens or intermittents, and may come and go as some wires are moved. These are caused by poor soldering technique and usually only require reflowing the solder. When one is found, isolate it by looking at the connections and moving the wires. The loose solder will move at the connection. Along with loose solder connections comes broken wires. These usually break at the connection, and may not be apparent except when the wire is moved. Broken wires are usually caused by wires nicked when stripping off the insulation.

Another common problem is the solder short. These are found where the solder flows between two pins. This is usually caused by using too much solder. Another type of short comes from bare or burned wire. This is caused by stripping too much insulation from the wire, applying excessive heat at the connection, or not being careful when soldering. Another type short is caused by bending the pins on the sockets.

A problem that is not as common, but still may appear, is defective socket pins. When the chips are plugged in, some types of pins may roll over and not make contact reliably. This is characterized by continuity to the socked pin but not to the IC pin and by the socket pin being loose in the socket after the IC is plugged in. This is caused by using a poor-quality IC socket.

A common problem that may give weird indications occurs when one or more of the power voltages is low. If the +5 volts is down to +4½ volts, or even up to +5½ volts, problems may appear. Usually, as long as the chip voltage is maintained within + 10%, the chip will not be damaged, but it may not operate correctly. Sometimes the power supply voltage may go down after the system is on for a while and the regulator has had a chance to heat up. Most regulators and semiconductors change characteristics when they are heated, so keep an eye on the voltages, and make sure the semiconductors do not heat up excessively.

SYSTEM CHECKOUT

Now let us start the checkout. The first step is to make sure all the wires are installed and go to the correct places. Give the wiring another inspection, looking for broken wires, bad solder joints, and shorts. Using an ohm meter, run continuity checks on the power and ground lines, again looking for opens and shorts to adjacent pins. When any problem is found, it must be cleared before proceeding.

Connect and apply the power-supply voltages, one at a time, with no chips installed. Measure at the socket pins, using a short piece of stripped wire inserted into the socket. Apply the ground first, then the voltages one at a time. Check for power supply heating, which indicates a short. Measure the voltages at the places where they are supposed to go. Check the socket pins and the resistor terminations where the voltages are routed.

Next, put in the chips for the hardware read/load circuit. With the hardware read/load switch off and the address and data switches off, turn on the +5 volts. All LEDs should come on. Set all the address and data switches on, and set the read/load switch to load. All the LEDs should be on. Operate the address and data switches, one at a time, observing that only the one LED goes off corresponding to the switch operated. Measure the voltage at the address and data bus terminal pins. When the LED is on, the voltage should be high. When the LED is off, the voltage should be low.

Repeat this routine for the read position of the read/load switch. It should operate the same except that the data switches are disabled. Measure the RW signal, it should be HIGH.

Next, insert the bottom RAM chip—the chip for D_7. Turn on all the power and read address 0000. Some of the data for bit 7 may be HIGH and some LOW. Set all address switches off and data switch 7 off. Place the read/load switch in the load position, and depress the write switch. Then place the read/load switch to read. Bit 7 should be off.

If problems arise here, it may be necessary to ground the select terminal for the RAM. If this is the case, install the

8205 address decoder and connect a jumper between output 1 and the RAM select terminals.

When the above RAM is checked out, insert the remaining RAM chips. Check these out in the same manner, loading each bit and reading it for both high and low. You don't need to write each memory location, but exercise each address line and each data line. This checks out the memory read and load circuitry as well as the RAM memory.

Turn the power off and insert the 8212s. These are the address bus drivers, and allow the address bus to drive several loads. Set the hardware read/load switch off and all the data and address switches to the open condition. All the LEDs should come on when power is applied. Ground the address pins on the 8080 chip, one at a time. The corresponding address LED should go off. Repeat this for all the address lines, making sure only the corresponding LED goes out.

Install the 8224 chip and turn on the power. Look at ϕ_2 TTL (pin 6 of the 8224) with a scope. The basic ϕ_2 waveshape should appear here. The main indication to look for is that the oscillator is working. Detailed examination of these pulses requires a good, high-frequency scope. Look for a LOW at pin 12 of the 8080 with a voltmeter. Depress the reset switch, this voltage should go HIGH.

If a scope is not available to observe the ϕ_2, a simple double LED monitor may be used. Such a circuit is shown in Fig. 5-1. This circuit indicates a HIGH level, a LOW signal, and a pulse train. The HIGH is indicated by the HIGH LED, and the LOW is indicated by the LOW LED. A pulse train is indicated by both LEDs on. This monitor can be used to indicate pulse trains, but it has difficulty indicating a single pulse.

Remember to turn off the power when removing or installing chips. Also keep an eye on the power for overheating, and measure the voltage levels often.

PUTTING IN THE MICRO

Now it is time to install the 8080 and the 8228 and see if the computer will run. Remove all the RAM chips, install the 8080 and the 8228, and turn on the power. The hardware

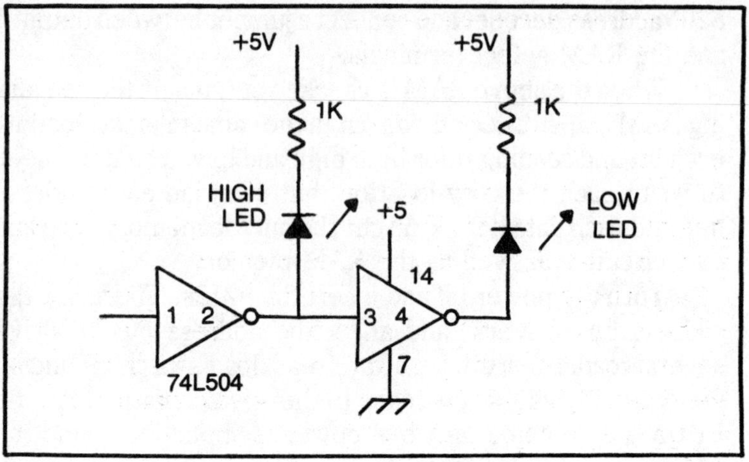

Fig. 5-1 Simple LED monitor for digital pulses or levels.

read/load switch should be off. The hold LED should be off. Depress the reset switch, all the address and data LEDs should be on as long as the reset switch is depressed. When it is released the address LEDs should flash. The high order LEDs will sequence on and off as the address is counting up. This indicates that the computer is running.

Insert all the RAM chips and turn on the system. Place the hardware read/load switch in the load position and load the following short program.

Address	Load in	Mnemonic
0000	00	NOP
0001	00	NOP
0002	00	NOP
0003	C3	JMP 0000
0004	00	
0005	00	

This program loops in the first 5 memory addresses. Place the hardware read/load switch off and depress the reset switch. The first 5 addresses LEDs and the 0, 1, 6, and 7 data LEDs should be on, but not at full brightness. This indicates that the computer is executing the above program.

Load in some short delay programs, and some loop programs, and play with the computer for a while. It is a major milestone that the computer is running, even if there is no indication that the computer can give, except the address and data LEDs.

It is time to review how the computer is loaded. The address and data switches load and read the buses and display the results in binary format. The addresses and instructions are given in hexadecimal format. Hex format simply means grouping 4 binary bits and taking their HEX equivalent. Table 5-1 gives the binary to hex conversation. To set up address 0005, place address switches 0 and 3 on, with the rest off. In the read or load position, these lights should be on. To load address 0123, the address switches 0, 1, 5, and 8 are on, with the remaining off. The address switches are broken up into 4 groups of 4 bits as shown in Fig. 5-2. The same applies for the data bus except that it is only 8 bits (or 2 hex bits) long. So for a C3, data switches 0, 1, 6, and 7 are on, with the remaining off.

SINGLE-STEP TEST

The next circuit to check out is the single-step circuit. Place the ICs in the sockets, turn on the power, and load the short loop given above. Verify that the loop is running, and place the free run/single step switch in the single step position. The computer should stop, and an address should

Table 5-1. Converting Binary Numbers to Hexadecimal Equivalents.

Binary	Hex
0000	0
0001	1
0010	2
0011	3
0100	4
0101	5
0110	6
0111	7
1000	8
1001	9
1010	A
1011	B
1100	C
1101	D
1110	E
1111	F

Address bits				
15 14 13 12 HIGH order bit	11 10 9 8 Second high order bit	7 6 5 4 Next to low order bit	3 2 1 0 low order bit	
0 1 1 1	0 1 1 1	1 0 0 1	0 0 0 1	binary
7	7	9	1	hex
1 0 1 0	1 0 1 1	1 1 0 0	1 1 0 1	binary
A	B	C	D	hex
0 0 0 0	1 1 1 0	1 1 1 1	0 1 1 1	binary
0	E	F	7	hex

Fig. 5-2. Address switch assignment and definition.

be displayed. Verify that it is one of the addresses being executed.

Depress the single step switch one time. The address should advance one. If the address LEDs advance by more than one address, the variable resistor needs adjusting. Turn down the pulse width until it advances only one address. If it advances one or more addresses when the switch is depressed, and one or more when it is released, there is excessive switch bounce and the switch must be replaced by a better switch. The debounce circuit will take care of most switch bounce. Switch bounce will cause the system to advance several addresses at once, and it is not adjustable. There is a wide range of adjustment where the circuit will work correctly.

Single stepping allows execution of one address or instruction. For two- or three-byte instructions, each memory fetch operation is displayed. Also, for memory read, memory write, and some other instructions, the operation which uses the bus will be displayed. More will be covered on this here and in the chapter on running simple programs.

Play with the single step and become familiar with its operation. Load up the simple loop program given previously, and single step through it. Notice that this program will single step forever. Depress reset to get out of the program.

Notice that the addresses and instructions are displayed for each step through the program.

Load in the following simple program:

Address	Load In	Mnemonic
0000	21	LXI H,0010
0001	10	
0002	00	
0003	36	MVI M,AA
0004	AA	
0005	23	INX H
0006	7D	MOV A,L
0007	FE	CPI,00
000A	00	
000B	C2	JNZ, 0003
000C	03	
000D	00	
000E	76	HALT

This program loads all the addresses from 0010 to 00FF with AA. When all the locations are loaded, the computer will go into the halt condition. The information loaded into address 0004 determines what is loaded into memory.

Load the program and execute it. Check some of the addresses between 0010 and 00FF to make sure they are loaded properly. Then change address 0004 to some other value, run the program, and read the locations again. This is

		Addresses	Data
	LXI H,	0000	21-10-00
Loop	MVI M,00	0003	36-00
	INX H	0005	23
	MOV A,H	0006	7C
	CPI,00	0007	FE-00
	JNZ,Loop	0009	C3-03-00
	HALT	000C	76

Note, where more than one data word is shown, the data is ioaded in sequential addresses.

Fig. 5-3. Filling a series of memory locations with zero.

the first indication that the computer is writing into memory. See Fig. 5-3.

Notice that when the computer is in the halt mode, all the displays are on.

Place the computer in single step and depress the reset switch. Single step through the program, making sure that the addresses and data are correct. Notice that after address 0004 is executed, the address LED's display 0010, and the data LED's indicate the data in address 0004 (AA). This indicates the actual loading of the data into the memory address. Continue single stepping, and notice that after address 000D is executed, the program jumps back to 0003. This is the loop which loads memory. Notice that when 0004 is executed the next time, that the address LED displays 0011.

The keyboard/display and the programmer circuits are checked out in chapter 7, after some of the instructions have been explained. This is because both of these sections require a program to check them out and to use them; at this point the instructions are not explained.

Always remember that the hardware read/load switch must be off and the read/write switch must be in the center off position for normal operation or when not using hardware read/load capability. Also, the single step switch must be off when not in use.

Chapter 6
The Instruction Set

A computer, no matter how smart it is, must be told what to do, for the computer does only what it is told. One tells the computer what to do via a series of coded instructions referred to as the program, sometimes called the software. Each instruction consists of a unique set of 1s and 0s which, when decoded set up the hardware to execute the desired instruction. A program consists of a series of instructions, arranged in logical order, which achieve some desired results. The instructions make up the individual steps of the program, and are the smallest operation programmable into the computer. The instructions control the hardware.

It's very important to understand what each instruction does and how it is used. Although the 8080's instruction set is somewhat limited, it is very powerful and can be used to perform almost any desired task.

TYPES OF INSTRUCTIONS

The four basic types of instructions are:

- Data movement
- Data manipulation
- Program manipulation
- Status management

Data Movement Instructions

These instructions move data around the computer. They can move data from one register to another, memory to a register, register to memory, from input circuits to a register, from a register to output circuits, or from one place to another within the system. For the data to be operated on by the computer, it must be in the proper place; these instructions are used to place the data where required.

Data Manipulation Instructions

The instructions manipulate, or operate on the data. Included in this type are arithmetic and logical instructions, which require the data to be in specific places (usually registers) in the computer. The result normally ends up in the accumulator.

Program Manipulation Instructions

These instructions alter the program flow, either conditionally or unconditionally. Normally sequential instructions are executed, but these instructions can change that. Unconditional instructions will cause the next instruction to be executed to be one at an address defined by the instruction. A conditional instruction will alter the program flow if its conditions are satisfied.

These instructions make the computer a thinking machine, capable of responding differently to different conditions.

Status Management Instructions

There are five condition flags associated with the 8080, as described previously. These flags are stored in the program status word (PSW), and are sampled by the conditional program-manipulation instructions. The flags are set by several of the data-manipulation instructions. They aren't individual instructions per se, but additional capabilities that affect some of the other instructions.

The flags are set as a result of the last instruction executed which affected the flags. They will remain as set

The second and third bytes of three-byte instructions comprise either 2 data words, or an address. The data words are used for register-pair immediate instructions. For example LXI D,2345 loads register pair D & E with 2345. That is, 23 is loaded into the D register and 45 is loaded into the E register. These bytes appear in sequential memory addresses, with the low-order in the second address and the high-order in the third location. This type of instruction is shown in Table 6-1 with (16) following the mnemonic, such as LXI D,(16). When an address is defined by bytes 2 and 3, it is shown as (adr) in Table 6-1, and requires that byte 2 be the low-order address and byte 3 be the high-order address. For example, LDA (adr) means to load the accumulator with the contents of the memory location specified by (adr). LDA 01F4 means to load the accumulator with the contents of memory address 01F4.

Data-Transfer Group. Move instructions are formatted MOV d,s where s is the source and d is the destination. Either d or s can be any single register of memory. As previously defined, any of the instructions which reference memory reference the memory address that is contained in the H & L registers, so this register pair must contain the desired address. The move instructions such as MOV A,A really accomplish very little, and are used only for delay loops. These instructions are listed because they are available due to the geometery and interconnect of the chip. It is easier to allow them than to change the interconnect for these unique conditions.

Eight-bit immediate instructions are formatted MVI d,data, or MVI d,(8). This moves the data in the second byte to the defined register or to memory. This type of instruction is used to load single registers and memory locations to a predetermined value.

Sixteen-bit immediate instructions are formatted LXI d,(16), and load the 16 bits (2 data words) defined by bytes two and three into the register pair. The LXI SP,(16) instruction is used to load the stack pointer with the high order address. This must be done in order to define the stack, and the stack information's location.

Table 6-1. The Instruction Set.

Op Code	Mnemonic	Flags affected	Clock cycles	Definition
DATA TRANSFER INSTRUCTIONS				
7F	MOV A,A	none	5	Move contents of A reg to A reg
78	MOV A,B	none	5	Move contents of B reg to A reg
79	MOV A,C	none	5	Move contents of C reg to A reg
7A	MOV A,D	none	5	Move contents of D reg to A reg
7B	MOV A,E	none	5	Move contents of E reg to A reg
7C	MOV A,H	none	5	Move contents of H reg to A reg
7D	MOV A,L	none	5	Move contents of L reg to A reg
7E	MOV A,M	none	7	Move contents of memory location defined by H & L reg to A reg
47	MOV B,A	none	5	Move contents of A reg to B reg
40	MOV B,B	none	5	Move contents of B reg to B reg
41	MOV B,C	none	5	Move contents of C reg to B reg
42	MOV B,D	none	5	Move contents of D reg to B reg
43	MOV B,E	none	5	Move contents of E reg to B reg
44	MOV B,H	none	5	Move contents of H reg to B reg
45	MOV B,L	none	5	Move contents of L reg to B reg
46	MOV B,M	none	7	Move contents of memory location defined by H & L reg to B reg
4F	MOV C,A	none	5	Move contents of A reg to C reg
48	MOV C,B	none	5	Move contents of B reg to C reg
49	MOV C,C	none	5	Move contents of C reg to C reg
4A	MOV C,D	none	5	Move contents of D reg to C reg
4B	MOV C,E	none	5	Move contents of E reg to C reg
4C	MOV C,H	none	5	Move contents of H reg to C reg
4D	MOV C,L	none	5	Move contents of L reg to C reg
4E	MOV C,M	none	7	Move contents of memory location defined by H & L reg to C reg
57	MOV D,A	none	5	Move contents of A reg to D reg
50	MOV D,B	none	5	Move contents of B reg to D reg
51	MOV D,C	none	5	Move contents of C reg to D reg
52	MOV D,D	none	5	Move contents of D reg to D reg
53	MOV D,E	none	5	Move contents of E reg to D reg
54	MOV D,H	none	5	Move contents of H reg to D reg
55	MOV D,L	none	5	Move contents of L reg to D reg
56	MOV D,M	none	7	Move contents of memory location defined by H & L reg to D reg
5F	MOV E,A	none	5	Move contents of A reg to E reg
58	MOV E,B	none	5	Move contents of B reg to E reg
59	MOV E,C	none	5	Move contents of C reg to E reg
5A	MOV E,D	none	5	Move contents of D reg to E reg
5B	MOV E,E	none	5	Move contents of E reg to E reg
5C	MOV E,H	none	5	Move contents of H reg to E reg
5D	MOV E,L	none	5	Move contents of L reg to E reg
5E	MOV E,M	none	7	Move contents of memory location defined by H & L reg to D reg
67	MOV H,A	none	5	Move contents of A reg to H reg
60	MOV H,B	none	5	Move contents of B reg to H reg
61	MOV H,C	none	5	Move contents of C reg to H reg

Table 6-1. The Instruction Set. (Continued from page 136.)

Op code	Mnemonic	Flags affected	Clock cycles	Definition
62	MOV H,D	none	5	Move contents of D reg to H reg
63	MOV H,E	none	5	Move contents of E reg to H reg
64	MOV H,H	none	5	Move contents of H reg to H reg
65	MOV H,L	none	5	Move contents of L reg to H reg
66	MOV H,M	none	7	Move contents of memory location defined by H & L reg to H reg
6F	MOV L,A	none	5	Move contents of A reg to L reg
68	MOV L,B	none	5	Move contents of B reg to L reg
69	MOV L,C	none	5	Move contents of C reg to L reg
6A	MOV L,D	none	5	Move contents of D reg to L reg
6B	MOV L,E	none	5	Move contents of E reg to L reg
6C	MOV L,H	none	5	Move contents of H reg to L reg
6D	MOV L,L	none	5	Move contents of L reg to L reg
6E	MOV L,M	none	7	Move contents of memory location defined by H & L reg to L reg
77	MOV M,A	none	7	Move contents of A reg to memory
70	MOV M,B	none	7	Move contents of B reg to memory
71	MOV M,C	none	7	Move contents of C reg to memory
72	MOV M,D	none	7	Move contents of D reg to memory
73	MOV M,E	none	7	Move contents of E reg to memory
74	MOV M,H	none	7	Move contents of H reg to memory
75	MOV M,L	none	4	Move contents of L reg to memory
EB	XCHG	none	7	Exchange D & E reg with H & L reg
3E	MVI A, (8)	none	7	Load A register with (8).
06	MVI B,(8)	none	7	Load B register with (8)
0E	MVI C,(8)	none	7	Load C register with (8)
16	MVI D,(8)	none	7	Load D register with (8)
1E	MVI E, (8)	none	7	Load E register with (8)
26	MVI H, (8	none	7	Load H register with (8)
2E	MVI L,(8)	none	10	Load L register with (8)
36	MVI M, (8)	none	10	Load memory with (8)
01	LXI B, (16)	none	10	Load B & C registers with (16)
11	LXI D, (16)	none	10	Load D & E registers with (16)
21	LXI H, (16)	none	10	Load H & L registers with (16)
31	LXI SP, (16)	none	7	Load stack pointer with (16)
0A	LDAX B	none		Load A reg with memory location defined by B & C registers
1A	LDAX D	none	7	Load A reg with memory location defined by D & E registers
	LHLD (adr)	none	16	Load H & L with contents of (adr)
2A	LDA (adr)	none	13	Load A reg with contents of (adr)
3A	STAX B	none	7	Store A reg in memory location
02				defined by B & C registers
12	STAX D	none	7	Store A reg in memory location defined by D & E registers
22	SHLD (adr)	none	16	Store H & L in (adr) & adr +1
32	STA (adr)	none	13	Store A in (adr)

Table 6-1. The Instruction Set. (Continued from page 137.)

Op code	Mnemonic	Flags affected	Clock cycles	Definition
ARITHMETIC AND LOGICAL GROUP INSTRUCTIONS				
87	ADD A	all	4	Add A register to A register
80	ADD B	all	4	Add B register to A register
81	ADD C	all	4	Add C register to A register
82	ADD D	all	4	Add D register to A register
83	ADD E	all	4	Add E register to A register
84	ADD H	all	4	Add H register to A register
85	ADD L	all	4	Add L register to A register
86	ADD M	all	7	Add contents of memory location defined by H & L to A register
8F	ADC A	all	4	Add A reg & carry to A reg
88	ADC B	all	4	Add B reg & carry to A reg
89	ADC C	all	4	Add C reg & carry to A reg
8A	ADC D	all	4	Add D reg & carry to A reg
8B	ADC E	all	4	Add E reg & carry to A reg
8C	ADC H	all	4	Add H reg & carry to A reg
8D	ADC L	all	4	Add L reg & carry to A reg
8E	ADC M	all	7	Add contents of mem location defined by H & L and carry to A reg
97	SUB A	all	4	Subtract A register from A reg
90	SUB B	all	4	Subtract B register from A reg
91	SUB C	all	4	Subtract C register from A reg
92	SUB D	all	4	Subtract D register from A reg
93	SUB E	all	4	Subtract E register from A reg
94	SUB H	all	4	Subtract H register from A reg
95	SUB L	all	4	Subtract L register from A reg
96	SUB M	all	7	Sub contents of memory location defined by H & L from A reg
9F	SBB A	all	4	Sub A reg & borrow from A reg
98	SBB B	all	4	Sub B reg & borrow from A reg
99	SBB C	all	4	Sub C reg & borrow from A reg
9A	SBB D	all	4	Sub D reg & borrow from A reg
9B	SBB E	all	4	Sub E reg & borrow from A reg
9C	SBB H	all	4	Sub H reg & borrow from A reg
9D	SBB L	all	4	Sub L reg & borrow from A reg
9E	SBB M	all	7	Sub contents of memory location defined by H & L and borrow from A reg.
09	DAD B	Carry	10	Add B & C reg to H & L reg
19	DAD D	Carry	10	Add D & E reg to H & L reg
29	DAD H	Carry	10	Add H & L reg to H & L reg
39	DAD SP	Carry	10	Add stack pointer to H & L reg
3C	INR A	Z,S,P,AC	5	Increment A reg
04	INR B	Z,S,P,AC	5	Increment B reg
0C	INR C	Z,S,P,AC	5	Increment C reg
14	INR D	Z,S,P,AC	5	Increment D reg
1C	INR E	Z,S,P,AC	5	Increment E reg
24	INR H	Z,S,P,AC	5	Increment H reg
2C	INR L	Z,S,P,AC	5	Increment L reg

Table 6-1. The Instruction Set. **(Continued from page 138.)**

Op code	Mnemonic	Flags affected	Clock cycles	Definition
34	INR M	Z,S,P,AC	10	Increment the memory location defined by H & L reg.
03	INX B	none	5	Increment BC reg pair
13	INX D	none	5	Increment DE reg pair
23	INX H	none	5	Increment HL reg pair
33	INX SP	none	5	Increment stack pointer
3D	DCR A	Z,S,P,AC	5	Decrement A reg
05	DCR B	Z,S,P,AC	5	Decrement B reg
0D	DCR C	Z,S,P,AC	5	Decrement C reg
15	DCR D	Z,S,P,AC	5	Decrement D reg
1D	DCR E	Z,S,P,AC	5	Decrement E reg
25	DCR H	Z,S,P,AC	5	Decrement H reg
2D	DCR L	Z,S,P,AC	5	Decrement L reg
35	DCR M	Z,S,P,AC	10	Decrement memory location defined by H & L reg
0B	DCX B	none	5	Decrement BC reg pair
1B	DCX D	none	5	Decrement DE reg pair
2B	DCX H	none	5	Decrement HL reg pair
3B	DCX SP	none	5	Decrement stack pointer
27	DAA	all	4	Decimal adjust A
2F	CMA	none	4	Complement A
37	STC	carry	4	Set carry flag
3F	CMC	carry	4	Compliment carry flag
07	RLC	carry	4	Rotate A reg left
0F	RRC	carry	4	Rotate A reg right
17	RAL	carry	4	Rotate A reg left through carry
1F	RAR	carry	4	Rotate A reg right through carry
A7	ANA A	all	4	Logically AND A reg with A reg
A0	ANA B	all	4	Logically AND B reg with A reg
A1	ANA C	all	4	Logically AND C reg with A reg
A2	ANA D	all	4	Logically AND D reg with A reg
A3	ANA E	all	4	Logically AND E reg with A reg
A4	ANA H	all	4	Logically AND H reg with A reg
A5	ANA L	all	4	Logically AND L reg with A reg
A6	ANA M	all	7	Logically AND the contents of the memory location with A reg
AF	XRA A	all	4	Exclusively OR A reg with A reg
A8	XRA B	all	4	Exclusively OR B reg with A reg
A9	XRA C	all	4	Exclusively OR C reg with A reg
AA	XRA D	all	4	Exclusively OR D reg with A reg
AB	XRA E	all	4	Exclusively OR E reg with A reg
AC	XRA H	all	4	Exclusively OR H reg with A reg
AD	XRA L	all	4	Exclusively OR L reg with A reg
AE	XRA M	all	7	Exclusively OR memory location defined by H & L with A reg
B7	ORA A	all	4	Logically OR A reg with A reg
B0	ORA B	all	4	Logically OR B reg with A reg
B1	ORA C	all	4	Logically OR C reg with A reg

Table 6-1. The Instruction Set. **(Continued from page 139.)**

Op code	Mnemonic	Flags affected	Clock cycles	Definition
B2	ORA D	all	4	Logically OR D reg with A reg
B3	ORA E	all	4	Logically OR E reg with A reg
B4	ORA H	all	4	Logically OR H reg with A reg
B5	ORA L	all	4	Logically OR L reg with A reg
B6	ORA M	all	7	Logically OR memory location defined by H & L reg with A reg
BF	CMP A	all	4	Compare A reg with A reg
B8	CMP B	all	4	Compare B reg with A reg
B9	CMP C	all	4	Compare C reg with A reg
BA	CMP D	all	4	Compare D reg with A reg
BB	CMP E	all	4	Compare E reg with A reg
BC	CMP H	all	4	Compare H reg with A reg
BD	CMP L	all	4	Compare L reg with A reg
BE	CMP M	all	7	Compare contents of memory defined by H & L with A reg
C6	ADI (8)	all	7	Add (8) to A reg
CE	ACI (8)	all	7	Add (8) and carry to A reg
D6	SUI (8)	all	7	Subtract (8) from A reg
DE	SBI (8)	all	7	Sub (8) and borrow from A reg
E6	ANI (8)	all	7	Logically AND (8) with A reg
EE	XRI (8)	all	7	Exclusively OR (8) with A reg
F6	ORI (8)	all	7	Logically OR (8) with A reg
FE	CPI (8)	all	7	Compare (8) with A reg
BRANCH CONTROL INSTRUCTIONS				
C3	JMP (adr)	none	10	Jump to (adr)
C2	JNZ (adr)	none	10	Jump to (adr) if Zero flag not set
CA	JZ (adr)	none	10	Jump to (adr) if Zero flag set
D2	JNC (adr)	none	10	Jump to (adr) if carry flag not set
DA	JC (adr)	none	10	Jump to (adr) if carry flag set
E2	JPO (adr)	none	10	Jump to (adr) if parity odd
EA	JPE (adr)	none	10	Jump to (adr) if parity even
F2	JP (adr)	none	10	Jump to (adr) if positive
FA	JM (adr)	none	10	Jump to (adr) if negative
E9	PCHL	none	5	Move H & L to program counter
CD	CALL (adr)	none	17	Call subroutine at (adr)
C4	CNZ (adr)	none	1117	Call sub at (adr) if zero flag not set
CC	CZ (adr)	none	11/17	Call sub at (adr) if zero flag set
D4	CNC (adr)	none	11/17	Call sub at (adr) if carry flag not set
DC	CC (adr)	none	11/17	Call sub at (adr) if carry flag set
E4	CPO (adr)	none	11/17	Call sub at (adr) if parity odd
EC	CPE (adr)	none	11/17	Call sub at (adr) if parity even
F4	CP (adr)	none	11/17	Call sub at (adr) if positive
FC	CM (adr)	none	11/17	Call sub at (adr) if negative
C9	RET	none	10	Return

Table 6-1. The Instruction Set. **(Continued from page 140.)**

Op code	Mnemonic	Flags affected	Clock cycles	Definition
C0	RNZ	none	5/11	Return if zero flag not set
C8	RZ	none	5/11	Return if zero flag set
D0	RNC	none	5/11	Return if carry flag not set
D8	RC	none	5/11	Return if carry flag set
E0	RPO	none	5/11	Return if parity odd
E8	RPE	none	5/11	Return if parity even
F0	RP	none	5/11	Return if positive
F8	RM	none	5/11	Return if negative
C7	RST 0	none	11	Restart at 0 interrupt location
	RST 1	none	11	Restart at 1 interrupt location
	RST 2	none	11	Restart at 2 interrupt location
DF	RST 3	none	11	Restart at 3 interrupt location
E7	RST 4	none	11	Restart at 4 interrupt location
EF	RST 5	none	11	Restart at 5 interrupt location
F7	RST 6	none	11	Restart at 6 interrupt location
FF	RST 7	none	11	Restart at 7 interrupt location
I/O AND MACHINE CONTROL INSTRUCTIONS				
C5	PUSH B	none	11	Place B & C reg on stack
D5	PUSH D	none	11	Place D & E reg on stack
E5	PUSH H	none	11	Place H & L reg on stack
F5	PUSH PSW	none	11	Place program status word on stack
C1	POP B	none	10	Place current stack in B & C reg
D1	POP D	none	10	Place Current stack in D & E reg
E1	POP H	none	10	Place current stack in H & L reg
F1	POP PSW	all	10	Place current stack in PSW
E3	XTHL	none	18	Exchange current stack with H & L
F9	SPHL	none	5	Move H & L to stack pointer
D3	OUT (port)	none	10	Output A reg to (port)
DB	IN (port)	none	4	Input (port) to A reg
F3	DI	none	4	Disable interrupts
FB	EI	none	4	Enable interrupts
00	NOP	none		No operation
76	HALT	none		Halt machine operation

Notes:
11/17: In the program transfer is not executed it takes 11 clock cycles, if it is executed it takes 17 clock cycles.
(adr): Three byte instruction requiring an address as bytes 2 & 3
(8): Two byte instruction requiring one 8 bit data word.
(16) Three byte instruction requiring two 8 bit data words.

The load accumulator and store accumulator, LDA (adr) and STA (adr), load the accumulator with the contents of the specified memory address, or store the contents of the accumulator in the specified memory address. These are direct memory addressing instructions, because the memory address effected is stored as bytes 2 and 3 of the instruction.

Two more direct-memory addressing instructions are the LHLD (adr) and SHLD (adr) instructions. LHLD (adr) loads the H & L register pair with the contents of the address specified by bytes 2 and 3, and the next address. That is, the L register is loaded with the contents of the address specified. The contents of the next address is moved to the H register. This instruction makes it convenient to store address pointers in RAM memory, and to load them with SHLD.

The LDAX rp and STAX rp instructions use indirect memory addressing. The address is located in the defined register pair—either the B & C register or the D & E register. STAX rp moves the contents of the accumulator to the defined address, and the LDAX rp moves the contents of the defined address to the accumulator. These one-byte instructions are used in reading, storing or updating strings of information.

The move instructions given above (MOV d,s, LDA (adr), STA (adr), LDAX rp, and STAX rp, do not change the data at the source, and can therefore be used repeatedly. There is one instruction left in the data transfer group. That is XCHG, or exchange H & L with D & E. This instruction does just that, it exchanges the contents of the two specified register pairs.

Arithmetic group: These instructions perform the arithmetic operations. Usually they operate on the accumulator, and most of them affect some or all flags.

The ADD r instruction adds the contents of the defined register to the contents of the accumulator and leaves the results in the accumulator. The ADD M instruction adds the contents of the memory location defined by the H & L register to the contents of the accumulator, leaving the results in the accumulator. The ADI (8) adds the data in byte 2 of the instruction to the accumulator, leaving the results in the accumulator. These instructions do not check the carry flag to determine if a carry must be added. This is not important for 8-bit operations, but when adding longer strings of numbers, such as a 32-bit number, the carry flag must be used for the second, third and fourth add operations.

The following three instructions do this. The ADC r instruction adds the contents of the defined register, and the carry flag, to the contents of the accumulator. The ADC M instruction adds the contents of the memory location defined by the H & L register, and the carry flag to the contents of the accumulator. The ACI (8) adds the data in byte two of the instruction, and the carry flag, to the contents of the accumulator.

The SUB r instruction subtracts the contents of the defined register from the accumulator, and the result is placed in the accumulator. The SUI M instruction subtracts the content of the memory location whose address is contained in the H & L registers from the accumulator. The result is placed in the accumulator. The SUI (8) instruction subtracts the content of byte 2 of the instruction from the accumulator. The result is placed in the accumulator. The SBB r, SBB M and SBI (8) are the three classes of subtract instructions utilizing the borrow in addition to the defined number.

The INR r instruction increments the defined register by one. The INR M increments the memory defined by the contents of the H & L register pair by one. The DEC r instruction decrements the defined register by one. The DCR M instruction decrements the memory location defined by the H & L register by one. These increment and decrement instructions add one to or subtract one from the register or memory. These affect 8-bit words, and can roll over zero. That is, if the contents is 11111111, an increment will make it 00000000, and vice versa.

The INX rp instruction increments the defined-register pair by one. The DCX rp decrements the defined-register pair by one. These instructions operate on a 16-bit register pair, and the lower order register of the pair must be filled before the high order register is affected.

The DAD rp instruction adds the defined-register pair to the H & L register, and places the result in the H & L register. This 16-bit add is used for double-precision data words. The DAA (decimal-adjust accumulator) instruction adjusts the accumulator to form two 4-bit binary-coded decimal words. This is a useful instruction when using BCD words in the data, or when driving BCD displays.

The ANA r instruction performs a bit-by-bit logical AND on the defined register and the accumulator. The ANA M instruction performs this between the memory location defined by the H & L register and the accumulator. The ANI (8) instruction does this between the data contained in byte 2 of the instruction and the accumulator. All three of these instructions place the result in the accumulator. When two numbers are logically AND'ed, a ONE appears in a bit position indicating if both numbers have a one in that bit position. For example:

```
     11110000          10100011
AND  01011101    and   00011010
     --------          --------
     01010000          00000010
```

The XRA r performs a logical Exculsive OR between the defined register and the accumulator. The XRA M does this between the memory location defined by the H & L register and the accumulator. The XRI (8) does this between the data in byte 2 of the instruction and the accumulator. The result for all three of these is placed in the accumulator.

When a logical-Exclusive OR is performed on two numbers a one appears in a bit position in the result if one and only one of the numbers in that bit position has a one. For example:

```
         11110000           10100011
Exc OR   01011101   Ex OR   00011010
         --------           --------
         10101101           10111001
```

The ORA r logically ORs the defined register with the accumulator. The ORA m logically ORs the data in the memory location defined by the contents of H & L and the accumulator. The ORI (8) logically ORs the data in byte 2 of the instruction and the accumulator. In all three of the above instructions the result is placed in the accumulator. When two numbers are logically ORd, a one appears in the bit position of the result when a one appears in that bit position for one or both of the numbers. For example:

	11110000		10100011
OR	01011101	OR	00011010
	11111101		10111011

The CMP r instruction does a bit-by-bit comparison between the defined register and the accumulator. This is done by subtracting the contents of the register from the accumulator without changing the register or the accumulator. The CMP M instruction compares the memory location defined by the H & L register with the accumulator's contents. The CPI (8) compares byte 2 of the instruction with the accumulator.

Because the compare is accomplished by a subtraction, setting the zero flag HIGH indicates a compare. These instructions are very useful because they do not change any of the data, they only set the flags, and the zero flag is used most often.

The RLC instruction rotates the contents of the accumulator to the left by one position. The low-order bit and the carry flag are both set to the value shifted out of the high-order bit position. The RRC instruction rotates the contents of the accumulator to the right by one position. The high-order bit and the carry flag are both set to the value shifted out of the low-order bit position. The RAL instruction rotates the contents of the accumulator left one position through the carry flag. The low order bit is set equal to the carry flag, and the carry flag is set to the value shifted out of the high order bit. The RAR instruction rotates the content of the accumulator right one position through the carry flag. The high-order bit is set equal to the carry flag, and the carry flag is set to the value shifter out of the low order bit.

The CMA instruction complements the contents of the accumulator. That is, all ones are changed to zeros, and all zeros are changed to ones. Similarly, the CMC instruction complements the carry flag. The STC instruction sets the carry flag to a one.

Branch Group: This group of instructions alters the normal sequential program flow. All except two of these instructions are either conditional and unconditional. The unconditional-branch instructions execute the branch without regards to the condition of the flags. The conditional branch either branch or execute the next sequential instruction depending on the condition of the branch and the state of the flags. The conditions available are given below, with the designation that appears as the second and sometimes third character in the mnemonic.

NZ——Zero flag = 0
Z——Zero flag = 1
NC——Carry flag = 0
C——Carry flag = 1
PO——Parity odd
PE——Parity even
P——Plus (sign flag = 0)
M——Minus (sign flag = 1)

The JMP (adr) instruction unconditionally jumps the program to (adr). The condition (adr) instruction jumps to the (adr) if its condition is satisfied. For example a JNZ 0124 will jump the program to address 0124 if the zero flag is zero. If the zero flag is one, the next sequential instruction is executed, and the jump is not executed.

The Call and Return instructions make it possible to use subroutines and not worry about specifying the return address. The call instructions place the address of the next sequential instruction on the processor's stack, then transfer program control to the address specified by bytes 2 and 3 of the instruction. The return instruction places the contents of the current stack address in the program counter, returning the program control to the place where it left it via the call instruction.

These instructions, both the conditional and unconditional, are used quite extensively to change program flow, and to call subroutines. For every call, however, there must be a return, or else it is quite possible that the program will lose track or the stack can become so large it overwrites part of the program or data. The stack is also used for other things, so care must be taken to keep track of what is placed on the stack. Remember, for every call there must be a return, and for every return there must have been a call executed previously. Do not leave the program flow using a jump instruction and expect to return to the proper point in the program flow using a return.

The RST n instruction transfers program control to the address indicated by the 3 bits specified by n, where n is a number from 0 to 7. The address is generated by taking the 3 bits of n and placing them as bits 5, 4, and 3 of the contents of the program counter, as shown.

Bit Position	15	14	13	12	11	10	9	8	7	6	5	4	3	2	1	0
Data	0	0	0	0	0	0	0	0	0	0	n	n	n	0	0	0

RST O transfers the program control to address 0000. RST 1 transfers to address 00008, RST 2 transfers to address 0010, etc.

The PCHL instruction moves the contents of the H & L register pair to the program counter. The next instruction executed resides at the address that was in the H & L register pair. This instruction allows program transfer to a location determined by the program.

Stack, I/O, and Machine Control Group: The PUSH rp instruction places the content of a designated register pair on the stack. The PUSH PSW places the contents of the accumulator (8 bits) and the program-status word (flags) on the stack. The POP rp instruction places the contents of the current stack location in the designated register pair. The POP PSW instruction places the current stack location contents in the accumulator and the flags. This group of four instructions allows temporary storage of information by placing it on the stack. Realize that the stack is a last-in-first-out type of storage. That is, the last information placed on the stack is the first taken off the stack. Thus, if several registers are stored on the stack, the last register pushed on must be the first popped off. The stack is also used for other purposes, namely the call and return instructions.

Realize that a POP instruction takes the last data that was placed on the stack, and moves it to the designated register pair. This last data can come from a PUSH instruction or from an executed CALL instruction. This applies to a RETURN instruction as well. So care must be taken to pop all data off the stack that was pushed on in a subroutine or the program may return to the wrong place.

The XTHL instruction exchanges the current stack data with the H & L register pair. So the last data on the stack is placed in the H & L register pair, and the data in the H & L register is placed in the current stack location. This instruction allows modification of the stack data in order to return to a different address.

The SPHL instruction moves the contents of H & L to the stack pointer. This allows redefining the stack address.

The IN (8) and OUT (8) are the input and output instructions. These instructions place the contents of the accumulator on the data bus, and the port address (8) on the low order 8 address lines. The input- or output-control signals are activated. This enables the computer to talk to input devices.

The EI instruction enables the system interrupt following the execution of the next instruction. This enables the microprocessor to receive and recognize interrupts. When the microprocessor is turned on, or when a reset is given, the interrupts are not enabled. So, if the program is looking for interrupts, this instruction must be executed.

The DI instruction disables interrupts following its execution. This disables the interrupt circuitry within the microprocessor so that it will not recognize interrupts.

The HLT instruction forces the microprocessor into its halt condition, so that the processor stops. This instruction is not normally used except under special circumstances. The normal exit from a halt condition is the system reset.

The NOP instruction does nothing except take up program space and time. This instruction is normally used when the program is changed and some extra addresses are left in the program. This is also used to mark time in program delay loops.

USING THE INSTRUCTIONS

A program consists of a logical series of instructions stored in sequential addresses. The program branch group can alter the normal program flow to change the sequential-

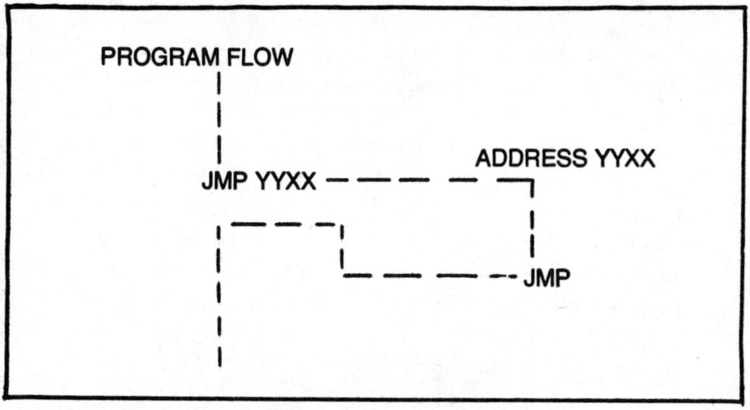

Fig. 6-1. Program patch to add instructions to a program.

address requirement. One of the convenient uses of the JMP instruction is to get a program running. You can use the JMP to add instructions to the program flow without rewriting the total program. Figure 6-1 shows how this is accomplished. A JMP instruction replaces three bytes of the normal program. This must replace either one, two or three total instructions, and the instructions that are replaced are moved to the address jumped to. The instructions required are added along with a jump instruction that jumps the program back to its normal program flow. Remember that the JMP instruction is a 3-byte instruction with bytes two and three being the destination address.

When using the PUSH and POP instructions to save register data during a subroutine, the information must be taken off the stack in the reverse order that it was put on. If the PUSH occurs within the subroutine, the POP must be inside the subroutine, or the subroutine's routine may be to the wrong place. Figure 6-2 illustrates use of the PUSH and POP instructions within the subroutine and before the call instruction.

There is a simple method to load two address pointers into two register pairs, such as to check for the end of data.

```
LHLD temp 2
XCHG
LHLD temp 1
```

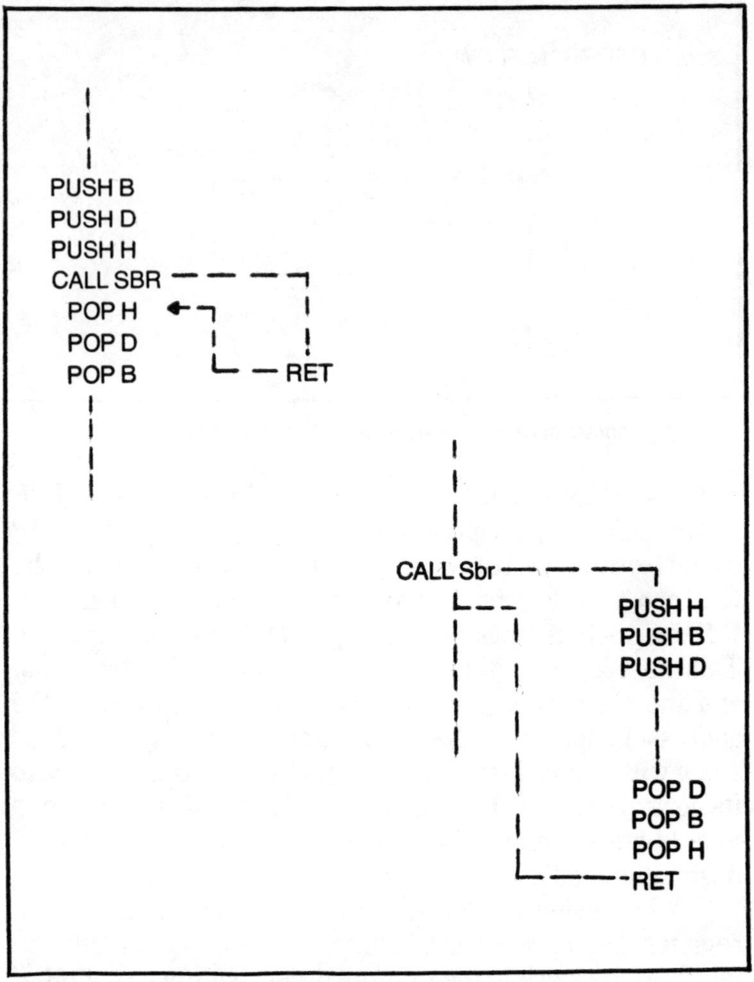

Fig. 6-2. Using the push and pop instructions.

This loads the contents of temp 2 into the D & E register pair and the contents of temp 1 into the H & L register pair.

When using memory instructions, such as MVI M, MOV M,r, and CMP M, the H & L registers must point to the memory address. This is usually done by setting these registers to the desired value in advance. There are times when it may be easier to use one of the other addressing forms, such as LDA (adr), but for a data string, or consective pointers, the LXI H (16) can be used, with an INX H between operations to keep the H & L registers pointing to the correct address.

When using the flags sample the flags immediately after setting them up. In this way the flags can't be changed before they are sampled. If there are instructions between the set up instruction and the sampling instruction, make sure they do not affect the flags.

Chapter 7
The Keyboard Display and EPROM Programmer

The keyboard and display circuits allow direct communication between the operator and the computer program. This requires a program for driving the displays and reading the keyboard. But it allows the operator to enter data into the program and memory simply by depressing keys. This takes place in real time and in no way compares to the hardware read, and load capability. These are two different applications.

The EPROM programmer allows the operator to program an EPROM and place it in the computer. Doing this allows the operator to write some programs, load them into memory, then program an EPROM with the program. Until the EPROM is programmed, the programs require the use of the hardware load circuit and procedure to get them into memory.

This chapter takes the reader through the checkout of these circuits using short, hand-loaded programs. The procedures for using the circuits and functions are given, both from the operator's point of view and that of the program.

Both circuits use the decoder shown in Fig. 3-34. This decodes the address bus to give port numbers 80 and 84. Since both circuits use 8255 input/output chips, which have the I/O read and write control signals as inputs the decoder does not require an I/O control signal to make sure that the circuits are selected only for the correct input and output port numbers. If the decoder is used to drive additional I/O ports the I/O control signals (I/O Read, and I/O Write) must be used as enable signals for the ports

KEYBOARD AND DISPLAY CIRCUITS

The keyboard-and-display circuit is shown in Fig. 3-31. Two 7-segment displays are driven by two ports from the 8255. The third port reads the keyboard.

The control word that sets ports A and B as output ports, bits 4 through 7 of port C as outputs, and low-order bits of port C as inputs, is 81. (See Table 3-5.) The port configuration is:

Output 80	Port A
Output 81	Port B
Output 82	Port C bits 4, 5, 6 & 7
Input 82	Port C bits 0, 1, 2, & 3
Output 83	Control word

Once the control word is written into the 8255 chip, it will retain that configuration until a reset is given, or a new control word is written into it.

When the system reset is generated, the 8255 is reset. The reset configures all ports as input ports to ensure that the outputs will be in their high-impedance state. This appears as a HIGH for the display drivers, turning on all segments of the display. Writing the control word into the 8255 sets ports A and B outputs LOW, turning all the displays off. By writing the proper output word at the proper port the desired segments are turned on. When an output port is written and set, it will remain that way until the port is rewritten. The port does not have to be continually written to display a character.

The first step in checking out the display is to double check the wiring to make sure it is correct. Then put in the following chips.

Chip	Shown in Figure	Function
8205	3-4	Decoder
8255	3-31	I/O chip
7406 (2)	3-31	Drivers for high order display
Display	3-31	High order display

Make sure the chips are installed correctly. Turn the power on and observe the display. All the segments of the high-order display should be on. If one or more of the segments is not on, check for proper connections. The end of the series limiting resistor connected to the driver can be grounded. This will turn on the segment, checking the display for that segment and the connection to the display. Do not ground any pin on the display, as this will subject the LED in the display segment to unlimited current, possibly burning it out.

Using the hardware read and load circuit, hand load the following program

Address	Mnemonic	Load into computer	
0000	MVI A, 81	36	Load control word
0001		81	
0002	Out 83	D3	Write control word
0003		83	
0004	MVI A, 00	36	Load word to be written
0005		00	
0006	OUT 80	D3	Output data word to
0007		80	Port 80
0008	JMP 0004	C3	Jump back
0009		04	
000A		00	

Using the single step function, step through the program. Notice that after address 0003 is executed, the address LEDs display 83 and the data LED' display 81. This same thing happens after address 0007 is displayed. This is because the data is transferred on the bus and the single step stops on the next bus transaction.

Table 7-1. The Bits Which Drive the Segments of The LED Display.

Bit	Segment	Data word
0	a	01
1	b	02
2	c	04
3	d	08
4	e	10
5	f	20
6	g	40

If the reset switch is depressed before starting the single step, all the segments and the individual LED will come on. When address 0003 is executed, all the segments and the individual LED will go off. Since the data loaded into the port is 00, they will stay off. After cycling through the program a few times, load 01 into address 0005, and depress reset. Again, single step through the program. At this time, segment a will come on after execution of address 0007. Refer to Fig. 3-34 for the placement of the segments. Table 7-1 shows the bits to drive the various segments, and the data word to be loaded into address 0005. Load these data words, one at a time, and make sure the proper segment comes on, using the single step capability.

Table 7-2 shows the data words required for the hex characters. This is derived from Fig. 3-34 and Table 7-1. Set up these characters, one at a time, by loading the data word into address 0005 in the above program. Then single step through the program to turn on the correct segments.

If the segments are sequenced properly during the above two tests, the wiring and circuitry is correct. If the wrong segments turn on during the execution of Table 7-1, there is a wiring error which must be corrected. The wiring shown in Fig. 3-31 is intended for the HP 5082-7740 display. Other displays may have different pin configurations. If a different type display is used, the wiring must be changed accordingly.

When the high-order display is checked out, install the low-order display and the remaining display driver. Using the hardware read and load circuit, load the following program.

Address	Mnemonic	Load into computer	
0000	MVI A, 81	36	Load control word
0001		81	
0002	OUT 83	D3	Write control word
0003		83	
0004	MVI A, 00	36	Load word to be written
0005		00	
0006	OUT 81	D3	Output data word to
0007		81	port 81
0008	JMP 0004	C3	Jump back
0009		04	
000A		00	

Using the single-step function, repeat the exercises given above for the high-order displays.

Notice that the only difference between the two programs is the output port, which defines which display is addressed.

To output one computer word to the displays requires breaking the 8-bit word into two 4-bit words. The high-order 4 bits are converted to segments using Table 7-2, then output to the high-order display. Then the low-order 4 bits

Table 7-2. Data Words and Segments Required to Display the Hex Characters.

Character	Segments	Data word
0	abcdef	3f
1	bc	06
2	abdeg	5B
3	abcdg	4F
4	bcfg	66
5	acdfg	6D
6	acdefg	7D
7	abc	07
8	abcdefg	7F
9	abcfg	67
A	abcefg	77
B	cdefg	7C
C	adef	39
D	bcdeg	5E
E	adegf	79
F	aefg	71

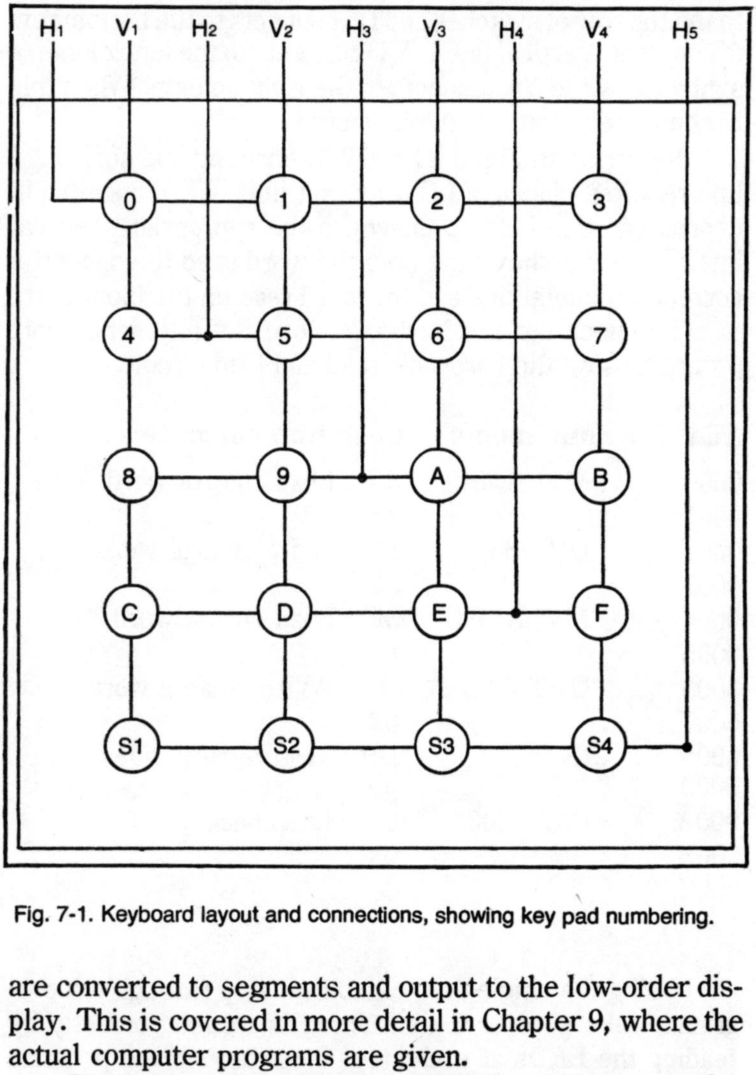

Fig. 7-1. Keyboard layout and connections, showing key pad numbering.

are converted to segments and output to the low-order display. This is covered in more detail in Chapter 9, where the actual computer programs are given.

The keyboard used by the author is a 20-button device arranged in a 4×5 matrix. The keyboard and connections are shown in Fig. 7-1. The wires come out the top of the keyboard, and are connected as shown in Fig. 3-31. You can use other keyboards by changing the wiring and programming as required, but it is advisable to use one similar to that shown in Fig. 7-1. Check with an ohmmeter to ensure that the connections are correct. Horizontal line 1 (H1) connects to the top row of switches and H5 connects to the bottom row of contacts. Vertical line 1 (V1) connects to the left column of switches, while V4 connects to the right column. When this is completed, connect the keyboard.

Referring to Fig. 3-31 and 7-1, enabling one horizontal line requires placing a LOW on that line. When a switch is depressed, this LOW connects to the appropriate vertical line. Table 7-3 shows the port and word used to enable the correct horizontal line and the word read on the input port.

To check out the keyboard, load the following short program using the hardware read and load circuit.

Address	**Mnemonic**	**Load into computer**	
0000	MVI A, 81	3E	Load control word
0001		81	
0002	OUT 83	D3	Write control word
0003		83	
0004	MVI A, EO	3E	Load enable word
0005		E0	
0006	OUT 82	D3	Write enable word
0007		82	
0008	IN 82	DB	Read vertical lines
0009		82	
000A	JMP 0008	C3	Jump back
000B		08	
000C		00	

Using the single-step capability, step through the program. Make sure each instruction is loaded correctly by reading the LEDs at each step. Step through the program until address 0009 is executed, and before 000A is displayed. The LEDs should display 82 on both high- and-low-order address LEDs and EF on the data lines. Depress the keyboard switch 0. The low-order 4 bits of the data word should be as shown in Table 7-3 under input word. Repeat for keys 1 through 3 and make sure the correct data word is received. Then change the enable word, loaded into address 0005 to that shown in Table 7-3 for keys 4 through 7 and read

Table 7-3. Enable and Read Bits for the Keys of the Keyboard.

Key	Enable word			Input Word			bits
	H	Port	Word	V	Port C	word	
0	1	82	EO	1	E		1110
1	1	82	EO	2	D		1101
2	1	82	EO	3	B		1011
3	1	82	EO	4	7		0111
4	2	82	DO	1	E		1110
5	2	82	DO	2	D		1101
6	2	82	DO	3	B		1011
7	2	82	DO	4	7		0111
8	3	82	BO	1	E		1110
9	3	82	BO	2	D		1101
A	3	82	BO	3	B		1011
B	3	82	BO	4	7		0111
C	4	82	70	1	E		1110
D	4	82	70	2	D		1101
E	4	82	70	3	B		1011
F	4	82	70	4	7		0111
S1	5	81	00	1	E		1110
S2	5	81	00	2	D		1101
S3	5	81	00	3	B		1011
S4	5	81	00	4	7		0111

the low-order 4 bits of the data word as above. Repeat for the keys up to F, checking out each key for the proper data word. Then check out the special keys, S1 through S4 by changing the port number, loaded into address 0007 to 81, and reading the data word while depressing the keys.

The detailed programming required for the keyboard is covered in Chapter 9, but the general concepts are given here. To read the keyboard, the horizontal lines must be enabled, one at a time. Then the input word must be read, and checked for a low bit. The port number and control word is decoded for the low bit to determine which key is depressed. If no keys are found LOW, the procedure must be repeated until the key is depressed. Table 7-4 shows the decoding of the enable word and input word for the various keys.

PROGRAMMER

The programmer, shown in Fig. 3-33, has two separate power switches. The 5-volt swtich allows turning off power to the EPROM. This facilitates removal and insertion of the EPROM to be programmed without turning off the computer. The 27-volt switch deactivates the programmer when not in use.

The programmer requires a program to generate the sequencing signals that set up the address and data and generate the program pulses. The programming is covered in the chapter on programming the system. This section checks out the programmer to ensure that the hardware works, and to gain understanding of how the circuit works.

Insert all the chips shown in Fig. 3-33, except the EPROM. Place a 1k resistor between pins 18 and 12 of the EPROM. This provides a load for the program pulse.

Load the following program using the hardware read and load capability.

Address	Mnemonic	Load into computer	
0000	MVI A, 80	3E	Load control word
0001		00	
0002	OUT 87	D3	Write control word
0003		87	
0004	MVI A, 00	3E	Load data word
0005		00	
0006	OUT 86	D3	Write data word
0007		86	
0008	Halt	76	

Turn on both power switches and single step through the program, stopping when you reach address 0008. Measure the voltage at pins 18 and 20. Pin 18 should be LOW and pin 20 should be about 12 volts. Measure the voltage at pins 22 and 23. They should both be LOW.

Next change the data loaded at address 0005 to FF. Again, measure pins 18 and 20. Pin 20 should be LOW and pin 18 should be about 25 volts. Look for HIGHS at pins 22 and 23.

The control word (80) configures all three of the 8255s ports as output ports. The chip is then programmed by setting up the data on the data bus. To verify the EPROM,

Table 7-4. Enable Words and Input Words for the Keys.

Enable Port	Bit low	Input Bit low	Key
82	4	0	0
82	4	1	1
82	4	2	2
82	4	3	3
82	5	0	4
82	5	1	5
82	5	2	6
82	5	3	7
82	6	0	8
82	6	1	9
82	6	2	A
82	6	3	B
82	7	0	C
82	7	1	D
82	7	2	E
82	7	3	F
81	7	0	S1
81	7	1	S2
81	7	2	S3
81	7	3	S4

requires configuring port A as an input port. This is accomplished by using the control word 90. First, change the output-port number to 85 and repeat the above, but looking for a voltage or ground at EPROM pins A_0 through A_7 pins. A ground for a 00 data word and HIGHS for a FF data word. Repeat this for output port 85, checking the D_0through D_7 pins.

When this is checked out, it is time to test the read capability. Load the following program using the hardware read and load capability. Using jumpers, ground all 8 data lines (Pins 9-11, and 13-17) at the EPROM socket.

Address	Mnemonic	Load into computer	
0000	MVI A, 90	3E	Load control word
0001		90	
0002	OUT87	D3	Write control word
0003		87	
0004	IN 84	DB	Read input word
0005		84	
0006	Jump 0004	C3	Jump back
0007		04	
0008		00	

Single step through the program until the input word is read and placed on the data bus, or until address 0005 is executed. All the data LEDs should be off. Remove the jumpers, one at a time, replacing them with 1k resistors between each data pin and +5 volts. The LED for that data line should come on. Repeat this for all 8 data lines.

Chapter 8
Programming

Programming is the writing of a series of instructions to control the computer in its performance of an assigned task. Programming is done in machine language—the actual hex number for the instruction is loaded into the computer from the keyboard by the switches. The programs in this book are written in and discussed using the mnemonic codes (the descriptive alphabetical code for each instruction). MOV A,B, for example, is the mnemonic for moving data from the B register to the A register, hex 78. Sometimes the hex machine code will be given, but even if it isn't remember that all computer inputs are in the hex format. It is advisable to make up a listing of the instructions, with the machine codes, as illustrated in Fig. 8-1, to place near the computer. This should be on two pieces of 11-inch by 17-inch paper. This sign, placed on the wall, will serve as a handy reference when programming or trouble-shooting the computer.

One of the nice things about microcomputers is that the user can understand both the hardware and the software. This allows the user to visualize what each instruction does as the program is written. Not in the intricate details of a microprocessor's operation, but in the overview—such as moving data from one register to another.

The ability to write good programs comes from a thorough understanding of the instructions and what they

DATA TRANSFER GROUP

Move

MOV	A,A	7F
	A,B	78
	A,C	79
	A,D	7A
	A,E	7B
	A,H	7C
	A,L	7D
	A,M	7E
MOV	B,A	47
	B,B	40
	B,C	41
	B,D	42
	B,E	43
	B,H	44
	B,L	45
	B,M	46
MOV	C,A	4F
	C,B	48
	C,C	49
	C,D	4A
	C,E	4B
	C,H	4C
	C,L	4D
	C,M	4E
MOV	D,A	57
	D,B	50
	D,C	51
	D,D	52
	D,E	53
	D,H	54
	D,L	55
	D,M	56

Move (cont)

MOV	E,A	5F
	E,B	58
	E,C	59
	E,D	5A
	E,E	5B
	E,H	5C
	E,L	5D
	E,M	5E
MOV	H,A	67
	H,B	60
	H,C	61
	H,D	62
	H,E	63
	H,H	64
	H,L	65
	H,M	66
MOV	L,A	6F
	L,B	68
	L,C	69
	L,D	6A
	L,E	6B
	L,H	6C
	L,L	6D
	L,M	6E
MOV	M,A	77
	M,B	70
	M,C	71
	M,D	72
	M,E	73
	M,H	74
	M,L	75
XCHG		EB

Move Immediate

MVI	A, byte	3E
	B, byte	06
	C, byte	0E
	D, byte	16
	E, byte	1E
	H, byte	26
	L, byte	2E
	M, byte	36

Load Immediate

LXI	B, dble	01
	D, dble	11
	H, dble	21
	SP, dble	31

Load/Store

LDAX B	0A
LDAX D	1A
LHLD adr	2A
LDA adr	3A
STAX B	02
STAX D	12
SHLD adr	22
STA adr	32

byte = constant, or logical/arithmetic expression that evaluates to an 8-bit data quantity. (Second byte of 2-byte instructions).

dble = constant, or logical/arithmetic expression that evaluates to a 16-bit data quantity. (Second and Third bytes of 3-byte instructions).

adr = 16-bit address (Second and Third bytes of 3-byte instructions).

* = all flags (C, Z, S, P, AC) affected

** = all flags except CARRY affected. (exception: INX and DCX affect no flags).

† = only CARRY affected.

ACCUMULATOR OPERATIONS

	Code	Function
XRA A	AF	Clear A and Clear Carry
ORA A	B7	Clear Carry
CMC	3F	Complement Carry
CMA	2F	Complement Accumulator
STC	37	Set Carry
RLC	07	Rotate Left
RRC	0F	Rotate Right
RAL	17	Rotate Left Thru Carry
RAR	1F	Rotate Right Thru Carry
DAA	27	Decimal Adjust Accum

Fig. 8-1. Programmers reference chart with instructions and op codes.

ARITHMETIC AND LOGICAL GROUP

Add*

Instruction	Register	Code
ADD	A	87
ADD	B	80
ADD	C	81
ADD	D	82
ADD	E	83
ADD	H	84
ADD	L	85
ADD	M	86
ADC	A	8F
ADC	B	88
ADC	C	89
ADC	D	8A
ADC	E	8B
ADC	H	8C
ADC	L	8D
ADC	M	8E

Subtract*

Instruction	Register	Code
SUB	A	97
SUB	B	90
SUB	C	91
SUB	D	92
SUB	E	93
SUB	H	94
SUB	L	95
SUB	M	96
SBB	A	9F
SBB	B	98
SBB	C	99
SBB	D	9A
SBB	E	9B
SBB	H	9C
SBB	L	9D
SBB	M	9E

Double Add †

Instruction	Register	Code
DAD	B	09
DAD	D	19
DAD	H	29
DAD	SP	39

Increment**

Instruction	Register	Code
INR	A	3C
INR	B	04
INR	C	0C
INR	D	14
INR	E	1C
INR	H	24
INR	L	2C
INR	M	34
INX	B	03
INX	D	13
INX	H	23
INX	SP	33

Decrement**

Instruction	Register	Code
DCR	A	3D
DCR	B	05
DCR	C	0D
DCR	D	15
DCR	E	1D
DCR	H	25
DCR	L	2D
DCR	M	35
DCX	B	0B
DCX	D	1B
DCX	H	2B
DCX	SP	3B

Specials

Instruction	Code
DAA*	27
CMA	2F
STC†	37
CMC†	3F

Rotate †

Instruction	Code
RLC	07
RRC	0F
RAL	17
RAR	1F

Logical*

Instruction	Register	Code
ANA	A	A7
ANA	B	A0
ANA	C	A1
ANA	D	A2
ANA	E	A3
ANA	H	A4
ANA	L	A5
ANA	M	A6
XRA	A	AF
XRA	B	A8
XRA	C	A9
XRA	D	AA
XRA	E	AB
XRA	H	AC
XRA	L	AD
XRA	M	AE
ORA	A	B7
ORA	B	B0
ORA	C	B1
ORA	D	B2
ORA	E	B3
ORA	H	B4
ORA	L	B5
ORA	M	B6
CMP	A	BF
CMP	B	B8
CMP	C	B9
CMP	D	BA
CMP	E	BB
CMP	H	BC
CMP	L	BD
CMP	M	BE

Arith & Logi Immediate

Instruction	Code
ADI byte	C6
ACI byte	CE
SUI byte	D6
SBI byte	DE
ANI byte	E6
XRI byte	EE
ORI byte	F6
CPI byte	FE

BRANCH CONTROL GROUP

Jump

Instruction	Code
JMP adr	C3
JNZ adr	C2
JZ adr	CA
JNC adr	D2
JC adr	DA
JPO adr	E2
JPE adr	EA
JP adr	F2
JM adr	FA
PCHL	E9

Call

Instruction	Code
CALL adr	CD
CNZ adr	C4
CZ adr	CC
CNC adr	D4
CC adr	DC
CPO adr	E4
CPE adr	EC
CP adr	F4
CM adr	FC

Return

Instruction	Code
RET	C9
RNZ	C0
RZ	C8
RNC	D0
RC	D8
RPO	E0
RPE	E8
RP	F0
RM	F8

I/O AND MACHINE CONTROL

Stack Ops

Instruction	Register	Code
PUSH	B	C5
PUSH	D	D5
PUSH	H	E5
PUSH	PSW	F5
POP	B	C1
POP	D	D1
POP	H	E1
POP	PSW*	F1
XTHL		E3
SPHL		F9

Input/Output

Instruction	Code
OUT byte	D3
IN byte	DB

Control

Instruction	Code
DI	F3
EI	FB
NOP	00
HLT	76

BRANCH CONTROL INSTRUCTIONS

Flag Condition	Jump		Call		Return	
Zero=True	JZ	CA	CZ	CC	RZ	C8
Zero=False	JNZ	C2	CNZ	C4	RNZ	C0
Carry=True	JC	DA	CC	DC	RC	D8
Carry=False	JNC	D2	CNC	D4	RNC	D0
Sign=Positive	JP	F2	CP	F4	RP	F0
Sign=Negative	JM	FA	CM	FC	RM	F8
Parity=Even	JPE	EA	CPE	EC	RPE	E8
Parity=Odd	JPO	E2	CPO	E4	RPO	E0
Unconditional	JMP	C3	CALL	CD	RET	C9

OP CODE VS. INSTRUCTION

Op	Instruction		Op	Instruction		Op	Instruction		Op	Instruction		Op	Instruction	
00	NOP		2B	DCX	H	56	MOV	D,M	81	ADD	C	AC	XRA	H
01	LXI	B,dble	2C	INR	L	57	MOV	D,A	82	ADD	D	AD	XRA	L
02	STAX	B	2D	DCR	L	58	MOV	E,B	84	ADD	H	AE	XRA	M
03	INX	B	2E	MVI	L,byte	59	MOV	E,C	85	ADD	L	AF	XRA	A
04	INR	B	2F	CMA		5A	MOV	E,D	86	ADD	M	B0	ORA	B
05	DCR	B	30	SIM*		5B	MOV	E,E	87	ADD	A	B1	ORA	C
06	MVI	B,byte	31	LXI	SP,dble	5C	MOV	E,H	88	ADC	B	B2	ORA	D
07	RLC		32	STA	adr	5D	MOV	E,L	89	ADC	C	B3	ORA	E
08	---		33	INX	SP	5E	MOV	E,M	8A	ADC	D	B4	ORA	H
09	DAD	B	34	INR	M	5F	MOV	E,A	8B	ADC	E	B5	ORA	L
0A	LDAX	B	35	DCR	M	60	MOV	H,B	8C	ADC	H	B6	ORA	M
0B	DCX	B	36	MVI	M,byte	61	MOV	H,C	8D	ADC	L	B7	ORA	A
0C	INR	C	37	STC		62	MOV	H,D	8E	ADC	M	B8	CMP	B
0D	DCR	C	38	---		63	MOV	H,E	8F	ADC	A	B9	CMP	C
0E	MVI	C,byte	39	DAD	SP	64	MOV	H,H	90	SUB	B	BA	CMP	D
0F	RRC		3A	LDA	adr	65	MOV	H,L	91	SUB	C	BB	CMP	E
10	---		3B	DCX	SP	66	MOV	H,M	92	SUB	D	BC	CMP	H
11	LXI	D,dble	3C	INR	A	67	MOV	H,A	93	SUB	E	BD	CMP	L
12	STAX	D	3D	DCR	A	68	MOV	L,B	94	SUB	H	BE	CMP	M
13	INX	D	3E	MVI	A,byte	69	MOV	L,C	95	SUB	L	BF	CMP	A
14	INR	D	3F	CMC		6A	MOV	L,D	96	SUB	M	C0	RNZ	
15	DCR	D	40	MOV	B,B	6B	MOV	L,E	97	SUB	A	C1	POP	B
16	MVI	D,byte	41	MOV	B,C	6C	MOV	L,H	98	SBB	B	C2	JNZ	adr
17	RAL		42	MOV	B,D	6D	MOV	L,L	99	SBB	C	C3	JMP	adr
18	---		43	MOV	B,E	6E	MOV	L,M	9A	SBB	D	C4	CNZ	adr
19	DAD	D	44	MOV	B,H	6F	MOV	L,A	9B	SBB	E	C5	PUSH	B
1A	LDAX	D	45	MOV	B,L	70	MOV	M,B	9C	SBB	H	C6	ADI	byte
1B	DCX	D	46	MOV	B,M	71	MOV	M,C	9D	SBB	L	C7	RST	0
1C	INR	E	47	MOV	B,A	72	MOV	M,D	9E	SBB	M	C8	RZ	
1D	DCR	E	48	MOV	C,B	73	MOV	M,E	9F	SBB	A	C9	RET	
1E	MVI	E,byte	49	MOV	C,C	74	MOV	M,H	A0	ANA	B	CA	JZ	
1F	RAR		4A	MOV	C,D	75	MOV	M,L	A1	ANA	C	CB	---	
20	RIM*		4B	MOV	C,E	76	HLT		A2	ANA	D	CC	CZ	adr
21	LXI	H,dble	4C	MOV	C,H	77	MOV	M,A	A3	ANA	E	CD	CALL	adr
22	SHLD	adr	4D	MOV	C,L	78	MOV	A,B	A4	ANA	H	CE	ACI	byte
23	INX	H	4E	MOV	C,M	79	MOV	A,C	A5	ANA	L	CF	RST	1
24	INR	H	4F	MOV	C,A	7A	MOV	A,D	A6	ANA	M	D0	RNC	
25	DCR	H	50	MOV	D,B	7B	MOV	A,E	A7	ANA	A	D1	POP	D
26	MVI	H,byte	51	MOV	D,C	7C	MOV	A,H	A8	XRA	B	D2	JNC	adr
27	DAA		52	MOV	D,D	7D	MOV	A,L	A9	XRA	C	D3	OUT	byte
28	---		53	MOV	D,E	7E	MOV	A,M	AA	XRA	D	D4	CNC	adr
29	DAD	H	54	MOV	D,H	7F	MOV	A,A	AB	XRA	E	D5	PUSH	D
2A	LHLD	adr	55	MOV	D,L	80	ADD	B				D6	SUI	byte

Fig. 8-1. Programmers reference chart with instructions and op codes. (Continued from page 165.)

HEX-ASCII TABLE

Hex	Instruction	Hex	Char		Hex	Char	Hex	Char		Hex	Char	
D7	RST 2	00	NUL		21	!	42	B		63	c	
D8	RC	01	SOH		22	"	43	C		64	d	
D9	---	02	STX		23	#	44	D		65	e	
DA	JC adr	03	ETX		24	$	45	E		66	f	
DB	IN byte	04	EOT		25	%	46	F		67	g	
DC	CC adr	05	ENQ		26	&	47	G		68	h	
DD	---	06	ACK		27	'	48	H		69	i	
DE	SBI byte	07	BEL		28	(	49	I		6A	j	
DF	RST 3	08	BS		29	)	4A	J		6B	k	
E0	RPO	09	HT		2A	*	4B	K		6C	l	
E1	POP H	0A	LF		2B	+	4C	L		6D	m	
E2	JPO adr	0B	VT		2C	,	4D	M		6E	n	
E3	XTHL	0C	FF		2D	-	4E	N		6F	o	
E4	CPO adr	0D	CR		2E	.	4F	O		70	p	
E5	PUSH H	0E	SO		2F	/	50	P		71	q	
E6	ANI byte	0F	SI		30	0	51	Q		72	r	
E7	RST 4	10	DLE		31	1	52	R		73	s	
E8	RPE	11	DC1	(X-ON)	32	2	53	S		74	t	
E9	PCHL	12	DC2	(TAPE)	33	3	54	T		75	u	
EA	JPE adr	13	DC3	(X-OFF)	34	4	55	U		76	v	
EB	XCHG	14	DC4	~~(TAPE)~~	35	5	56	V		77	w	
EC	CPE adr	15	NAK		36	6	57	W		78	x	
ED	---	16	SYN		37	7	58	X		79	y	
EE	XRI byte	17	ETB		38	8	59	Y		7A	z	
EF	RST 5	18	CAN		39	9	5A	Z		7B	{	
F0	RP	19	EM		3A	:	5B	[		7C	|	
F1	POP PSW	1A	SUB		3B	;	5C	\		7D	}	
F2	JP adr	1B	ESC		3C	<	5D	]				(ALT MODE
F3	DI	1C	FS		3D	=	5E	^	(↑)	7E		
F4	CP adr	1D	GS		3E	>	5F	—	(←)	7F	DEL	
F5	PUSH PSW	1E	RS		3F	?	60	`				(RUB OUT
F6	ORI byte	1F	US		40	@	61	a				
F7	RST 6	20	SP		41	A	62	b				
F8	RM											
F9	SPHL											
FA	JM adr											
FB	EI											
FC	CM adr											
FD	---											
FE	CPI byte											
FF	RST 7											

do—and from experience. First study the instructions, visualize what they do, and where they are used. There's no need to memorize the machine code—that can be looked up—but the types of instructions, what they do, and what tools are available must be known.

THE BASIC PROGRAMMING STEPS

Listed below are several steps used in writing a program. The order in which they are used and which steps are used depends on the size and complexity of the program. Some of the steps are discussed in detail later.

1. Define the program objective.
2. Break the objective up into logical parts. Visualize how each of these parts can be accomplished.
3. Draw a simplified flow diagram.
4. Check the flow diagram to ensure that it flows logically and that the overall objective is accomplished.
5. Visualize how each block in the simplified flow diagram can be accomplished.
6. Compile this into a detailed flow diagram. This is the first time that the instructions and how the computer works enters into programming.
7. Assign labels (alphanumeric designations) to addresses, program variables, and constants not yet determined.
8. Examine the program, one block at a time, and investigate the effects of the different variables and program transfers. Make sure each block does only what it is supposed to do.
9. Examine the program, looking for the possibility of undesirable program loops or of the program recognizing unwanted conditions.
10. Block by block, assign mnemonic codes for the instructions required to complete each block. Labels can be assigned to program variables and jump to addresses.
11. Make sure each instruction works in the manner desired, and that the results are as desired.

12. Ensure that each flag is set by the conditions desired before the flags are used, and that they are not changed before they are used.
13. Make sure each call instruction has a return instruction, or that provisions are made to account for the required return.
14. Keep track of the program-initialization requirements.
15. Make sure each conditional transfer instruction transfers only on the conditions desired.
16. Talk the program through several times, setting up all possible conditions to verify that the program works as desired.
17. Make sure that there is a POP instruction, or some means of adjusting the stack, for each PUSH instruction. The converse also applies.
18. Remember that the last information placed on the stack by a PUSH instruction is the first information off the stack by a POP instruction.
19. Make sure the program has some place to go when it is finished. Otherwise it will wander aimlessly, destroying programs and data.
20. Determine the initialization requirements. Make sure that the stack pointer and all the required conditions and all program variables are initialized to the proper conditions.

USING THE STACK

The stack is used by the hardware to store the return addresses for the CALL-type instructions. When a CALL-type instruction is executed the address of the next sequential instruction is placed at the current stack location, and the stack pointer is decremented twice. Thus, the stack pointer is always pointing to the next stack address. Depending on the number of unexecuted returns and the amount of data stored on the stack, the stack pointer may be several addresses down from the value originally assigned. This must be taken into account when the stack is initialized. That is, the stack pointer is loaded with the top stack address using the LXI SP instruction. The stack is normally placed in some area of RAM that is not used by the program, and usually at the upper end of the memory area.

The PUSH and POP instructions save data and free registers for usage by subroutines. If data is in the registers that are to be used by the subroutine, this data must be saved if it is to be retained. The easiest way to save it is to place it on the stack using one of the two methods shown in Fig. 8-2. The first method stores the information on the stack before calling the subroutine, and retrieves it after the return is executed. The second method stores the information on the stack in the subroutine, and retrieves it before returning. Both methods have their uses but the second method uses fewer instructions; the push and pop instructions are required only once in this subroutine, and the first method requires these instructions whenever the subroutine is called.

Realize that the informtion at the current-stack location can be changed by popping it into a register pair, altering it, and pushing it back on the stack. This method is often used to change the return address under certain conditions. For example, the instructions required to rerun the subroutine are:

```
POP rp
DCX rp
DCX rp
DCX rp
PUSH rp
RET
```

Place this in the branch of the subroutine when it is desired to call the same subroutine. There must be another branch in which the program exits in some other manner. The rp used above designates a register pair. When this instruction set is executed, it decrements the current stack location by three—the address of the call instruction for the subroutine.

THE SIMPLIFIED FLOW DIAGRAM

The simplified flow diagram provides the overall picture of the logical steps required to accomplish the program

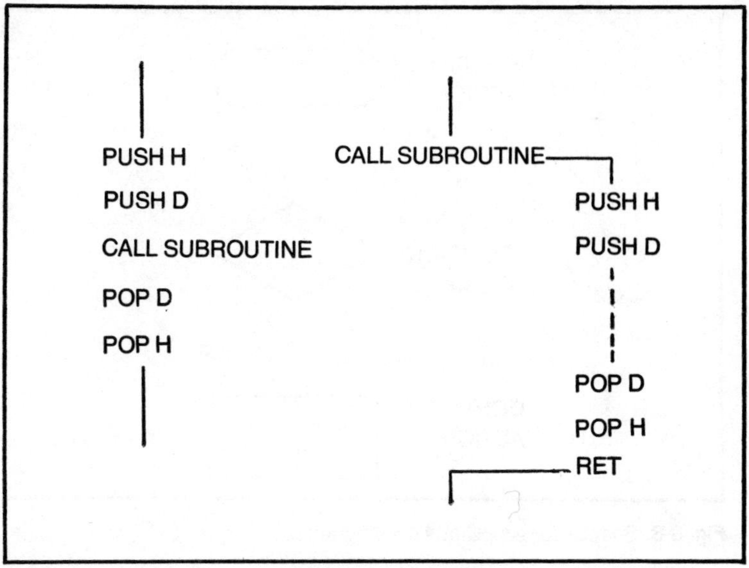

Fig. 8-2. Using the PUSH and POP instructions within subroutines.

objectives. The instruction types available and the computer used are not considered, only what the program is to accomplish. There are three different types of operations to be considered here. These are:

- Operator actions: These are actions which require an operator input, such as an execute input.
- Decision blocks: These are decisions made by the program and have more than one possible output. These blocks are usually represented by diamonds.
- Computer operations: These blocks represent computer action in general terms.

Figure 8-3 shows the shapes used in this book for both the simplified and detailed flow diagrams. Any shapes can be used, and the decision blocks should be different than the other two. Some programmers use rectangles for both operator inputs and computer operations, and diamonds for decision blocks.

Figure 8-4 shows the simplified flow diagram for a simple countdown loop for decrementing counter n times. The first block sets up a second counter with the number of passes (n). The second block decrements both counters and

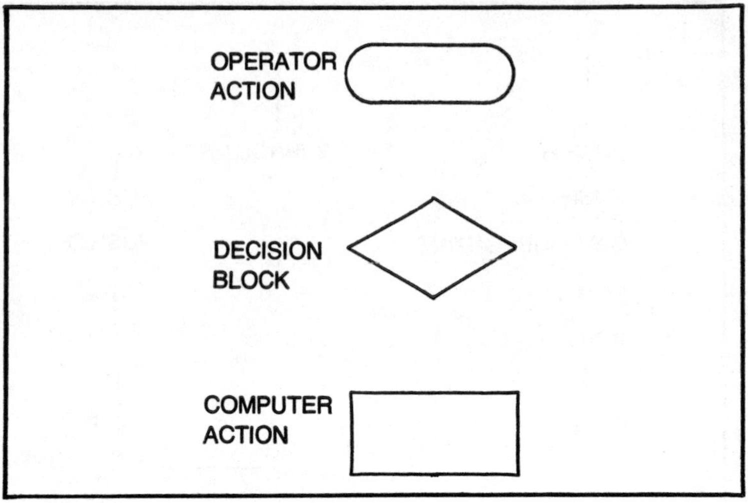

Fig. 8-3. Shapes for simplified flow diagrams.

the third block checks for the second counter equal to zero. This indicates the end of the loop.

Sometimes the simplified flow diagram is visualized but not written down. This decision depends on the complexity of the program and the programmer's experience. The starting programmer is advised to write the simplified flow diagram on paper. This forces visualization of the program.

THE DETAILED FLOW DIAGRAM

The detailed flow diagram is the first step in bringing the program and the computer together. The detailed flow diagram consists of the blocks required to execute the program in the computer. General terms can be used to describe the action of each block, or the actual mnemonics can be used for some of the blocks. A combination of both are used in this book. See Fig. 8-6. Figure 8-5 shows the detailed flow diagram for the countdown loop shown in Fig. 8-4. This flow diagram assumes that the counter is one data word in memory, and it is to be returned to memory.

The first block moves the counter to the A register; the second block sets up the B register as the second counter (the pass counter); the third block decrements both the A and

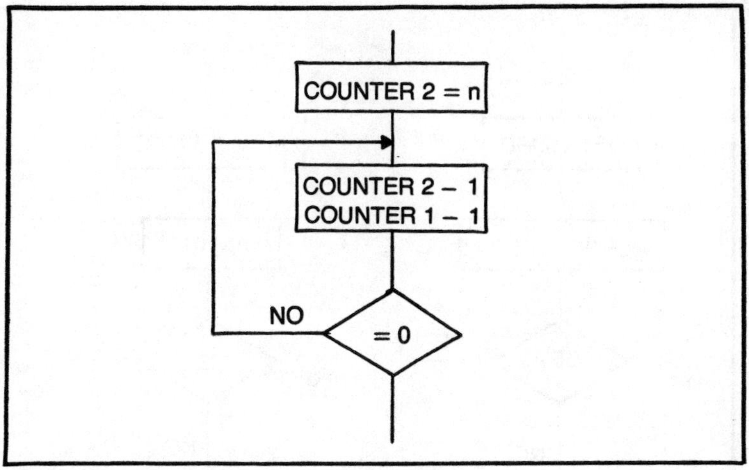

Fig. 8-4. Simple countdown loop flow diagram.

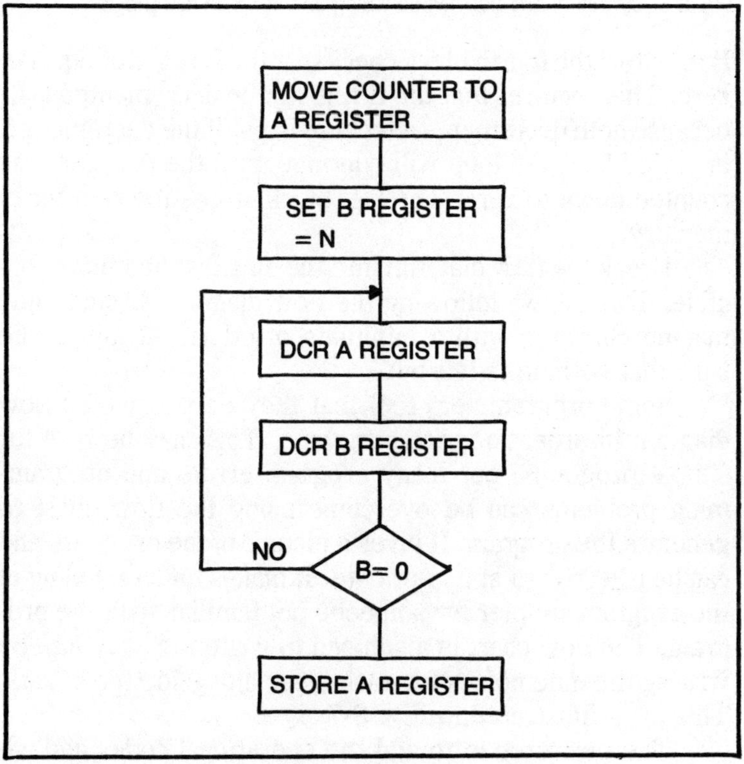

Fig. 8-5. Detailed flow diagram for Fig. 8-4.

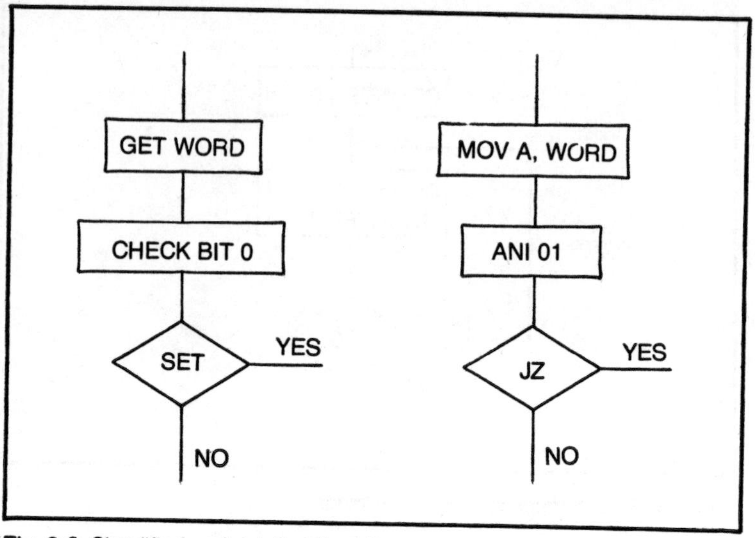

Fig. 8-6. Simplified and detailed flow diagrams for a bit test program.

B register; the fourth block checks for the B register equal to zero. This requires that the B register be decremented last, because both decrements affect the flags. If the decrement A is placed last, the loop will continue until the A register is counted down to zero. The last block stores the counter in memory.

Break the flow diagram into the smallest functions possible. This allows following the flow diagram through, and making changing with a minimum of effort. Always make sure that nothing is left out.

Some programmers feel that they do not need a flow diagram in order to write programs. This may be true for simple programs, but many program errors and programming problems can be overcome using the flow chart to generate the program. It gives a picture of the program, and can be referred to at a later date. It makes understanding of the program simpler for someone not familiar with the program. The flow chart is also used to write the program, by writing the mnemonics for each block alongside the blocks. This is as illustrated in Fig. 8-7.

The next step is to add the operational codes and addresses to the flow diagram. The addresses may be absolute,

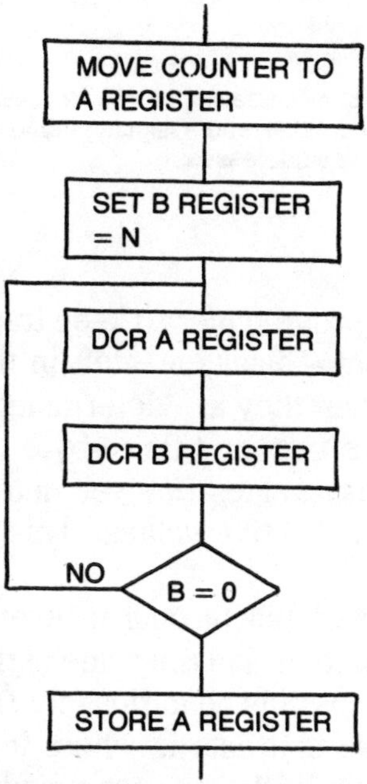

ADDRESS	MNEMONIC	OP CODE
0100	LDA 0150	3A
0101		50
0102		01
0103	MVI B,n	06
0104		n
0105	DCR A	3D
0106	DCR B	05
0107	JNZ 0105	C2
0108		05
0109		01
010A	STA 0150	32
010B		50
010C		01

Fig. 8-7. Flow diagram with program listing.

as shown in Fig. 8-7, or relative addresses with labels, as shown in Fig. 8-8. If relative addresses are used, they must be converted to absolute addresses when loaded into the computer. Some programmers write the program operational code on a separate piece of paper. But this means that the program is documented with two pieces of paper instead of just one.

```
        ORIGIN  LDA   0150
        03      MVI   B,n
LOOP:   05      DCR   A
        06      DCR   B
        07      JNZ   Loop
        0A      STA   0150
```

Fig. 8-8. Using relative addresses and labels.

```
LDA, TEST   3A
            —
            —
ANA B       A0
JNZ YES     C2
            —
            —
```

Fig. 8-9. Leaving blanks for relative addresses and assigning labels for these addresses.

The flow diagram allows the programmer to keep track of two- and three-byte instructions—blanks are left in the mnemonics which are filled in when they are determined.

Always leave space for these two- and three-byte instructions. Leave blanks for those values not yet determined, and fill in labels for those relative values. This is illustrated in Fig. 8-9.

Once the flow chart is completed, talk through it several times keeping track of register contents and the value of the program variables. Set up all the possible conditions for the program variables, and make sure that data is where it is required. Also check for the intregity of the data contained in any of the registers used.

USING THE CONDITIONAL INSTRUCTIONS

The conditional program-transfer instructions give the program the ability to make decisions as a result of program operation. These transfer instructions change the program flow depending on the condition of the program flags. In the example shown in Fig. 8-5, the JUMP NON ZERO (JNZ) instruction makes the decision when it is time to exit the program loop. If the zero flag is not set, the program jumps back, and if the flag is set, the program exits the loop.

There are conditional program transfer instructions which alter the program flow depending on the condition of each of the program flags. These are described in Table 8-1. Any of the returns, conditional or unconditional, will work with any of the call instructions. When using conditional returns, make sure that the condition will be met, or that some other loop exists which allows the program to return if the conditional return is not satisfied. In Fig. 8-5, the A register count down to zero, so eventually the zero flag will be set allowing the program to exit the loop and execute the return or the following program. It is possible, if you aren't careful, to end up with a program loop from which there is no exit.

Figure 8-10 illustrates use of the conditional and unconditional transfer instructions. Figure 8-11 shows a program loop which can cause trouble. The loop intends to find a data word with the low-order bit HIGH. If none of the data words has this bit HIGH, the program will remain in the loop until it does find HIGH in this bit position, which may be out of the data field. Remember that the next sequential address after FFFF is 0000, so the program may find this out of the program data area.

You can, however, set the low-order bit in the last word of the data field HIGH. If no word is found, the program still exits when it reads the last data word. Another method is to check for the last data address, as illustrated in Fig. 8-12. In

Table 8-1. The Conditional Program Transfer Instructions.

MNEMONIC	OP CODE	DESCRIPTION
JNZ	C2	Jump if zero flag not set
JZ	CA	Jump if zero flag set
JNC	D2	Jump if carry flag not set
JC	DA	Jump if carry flag set
JPO	E2	Jump if parity flag not set
JPE	EA	Jump if parity flag not set
JP	F2	Jump if minus flag not set
JM	FA	Jump if minus flag set
CNZ	C4	Call if zero flag not set
CZ	CC	Call if zero flag set
CNC	D4	Call if carry flag not set
CC	DC	Call if carry flag set
CPO	E4	Call if parity flag not set
CPE	EC	Call if parity flag set
CP	F4	Call if minus flag not set
CM	FC	Call if minus flag set
RNZ	C0	Return if zero flag not set
RX	C8	Return if zero flag set
RNC	D0	Return if carry flag not set
RC	D8	Return if carry flag set
RPO	E0	Return if parity flag not set
RPE	E8	Return if parity flag set
RP	F0	Return if minus flag not set
RM	F8	Return if minus flag set

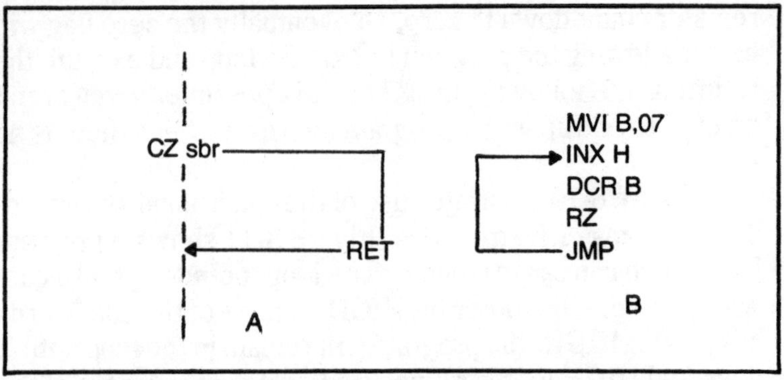

Fig. 8-10. Entering and returning from subroutines using conditional call and return instructions.

this figure, the zero flag will be set if it finds the end of data so the program can determine which program exit was used.

When trying to determine if a data value falls between two values, it is advisable to use the carry flag. If the minus flag is used, problems can arise if the data or the limits have data-bit 7 high. This is illustrated in Fig. 8-13. The high-order limit is subtracted from the data. Normally the minus flag would be set only if the data is smaller than the high order limit. But if data has bit 7 high and the high order limit does not, the minus flag will be set, and, as a result, the minus flag will be set. Using the carry flag gets around this problem.

SUBROUTINES

Subroutines comprise a series of instructions which the program uses over and over again. These subroutines are accessed by the call instructions. Using subroutines saves program addresses, and simplifies programming. If data is stored in a register and the subroutine uses the register, the

```
LXI H, DATA ADDRESS
MOV A,M
ANI 01
RNZ
INX H
JMP
```

Fig. 8-11. Reading a series of addresses to find a bit 0.

```
LXI H, DATA ADDRESS
MOV A,M
ANI 01
RNZ
MOV A,L
CPI LOW ORDER ADDRESS LIMIT
JNZ
MOV A,H
CPI HIGH ORDER ADDRESS LIMIT
RZ
INX H
JMP
```

Fig. 8-12. Restricting the program of Figure 8-11 to an upper address limit.

data is lost. If this data is to be used later in the program, it must be saved. One easy method of saving it is to store it on the stack.

Subroutines can be nested several levels, providing there is a return from each subroutine. Subroutines nesting is the calling of one subroutine from another subroutine. The limits on the number subroutines that can be nested is the size of the available stack area. Each call requires two stack locations to store its return address.

When a call-type instruction is executed, the next instruction address is automatically placed on the stack. The

```
MOV A, DATA
SUI HIGH ORDER LIMIT
JP
MIV A, DATA
SUI LOW ORDER LIMIT
RP
SET OUT OF LIMITS INDICATOR
RET
```

Fig. 8-13. Program to determine if the data falls between two values.

return-type instruction takes the last two words off the stack and uses them as its return address, and when the return is executed, the program flow transfers to this location.

Because the return instruction does not change the condition of the flags, the flags can be set in the subroutine and sampled after the return, as illustrated by:

```
RCY  CALL
           CPI
           RET
      JZ RCY
```

This is especially useful if the program is to transfer to various points in the program depending on the condition of the flags. Another trick is to replace the return address with another address for certain conditions. This can be done by:

```
POP H
LXI H, new address
PUSH H
RET
```

This will return the program to the new address. This is especially useful when an error condition has been detected. This allows the operator to cycle the program to the error location, and recycle for new input.

Always keep track of the registers and temporary storage locations used within the subroutines. It is advisable to make up a subroutine listing that gives the address, function of the subroutine, set up conditions required, registers used, temporary storage locations used, and where to find the results. This provides a quick reference for writing programs.

It takes three memory locations to call a subroutine; any repeated sequence of more than three memory locations, therefore, can be replaced by a call. The number of locations saved is determined by the amount of addresses in the subroutine, and the number of times it is used. If a sequence of six locations is used only twice, it is not efficient to replace it with a subroutine; but if it is used several times, it is efficient.

MONITOR AND CONTROL PROGRAMS

Any general-purpose computer requires a monitor or control program as its resident program starting at the initialization address (address 0000 for this computer). This program allows the operator to talk to the computer and to input programs. The monitor may contain subroutines which can be used by the operator within other programs. The basic requirements for the monitor for this computer are:

Initialize: Initialize the computer and reset all the I/O ports.

Load: A keyboard program which allows the operator to input data into the program by the keyboard.

Read: To allow the operator to read specified memory addresses and display on the LED display.

Go To To allow the operator to specify a memory address and transfer program flow to that address. This program allows execution of operator programs.

These are the minimum requirements, and they can be expanded at a later time. Figure 8-14 illustrates the flow diagram for this program. The program listing is given in Chapter 9. This program loops back on itself for the read and local branches, and is open loop for the GOTO branch. The program executed by the GOTO must loop to a place that provides a program termination.

The monitor program must start at address 0000, because this is the first address executed when the computer is turned on or reset. During the initialization the stack pointer must be set to the address of the top of the stack by the LXI,SP instruction. Initialization also reset all the ports and, if required, initialize the program variables.

PROGRAM DEBUGGING

When a program is loaded into the computer, it's tempting to execute it and let it run. If the program runs correctly, everything is fine. But the odds are that it will not run as desired. If there are program bugs, weird things can happen. The program might be completely destroyed, some addresses might be changed or shifted, or nothing at all might happen. For this reason it is advisable to check the

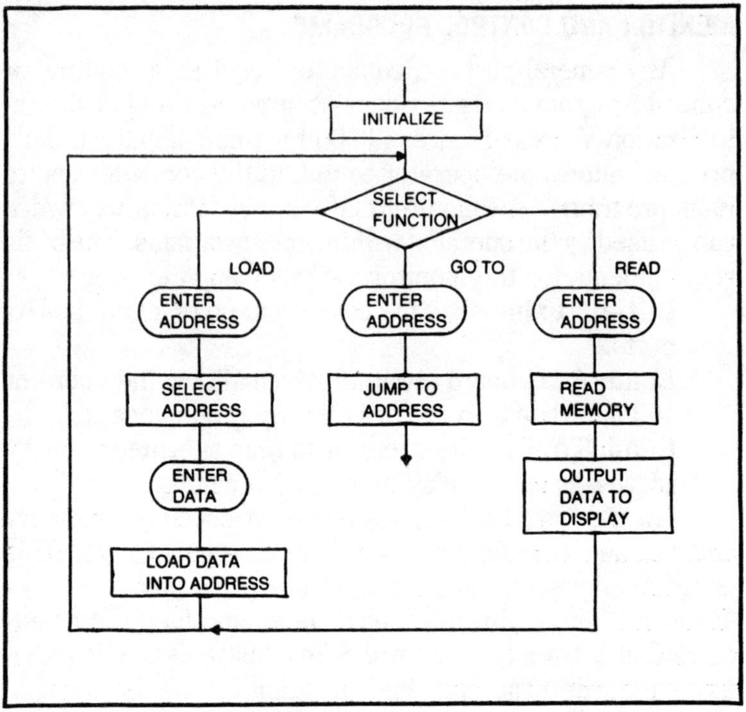

Fig. 8-14. Simplified flow diagram for a monitor program.

program first. It will take only a few minutes and can save reloading the program several times. Among the things to be checked are:

1: Single step through the program and verify that the program is loaded.
2: Make sure all the jump-destination addresses are correct.
3: Make sure the conditional transfers occur on the correct conditions.
4: Make sure that the flags are set by the desired instructions, and not changed before they are sampled.
5: Make sure that registers are not changed erroneously.
6: Make sure that the data is where it is supposed to be.
7: Make sure the count down loops are correct.
8: Make sure there are no loops where it is possible to exit in an undesirable conditions.

9: Make sure there is no conditions where an infinite loop can exist.

If the program contains complex subroutines, set up conditions to execute and check these subroutines. This is done by writing short test programs setting up the conditions for the subroutine, then executing the subroutine and checking the results.

When the program has been checked, it can be executed. Kick it off and let it run. If it runs, well and good. But if it don't run it must be debugged. Remember that the computer does only what it is told to do. If it don't run, the program must be in error. If the program seems to go into a loop, or just stop someplace, use the single step to stop the computer and display the address.

To begin single stepping the program at its start, reset the computer and select and enter the GOTO address. *Do not execute the GOTO until after the single step is selected.* Then the program can be single stepped to find where it goes astray.

If instructions are left out of the program, program patches can correct omission. Use jump instructions to go to a memory location where the replaced instruction and the instruction that was left out, are executed along with a jump back to the program. This is illustrated by Fig. 8-15, where the MOV A,M instruction was left out of the original program. The LHLD instruction is replaced with a JUMP in-

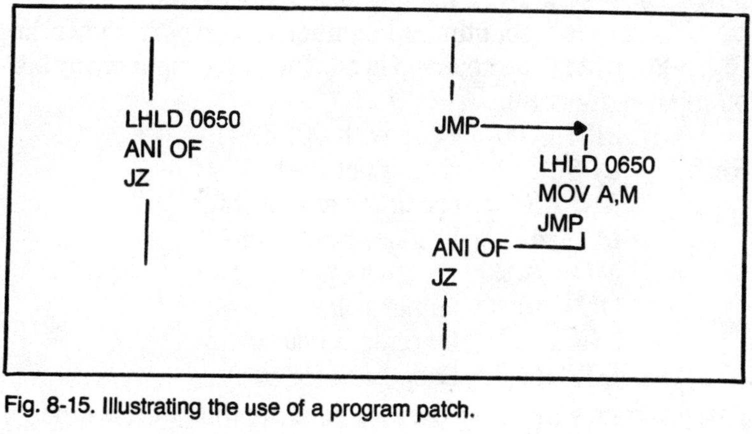

Fig. 8-15. Illustrating the use of a program patch.

struction. The LHLD instruction and the MOV A,M instruction is placed at the jump-to address. Next the JUMP instruction transfers the program back to the main program. Note that a call and return instruction can be used with the savings of two memory locations.

One method of reading the registers involves inserting temporary program patches in the program. These patches store the registers' contents so that they can be read later. This allows reading the register contents after program execution is complete. Another debugging tool is the HLT instruction. This instruction stops the computer execution. When the halt is executed, reset the computer and read the program variables and temporary storage locations.

Talk the program through, using the program listing and keeping track of the program variables and register contents. Set up all the conditions and verify that the program will talk through correctly. It should talk through, and if all the instructions are understood, the problem should become apparent.

If all else fails, try a different approach. But remember that if the program is executable, it will work.

SOME PROGRAMS

Now let us look at some real programs. These simple programs are given as program listings in mnemonics, while flow charts—are given for the longer programs.

To output a counting up number to the port shown in Fig. 3-20, where the count up is one for every input of any bit on input-outport 80.

```
        MVI C,00    Start with 00
Read    IN 80       read input port
        ANI FF      check for any bit high
        JZ read     If none, read again
        MOV A,C
        OUT 40      output count
        INR C       Increment count
        JMP Read    Loop back for next
```

This program will stay in the loop until the computer is reset.

A program to output one pulse on port 40 bit 4 for each input on port 20 bit 0. The output pulse's length is the same as the length of time that the input pulse is available.

```
Read    IN 20        Read input port
        ANI 02       Check  for bit 1
        JZ Exit      Exit if set
        ANI 01       Check  for bit 0
        JNZ low      Jump if not set
        MVI A,10     Bit  4  set high
Write   OUT 40
        JUMP read
Low     MVI A,00     Bit 4 set low
        JMP Write
```

There are times when you'll need loops. The delay time is calculated from the clock cycles required to execute one pass through the loop, the basic clock-cycle time, and the number of times the loop is executed. The basic processor speed is 1/9 of its crystal frequency, which works out to be 500 nanoseconds for the 18 MHz crystal. This gives a 500nsec clock-cycle time. The number of clock cycles required for each instruction are given in Chapter 6.

If the delay time is as long as 50msec, dummy instructions may be used in the loop to kill time. Loops may also be nested to allow even longer delays. Figure 8-16 shows a

```
                          CLOCK
                          CYCLES

START   MVI C,84            7   SET UP FOR 132 PASSES
LOOP    DCR C               5   DECREMENT PASSES
        JNZ LOOP           10   LAST PASS?
        DCR B               5   DECREMENT NUMBER OF PASSES
        JNZ START          10   COMPLETED?
```

Fig. 8-16. A program delay loop.

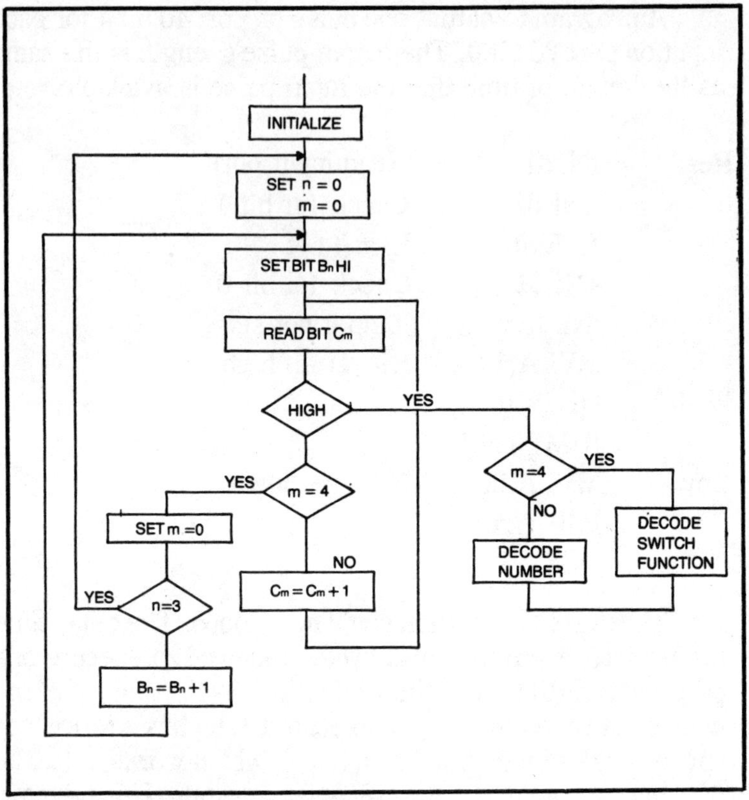

Fig. 8-17. Keyboard read flow diagram.

basic 1-millisecond delay loop, with the number of milliseconds delay stored in the B register when entering the loop.

The requirements for use of the keyboard shown in Fig. 3-31 are:

1: Set one vertical line HIGH
2: Read the horizontal lines, one at a time, looking for a HIGH
3: Sequence through all the vertical lines until a HIGH is found.

When the HIGH is found, the number is decoded to find the number of the input.

The flow chart for the keyboard read program is shown in Fig. 8-17. This flow chart refers to Fig. 3-31 for the port numbers and pin numbers. B is the B port and B_n refers to one line (n) on the B port. The C port is referenced as C, with C_m representing one line of the C port. The actual decoding of the input is the conversion from B_n and C_m to a hex number.

The program remains in the loop until it detects a HIGH on either one of the number lines or the control line. H_5 is used as the control line which allows special inputs to the program. These inputs are programmable, and are defined by the programmer. To output one hexadecimal character to

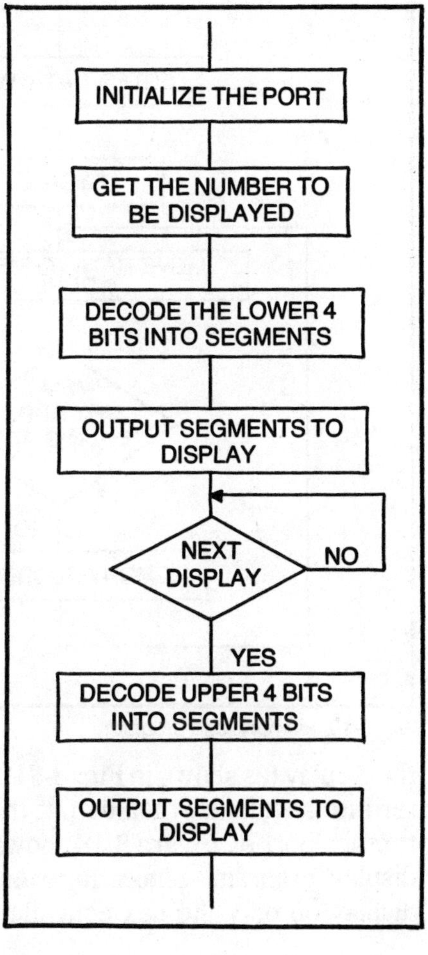

Fig. 8-18. Display flow diagram.

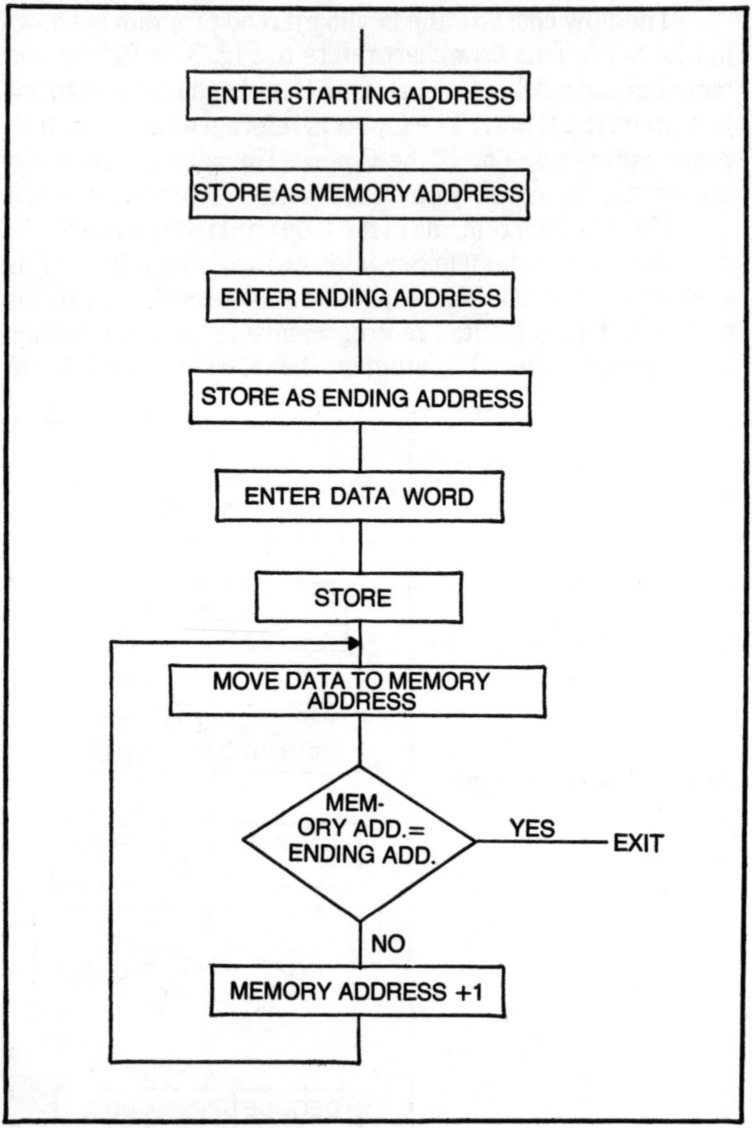

Fig. 8-19. Memory load program.

the display (as shown in Fig. 3-31) simply decode the character into segments, then output the segments to the display through port A. Figure 8-18 shows the flow diagram for this display program. Since there is only one display, it can display on only the hex equivalent for 4 bits. It takes two displays to accomodate one 8-bit word. One of the keyboard control keys is used to display the upper 4 bits, after the lower 4 bits are displayed. The decoding requirements and the program listing are given in Chapter 9.

Another useful program loads an area of memory with a data word. Typically this program is used to fill a memory area with zeros. The flow diagram for this program is shown in Fig. 8-19. The starting address, ending address, and data are input from the keyboard.

Chapter 9
Programming the Microcomputer

Once the computer is checked out and running, it is time to seriously consider programming it. This will be done in two stages— the first stage consists of the basic programs required to use the keyboard, display and EPROM programmer, and to allow the operator the capability of generating programs. This is a minimum type program, and part of it must be loaded with the hardware read and load capability every time the computer is powered up. Since the entire program is stored in RAM memory until the first EPROM is programmed, the total program is lost when power is turned off. At this point, the address decoder output 1 is connected to the RAM enable.

When this program is developed and written into EPROM, the second stage of development begins. This includes more capability, and refinements to the basic programs. As new programs are developed they are written into EPROMS so that they are available for use.

The basic program, the monitor, which resides in the computer, is the first program the computer enters when it is powered up. It has three capabilities, keyboard input and output, the EPROM-driver program, and GOTO. The keyboard input and output program allows the operator to read and display information under program control and to input information into the program. It is set up so that the operator can read or load any memory location under program control. The EPROM programmer software controls the EPROM programmer, accepting data from desired addresses. For the first-stage programing, the verify capability isn't included. Instead, the EPROM must be placed in the computer and read. The GOTO program allows the operator to begin program execution from any desired address.

Figure 9-1 shows a simplified flow diagram for the monitor program. When the computer is turned on, or reset, the program execution begins at the top, or address 0000. It looks for one of three inputs from the keyboard. Each of these numbers transfers the program to one of the three monitor programs. When the EPROM programmer software or the keyboard load and read program is exited, the program returns control as shown. The GOTO program is termed open ended because the program control is transferred to the desired address.

The initialization must set the stack pointer and initialize the ports. The stack pointer defines the top of the stack, and is usually set to high order RAM. Since the RAM addresses are 0000 through 03FF, the stack pointer is set to 03F0. Addresses 03F1 through 03FF are reserved for pro-

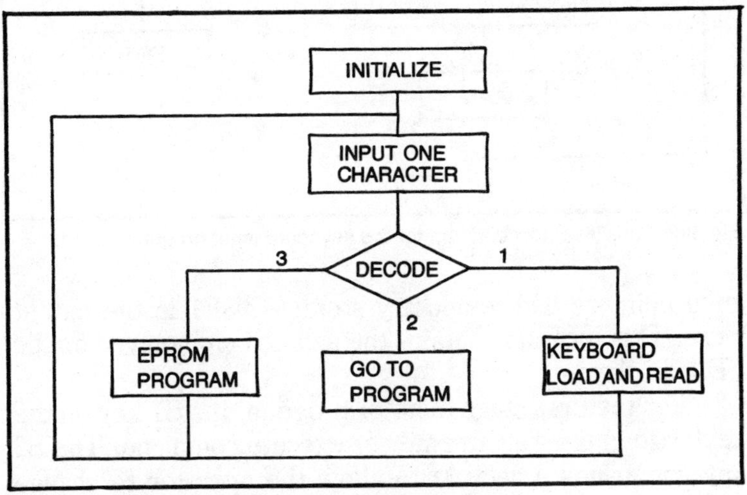

Fig. 9-1. Basic monitor program simplified flow diagram

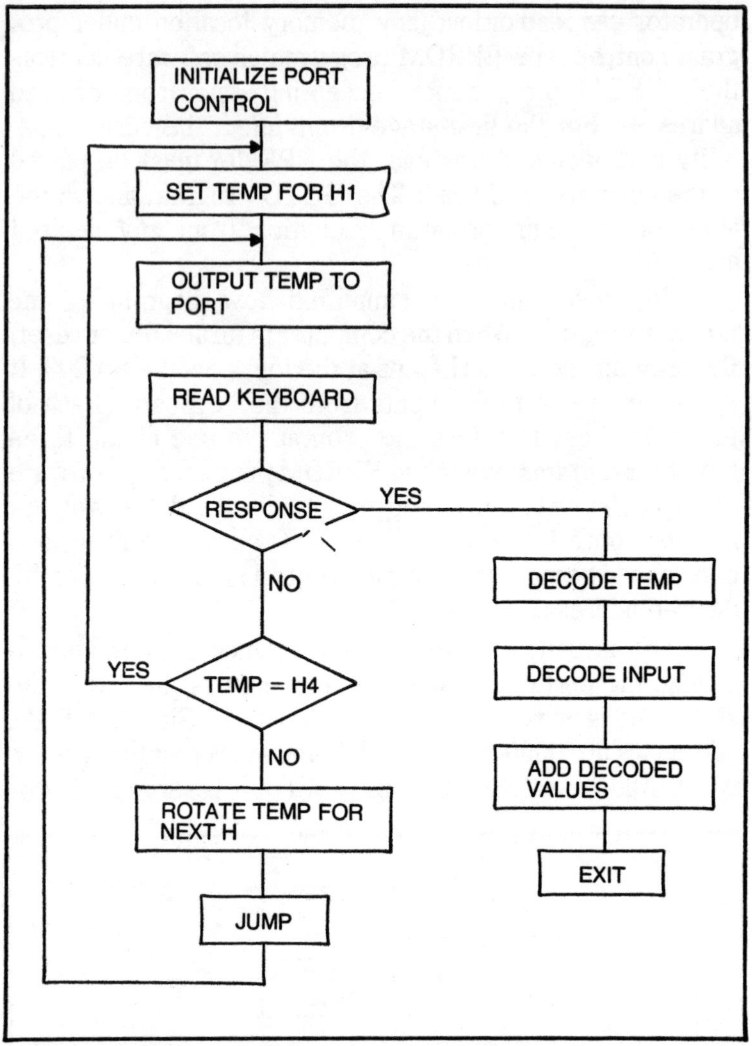

Fig. 9-2. Simplified flow diagram for the keyboard input program.

gram pointers and temporary storage. 03F1 is the output word. This location contains the data to be displayed on the LED displays.

For the first-stage monitor program, the S1 key on the keyboard is used as an enter or execute command. The S2 key commands a recycle to allow the operator to change previously entered data. The individual LED indicates that an operator input is required, and goes out when it is received. S3 and S4 are not used in this monitor.

MONITOR SUBROUTINES

The monitor requires subroutines for:

- Keyboard Input
- Display data on LEDs
- Delay
- Reading S1 and S2
- Individual LED on
- Individual LED off

Keyboard input

The keyboard-input subroutine reads and decodes the keyboard input for hex inputs. The special keys are not read. Figure 9-2 shows the simplified flow diagram for this subroutine. Each horizontal line is enabled, one at a time, and the vertical lines are read. The program loops until it finds an input. When a response is received, the response is com-

ADDRESS	FUNCTION
0000	CONTROL PORTION OF MAIN
0038	GO TO PROGRAM
00A0	CHANGE TABLE
0100	KEYBOARD READ SUBROUTINE
0148	DISPLAY SUBROUTINE
0179	CONVERSION TABLE
0189	READ SPECIAL KEYS SUBROUTINE
019C	LED ON SUBROUTINE
01A3	LED OFF SUBROUTINE
01AC	DELAY SUBROUTINE
01B9	INPUT 2 SUBROUTINE
0200	KEYBOARD READ AND LOAD MAIN PROGRAM
0300	EPROM PROGRAMMER MAIN PROGRAM
03f0	STACK POINTER
03f1	DISPLAY ADDRESS

Fig. 9-3. Memory allocation for the phase 1 monitor.

bined with the H output number, and decoded for its hex equivalent. Then the program exits the subroutine with the result stored in the accumulator. When the program is exited, the accumulators data must be stored if the input data is need later.

Figure 9-3 shows the memory allocation for the first-stage monitor. The main is placed to start at address 0000, with its subroutines beginning at 0100. Thus, the keyboard read program starts at 0100. Figure 9-4 shows the program listing for the keyboard-entry program. The H lines are enabled, one at a time, while looking for a vertical input. When a vertical input is received, its value is decoded, and added to the decoded value of the H number. The vertical is decoded by counting the number of rotate instructions it takes to generate a carry from the input bit. The horizontal input is decoded the same way, except 04 is added for each rotation.

As with all program modules, it is advisable to check out the subroutine before incorporating it into another program. The following short program will check out the keyboard entry program by storing the data read in address 0300.

Address	Mnemoni	Load into computer	
0000	KLXI SP,03f0	31	Load stack pointer
0001		F0	
0002		03	
0003	MVI A, 81	3E	Load control word
0004		81	
0005	OUT 83	D3	Output control word
0006		83	
0007	Call, 0100	CD	Call input
0008		00	
0009		01	
000A	STA,0300	32	Store input
000B		00	
000C		03	
000D	HALT	76	

Single step through the program the first time, making sure that the program executes correctly. When the input instruction is executed, depress a key and single step a couple more instructions holding the key down. When the halt is reached, all the LED's will come on indicating that the computer has executed the halt. Read address 0300 for the correct value for the key depressed. Reset the program and let it run. It should run in a loop, indicated by several of the LEDs being dim due to rapid cycling on and off. When a key is depressed the computer should go to the halt condition.

Check each key, making sure the correct answer is received for each key. Remember that the first key, the one in the upper left corner, is 0. That will be the value loaded into location 0300 for that key.

Display subroutine

The function of the display subroutine is to display each desired computer word as two hex digits. The computer word is stored at address 03F1, and is broken up into two hex digits, one for each of the two LED displays. Figure 9-5 shows the program listing for this program. The program takes the high-order four bits, converts them to segments, and outputs them to the high-order display. Then the low-order 4 bits are converted and displayed on the low-order display.

Figure 9-6 gives the program listing for this program. The display word is loaded into the accumulator, then masked and rotated to the low-order 4 bits. These bits are converted to segments by loading the H and L register pair with the starting address of the conversion table (0179). The H and L register pair is incremented and the accumulator is decremented until the address is achieved. Then this value is output to the proper display.

For the low-order display, the low order 4 bits are converted and output on the display for the low-order portion. Figure 9-7 gives the conversion table which must also be loaded into the computer.

Address	Mnemonic	Load into computer	
0100	IN,81	Db	READ CURRENT LED DISPLAY
0101		81	
0102	ORI,80	F6	DISABLE SPECIAL KEYS
0103		80	
0104	OUT,81	D3	
0105		81	
0106	MVI A,10	3E	SET UP OR H1
0107		10	
0108	CMA	2F	
0109	MOV D,A	57	SAVE H
101A	OUT,82	D3	OUTPUT H
010B		82	
010C	IN 82	DB	READ VERTICALS
010D		82	
010E	CMA	2F	
010F	ANI,OF	E6	MASK INPUT
0110		0F	
0111	ORA A	B7	SET FLAGS
0112	JNZ,0122	C2	JUMP IF RESPONSE ON
0113		22	VERTICALS
0114		01	
0115	MOV A,D	7A	GET H
0116	CMA	2F	
0117	CPI,80	FE	CHECK FOR H4
0118		80	
0119	JZ,0106	CA	RECYCLE IF H4
011A		06	
011B		01	
011C	RAL	17	ROTATE H FOR NEXT VALUE
011D	ANI,FO	E6	
011E		F0	
011F	JMP,0108	C3	JUMP BACK FOR NEXT H
0120		08	
0121		01	
0122	MVI B,00	06	
0123		00	
0124	MOV C,A	4F	SAVE VERTICAL
0125	MOV A,D	7A	GET H
0126	CMA	2F	

Fig. 9-4. The keyboard read program listing.

Address	Mnemonic	Load Into Computer	
0127	ANI F0	E6	MASK
0128		F0	
0129	RAR	1F	DECODE H
012A	RAR	1F	
012B	RAR	1F	
012C	RAR	1F	
012D	RAR	1F	
012E	JC,013A	DA	
012F		3A	
0130		01	
0131	MOV D,A	57	
0132	MOV A,B	78	
0133	ADI,04	C6	ADD 4 FOR EACH BIT LOCATION
0134		04	
0135	MOV B,A	47	SAVE
0136	MOV A,D	7A	
0137	JMP,012D	C3	JUMP BACK IF NOT DONE
0138		2D	
0139		01	
013A	MOV A,C	79	
013B	MVI C,00	0E	
013C		00	
013D	RAR	1F	
013E	JC,0145	DA	CONVERSION FINISHED
013F		45	
0140		01	
0141	INR C	0C	
0142	JMP,013D	C3	JUMP BACK IF NOT DONE
0143		3D	
0144		01	
0145	MOV A,C	79	COMBINE DECODED VALUES
0146	ADD B	80	
0147	RET	C9	

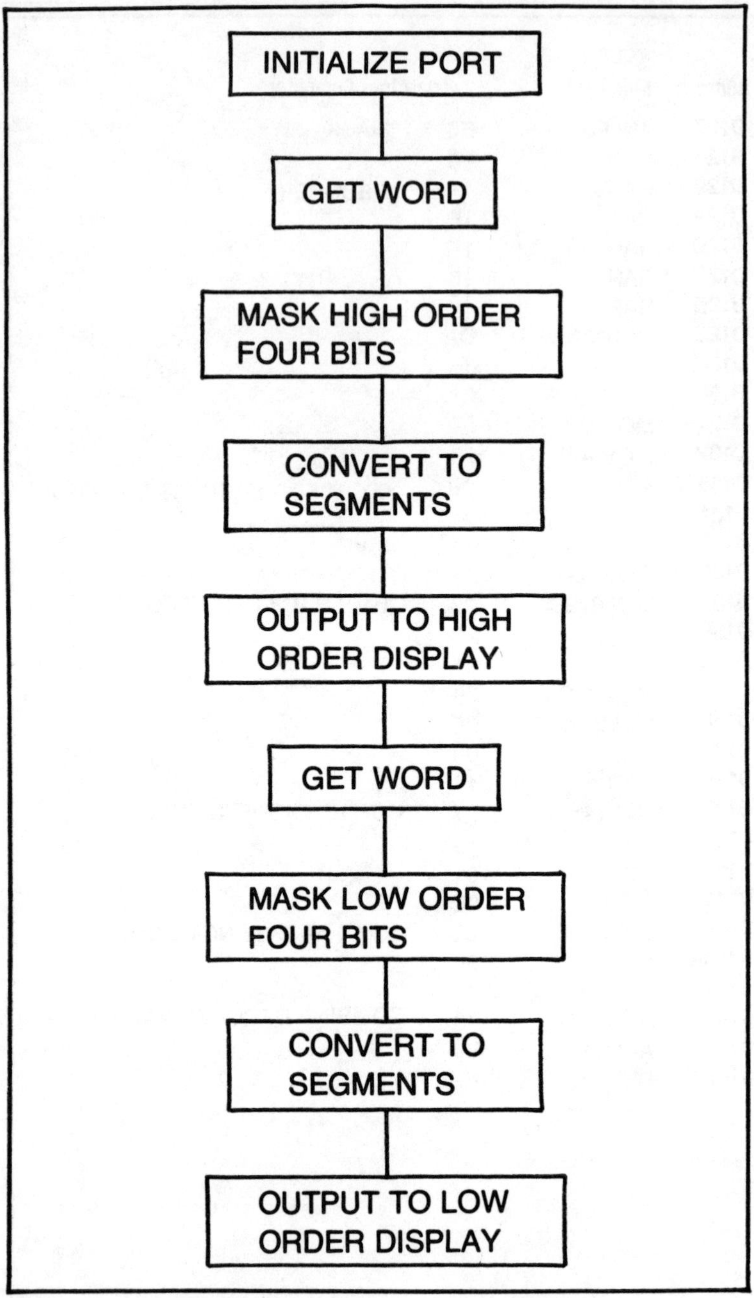

Fig. 9-5. Simplified flow diagram for the display program.

ADDRESS	MNEMONIC	LOAD INTO COMPUTER	
0148	MVI A,81	3E	Load control word
0149		81	
014A	OUT 83	D3	Output control word
014B		83	
014C	LDA 03F1	3A	Load word to be displayed
014D		F1	
014E		03	
014F	RAR	1F	Move high order 4 bits
0150	RAR	1F	to low order
0151	RAR	1F	
1052	RAR	1F	
0153	ANI OF	E6	Mask
0154		OF	
0155	LXI H,0179	21	Load starting address
0156		79	of conversion table
0157		01	
0158	ORA	B7	Set flags
0159	JZ,0161	Ca	If zero, jump to read
015A		61	
015B		01	
015C	INX H	23	Get number from table
015D	DCR A	3D	
015e	JNZ 015C	C2	
015F		5C	
Address	Mnemonic	Load into computer	
0160		01	
0161	MOV A,M	7E	Read segment number
0162	OUT 80	D3	Output to high order display
0163		80	
0164	LDA 03F1	3A	Read word
0165		F1	
0166		03	
0167	ANI OF	E6	Mask low order 4 bits
0168		OF	
0169	LXI H,0179	21	Load starting address of
016A		79	conversion table
016B		01	
016C	ORA A	B7	Set flags
016D	JZ,0175	CA	Jump if zero
016E		75	
016F		01	
0170	INX H	23	
0171	DCR A	3D	
0172	JNZ 0170	C3	Jump back
0173		70	
0174		01	
0175	MOV A,M	7E	Read segment
0176	OUT 81	D3	Output to low order display
0177		81	
0178	RET	C9	

Fig. 9-6. Program listing for the display program.

ADDRESS	VALUE
0179	3F
017A	06
017B	5B
017C	4F
017D	66
017E	6D
017F	7D
0180	07
0181	7F
0182	67
0183	77
0184	7C
0185	39
0186	5E
0187	79
0188	71

Fig. 9-7. Display conversion table.

To test out this subroutine, load the following simple program into the computer using the hardware read and load function.

Address	Mnemonic	Load into computer	
0000	LXI SP, 03F0	31	Load stack pointer
0001		F0	
0002		03	
0003	CALL 0148	CD	Call output subroutine
0004		48	
0005		01	
0006	HALT	76	

Before executing the program, load address 03F1 with 00. When the program is executed, the displays should show 00. Then load in other numbers into address 03F1 and check for all displays of all digits.

To use the program, make sure that the information is loaded into the address 03F1, and call location 0148. This is done to facilitate reading the special keys, S1 through S4, and the use of the individual LED. Because these both use the same ports as the 7 segment displays.

Read Special Keys

The special keys furnish the operator with direct communication with the program for control functions. The S1 and S2 keys are used for execute and repeat keys. Figure 9-8 shows the flow diagram, and Fig. 9-9 gives the program listing.

Basically, this program enables keyboard line H5 and looks for a response. When a response is received, the program is exited with the response stored in the low-order 4 bits of the A register. The main program must decode the response to determine if it is the correct one.

Set Individual LED On or Off

The individual LED tells the operator it is time for an input, or that an operation is in progress. This LED is turned on and off by program control.

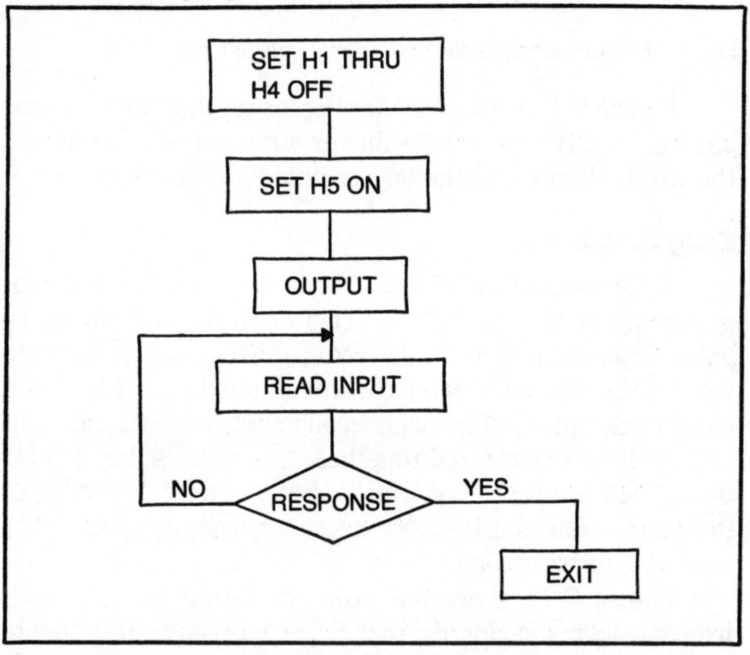

Fig. 9-8. Simplified flow diagram for the program to read the special keys.

ADDRESS	MNEMONIC	LOAD INTO COMPUTER	
0189	MVI A,F0	3E	Set H1 thru H4 off
018A		F0	
018B	OUT,82	D3	
018C		82	
018D	IN,81	DB	Read LED display
018E		81	
018F	ANI,7F	E6	Enable H5
0190		7F	
0191	OUT,81	D3	
0192		81	
0193	IN,82	DB	Read verticals
0194		82	
0195	CMA	2F	
0196	ANI,OF	E6	Mask
0197		OF	
0198	JZ,0193	JA	If no response, jump back
0199		93	
019A		01	
019B	RET	C9	

Fig. 9-9. Program listing for the read special keys program.

Figure 9-10A gives the listing for turning the LED on, and Fig. 9-10B gives the listing for turning it off. To operate the LED, simply call the appropriate subroutine.

Delay Subroutine

A 50-millisecond delay loop is required for the programming of the EPROM's. This controls the program's pulse time, and is directly dependent on the cycle time of the various instructions used to create the loop. The basic clock-cycle time is 500 nanoseconds but, because the wait and ready are connected together, this time is doubled for every memory access operation. Since the fetch portion of the instruction is a memory access, the basic clock-cycle time is 1 microsecond.

Figure 9-11 gives the program listing for a 50 millisecond delay loop for use with the programmer. It is double count-down loop, and its delay lasts a few microseconds

Address	Mnemonic	Load into computer	
019C	IN,80	DB	Read LED display
019D		80	
019E	ORI,80	f6	Add LED on
019F		80	
01A0	OUT,80	D3	Output
01A1		80	
01A2	RET	C9	

A

Address	Mnemonic	Load into computer	
01a3	IN,80	DB	Read LED display
01A4		80	
01A5	ANI,7F	E6	Add LED off
01A6		7F	
01A7	OUT,80	D3	Output
01A8		80	
01A9	RET	C9	

B

Fig. 9-10. Program lising for the LED on program (A) and the LED off program (B).

ADDRESS	MNEMONIC	LOAD INTO COMPUTER	
01AC	MVI C, 02	0E	Load outer loop constant
01AD		02	
01AE	MVI B,19	06	Load inner loop constant
01AF		19	
01B0	DCR B	05	Decrement inner loop
01B1	JNZ 01B0	C2	Inner loop
01B2		B0	
01B3		01	
01B4	DCR C	0D	Decrement outer loop
01B5	JNZ,01AE	C2	Outer loop
01B6		AE	
01B7		01	
01B8	RET	C9	

Fig. 9-11. Program listing for the delay subroutine.

longer than required. This is of no consequence since there is a larger tolerance on the program pulse width.

Input Two Characters

A subroutine which is an expansion of the input subroutine, inputs two characters. This subroutine, shown in Fig. 9-12, inputs the two characters, high-order first, and exits with the information in the A register. Address 03F2 serves as temporary storage.

THE MAIN PROGRAM

The simplified flow program for the main program is shown in Fig. 9-1. This program initializes the computer and allows the operator to choose one of the three resident programs. These are:

Keyboard read and load—allows the operator to read and change memory from the keyboard.

GOTO—allows the operator to start execution of a program at any desired location.

Program EPROM—allows the operator to program EPROMS, to create permanent memory.

These three programs allow the operator to write programs, execute them, and program them on EPROM's. The phase-1 programmer program is simple program, so the first program developed in phase 2 is the EPROM programmer driver, which allows more complete definition of the portion to be programmed.

The initialize portion sets the stack pointer to 03F0, and sets all ports. The LED then turns on, indicating that it is time for the operator to select which program to execute by entering 1, 2, or 3 from the keyboard. The keyboard entry is decoded, after the operator has a chance to check the entry. If the 1 is depressed, the keyboard read and load program is entered.

Figure 9-13 shows the flow diagram for the keyboard read and load program. All four special keys are used in this program as defined below.

- S1 Execute, and exit at end of program

ADDRESS	MNEMONIC	LOAD INTO COMPUTER	
01B9	MVI A,00	3E	Zero pointers
01BA		00	
01BB	STA,03F2	32	
01BC		F2	
01BD		03	
01BE	STA,03F1	32	
01BF		F1	
01C0		03	
01C1	CALL,0100	CD	Get first number
01C2		00	
01C3		01	
01C4	RAL	17	Position first number
01C5	RAL	17	
01C6	RAL	17	
01C7	RAL	17	
01C8	ANI,F0	E6	Mask
01C9		F0	
01CA	STA 03F2	32	Save high order
01CB		F2	
01CC		03	
01CD	IN,82	DB	Read keys for key
01CE		82	release
01CF	CMA	2F	
01D0	ANI,OF	E6	
01D1		0F	
01D2	ORA A	B7	Set flags
01D3	JNZ,01CD	C2	Jump back if key not
01D4		CD	released
01D5		01	
01D6	CALL,0100	CD	Get second number
01D7		00	
01D8		01	
01D9	ANI,OF	E6	
01DA		0F	
01DB	MOV B,A	47	Save second number
01DC	LDA,03F2	3A	Get first number
01DD		F2	
01DE		03	
01DF	ADD B	80	Add second number
01E0	STA,03F2	32	Save combined number
01E1		F2	
01E2		03	
01E3	IN,82	DB	Check for key released
01E4		82	
01E5	CMA	2F	
01E6	ANI,OF	E6	Mask
01E7		0F	
01E8	ORA A	B7	Set flags
01E9	JNZ01E3	C2	Jump back until key
01EA		E3	released
01EB		01	
01EC	LDA,03F2	3A	Load data into accumulator
01ED		F2	
01EE		03	
01EF	RET	C9	

Fig. 9-12. Program listing for the input 2 program.

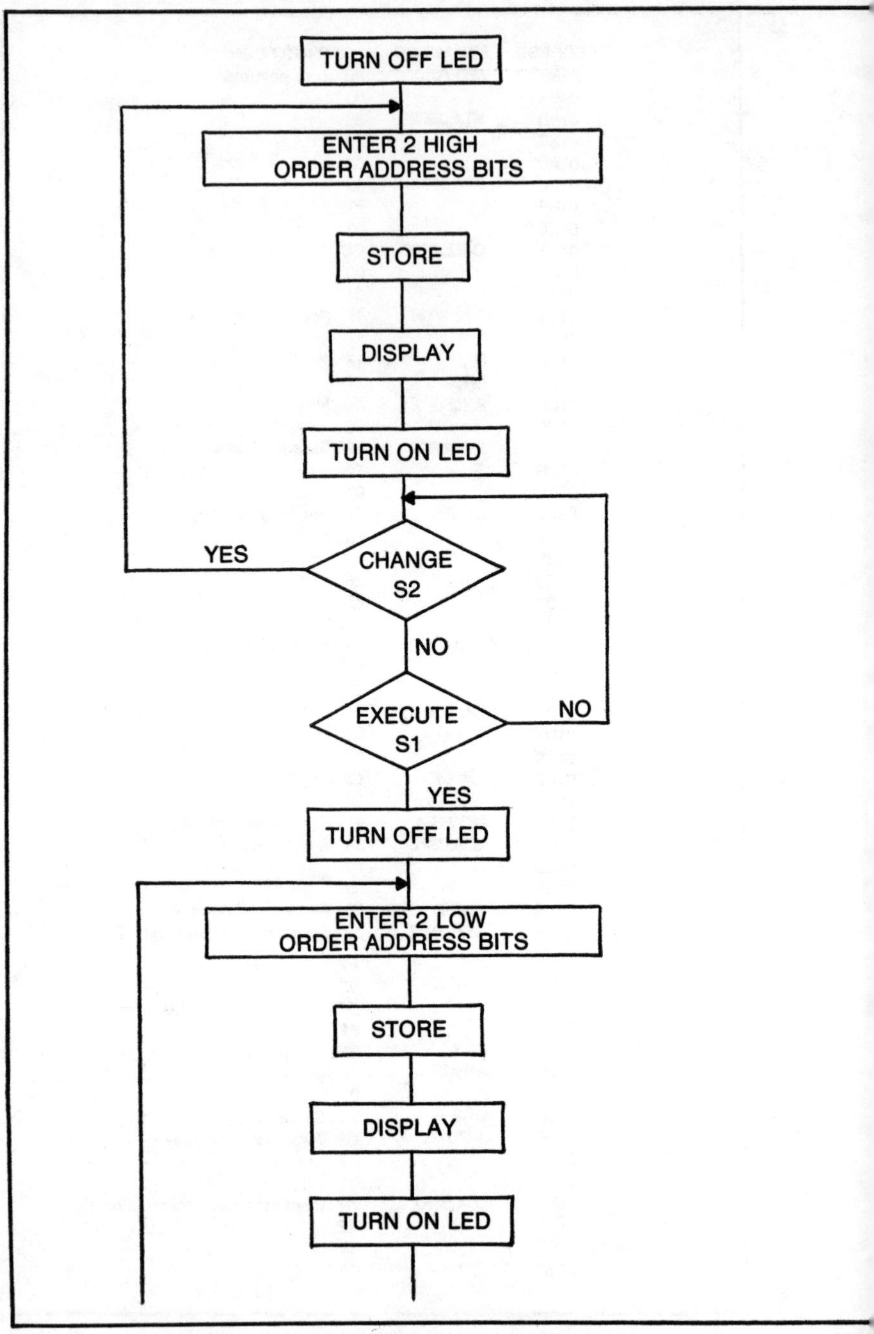

Fig. 9-13. Simplified flow for the keyboard read and load program.

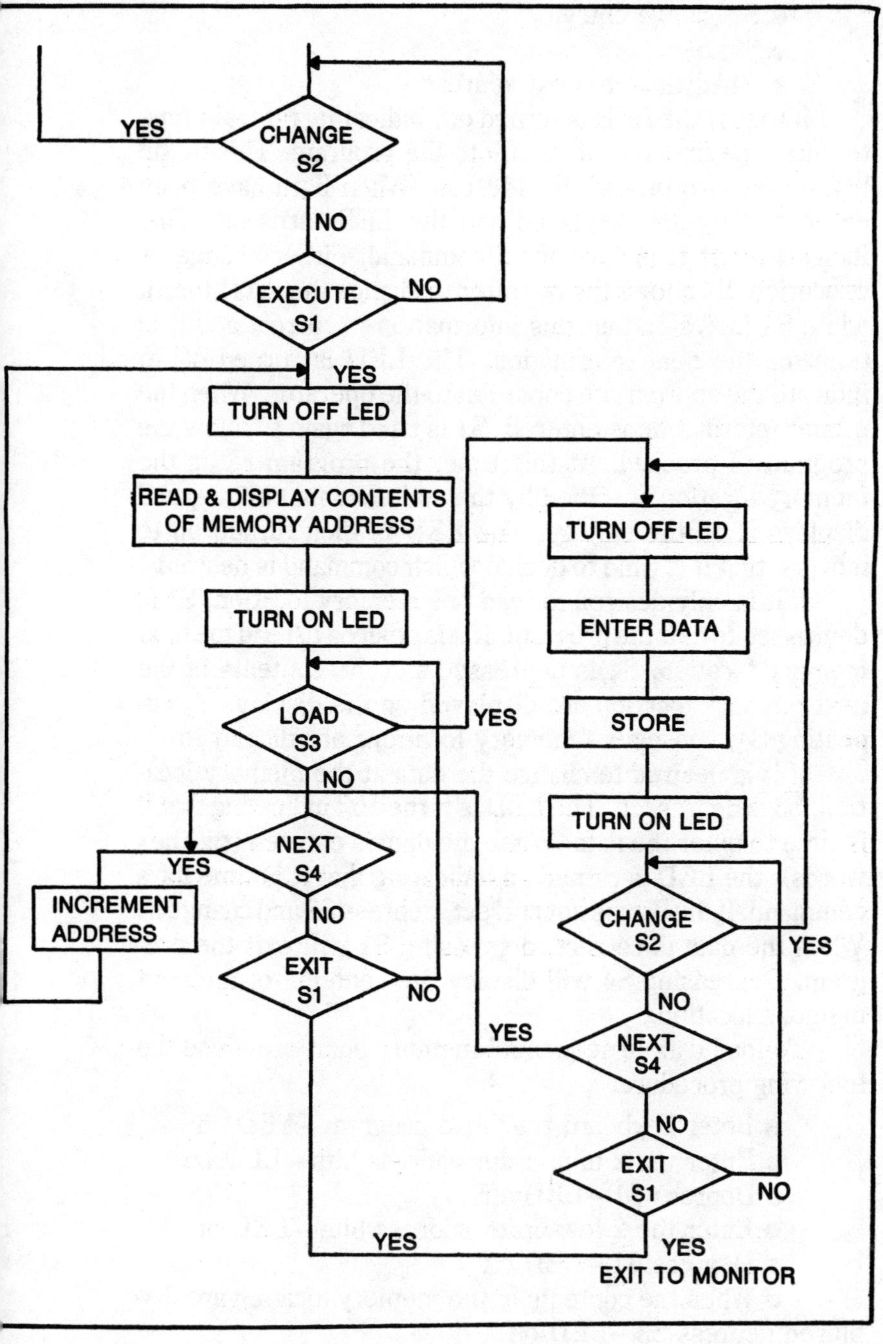
YES
CHANGE S2
NO
EXECUTE S1
NO
YES
TURN OFF LED
READ & DISPLAY CONTENTS OF MEMORY ADDRESS
TURN ON LED
LOAD S3
YES
NO
NEXT S4
YES
INCREMENT ADDRESS
NO
EXIT S1
NO
TURN OFF LED
ENTER DATA
STORE
TURN ON LED
CHANGE S2
YES
NO
NEXT S4
YES
NO
EXIT S1
NO
YES
YES
EXIT TO MONITOR

- S2Change entry
- S3Load
- S4Advance to next address

Initially, the LED is turned off, indicating that it is time to enter the first information into the program. This is the high-order two bits of the address. When both have been entered, they are displayed and the LED turns off. This indicates that it is time for a command, either change or execution. S2 allows the operator to change the data stored, while S1 indicates that this information is correct and it is time for the next information. The LED is turned off to indicate the appropriate condition to the operator. When the proper information is entered, S1 is used again to allow the program to proceed. At this time, the program reads the memory location specified by the address input above, and displays it on the display. The LED is then turned on to indicate that it is time to decide which command is desired.

If it is only desired to read one memory location, S1 is depressed to exit the program. If it is desired to read the next memory location, S4 is depressed and the contents of the next memory location are displayed on the display. By repeating S4, consective memory locations are displayed.

If it is desired to change the data at the memory location, S3 is depressed. The LED is turned off indicating that it is time to enter the data. When the data is entered (two hex words), the LED is turned on indicating that it is time for a command. If the data is not correct, depress S2 and change it. When the data is correct, depressing S1 will exit the program. Depressing S4 will display the contents of the next memory location.

To load data in sequential memory addresses, use the following procedure:

- Enter keyboard read load program—LED off
- Enter the 2 high-order address bits—LED on
- Depress S1—LED off
- Enter the 2 low-order address bits—LED on
- Depress S1—LED off
- When the contents of the memory location are displayed depress S3—LED off

- Enter two data bits to be loaded into memory location—LED on
- Depress S4—Contents of next memory location displayed—LED off momentarily then on.
- Depress S3 to load the next location—LED off
- Repeat steps 7, 8, and 9 until all the desired memory locations are loaded.

Figure 9-14 shows the sequence of events (in general terms) for this program. Remember when the LED is off it is time to enter data, and when it is on it is time to enter a command.

The GOTO program allows the operator to execute a program entered into RAM memory. Figure 9-15 is the flow diagram for the GOTO program. In essence, the address is entered, loaded into the program counter, and the program control transfers to this location.

Special switches S1 and S2 are used. Their function is:

S1—Execute, or proceed to the next step

S2—Change the last entry

Here again, the LED indicates when data entry or a command is required. First the LED is turned off, indicating that it is time to enter the high-order two address bits, then the LED is turned on, and the entry is displayed. To change

LED	OPERATION OR ACTION
OFF	ENTER TWO HIGH ORDER ADDRESS BITS
ON	ENTER EITHER CHANGE (S2) TO CHANGE, DATA OR EXECUTE (S1) TO CONTINUE
OFF	ENTER TWO LOW ORDER ADDRESS BITS
ON	ENTER EITHER CHANGE (S2) TO CHANGE DATA, OR EXECUTE (S1) TO CONTINUE
OFF	DISPLAY CONTENTS OF MEMORY ADDRESS
ON	ENTER S1 TO RETURN TO MONITOR, OR S4 TO READ NEXT MEMORY ADDRESS, OR S3 TO CHANGE CONTENTS OF MEMORY LOCATION.
OFF	ENTER DATA
ON	ENTER S1 TO RETURN TO MONITOR, S4 TO READ NEXT ADDRESS, OR S2 TO CHANGE DATA AT SAME ADDRESS

Fig. 9-14. Sequence chart for the keyboard read and load program.

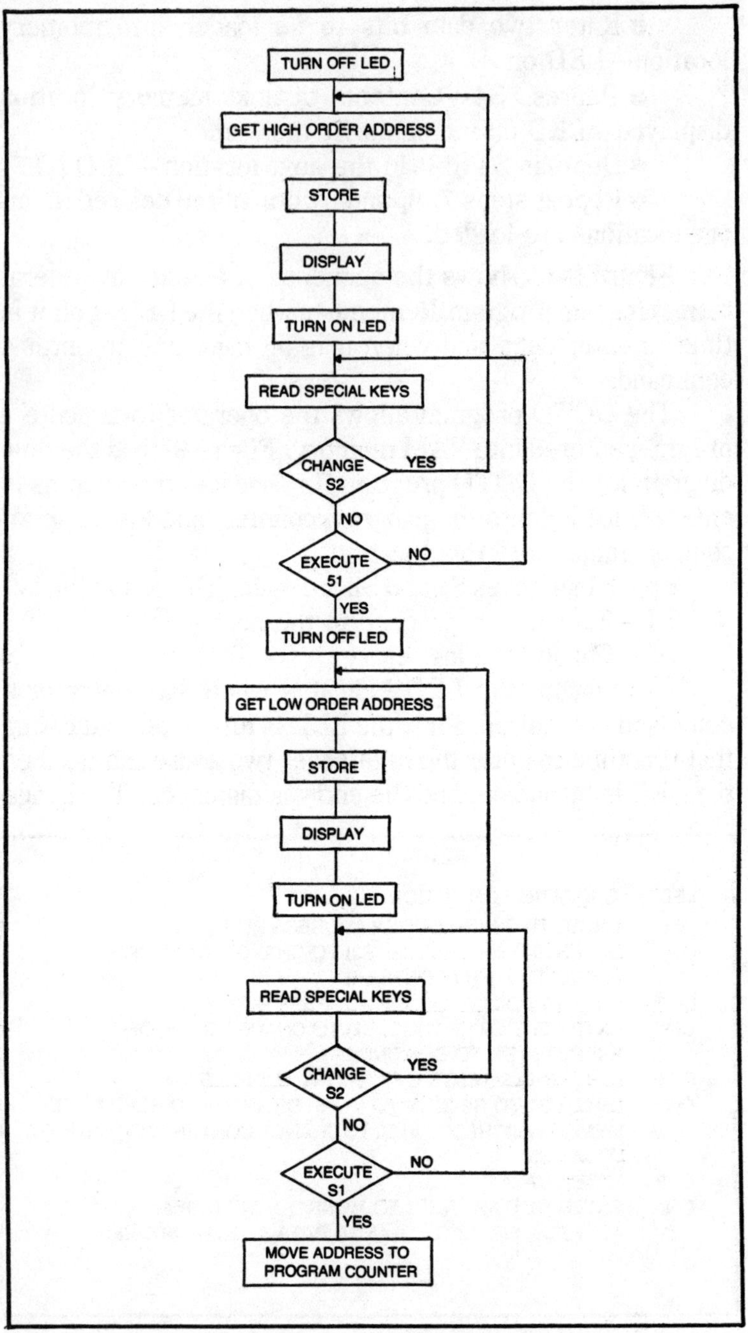

Fig. 9-15. Simplified flow diagram for the GOTO program.

the entry, depress S2 and enter the new address. If the entry is correct, depress S1 to proceed. The LED is then turned off indicating that it is time to enter the low-order two address bits. When these are entered, they are stored, displayed, and the LED is turned off. This indicates that it is time for a command. If the address is not correct, depress S2 and

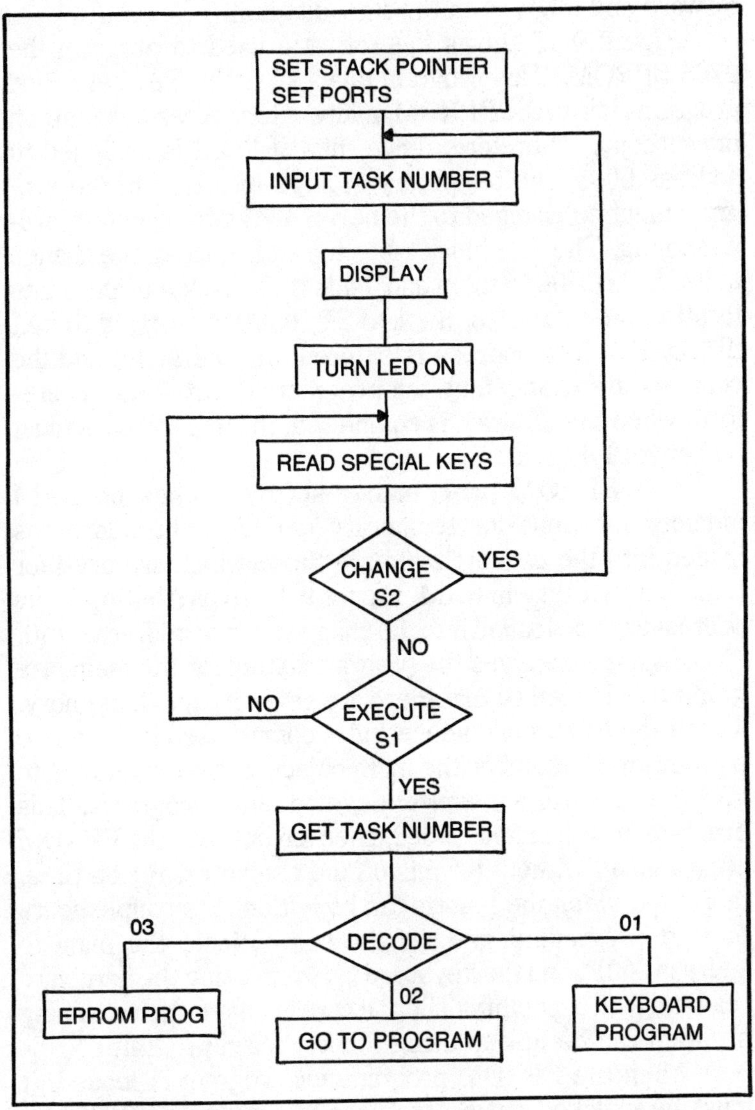

Fig. 9-16. Simplified flow diagram for the control portion of the monitor.

change the address. If the address is correct, depress S1 to transfer the program control to the address entered.

Figure 9-16 is a detailed flow diagram for the control portion of the main program. Here again, special keys S1 and S2 are used to change the data and execute the chosen program. The sequence of operations required is straight forward and is given in the flow diagram.

Figure 9-17 shows the software used to program the 2708 EPROM. This program takes all of the RAM area and programs it into the EPROM, address for address, making an image copy. Therefore, since this EPROM is assigned to address 0000, the temporary storage locations in the program must be changed to the new RAM address before programming. The first block takes the addresses in the change table, adds 0C00 to them and loads them back into the same location. For example, the LXI SP, 03F0 is changed to LXI SP, OFFO. The address is entered into the table, and the contents are changed by the programmer program. Therefore, when the program is completed, these addresses must be converted back.

The EPROM programmer software uses no RAM memory locations for temporary storage. The addresses loaded into the convert table are those which are used for temporary storage in RAM. Figure 9-18 gives a listing of the addresses to be loaded into the change table at address 00A0.

Figure 9-19 gives the program listing for the main program. It is loaded so that there are several gaps in memory. This is done for convenience and is compressed in the phase 2 program. Remember the main object of this program is to give the operator a means to develop other programs. This program must be hand loaded, checked out, and the EPROM programmed without turning off the computer. Pick a time, therefore, when the system can be left on for a couple hours to start programming. Load the subroutines, the main to address 002E, and the keyboard program using the hardware read and load capability. Then, if care is taken, the remaining program can be loaded using the keyboard program.

When the EPROM programmer program is loaded, it must be checked out before trying to program EPROMs.

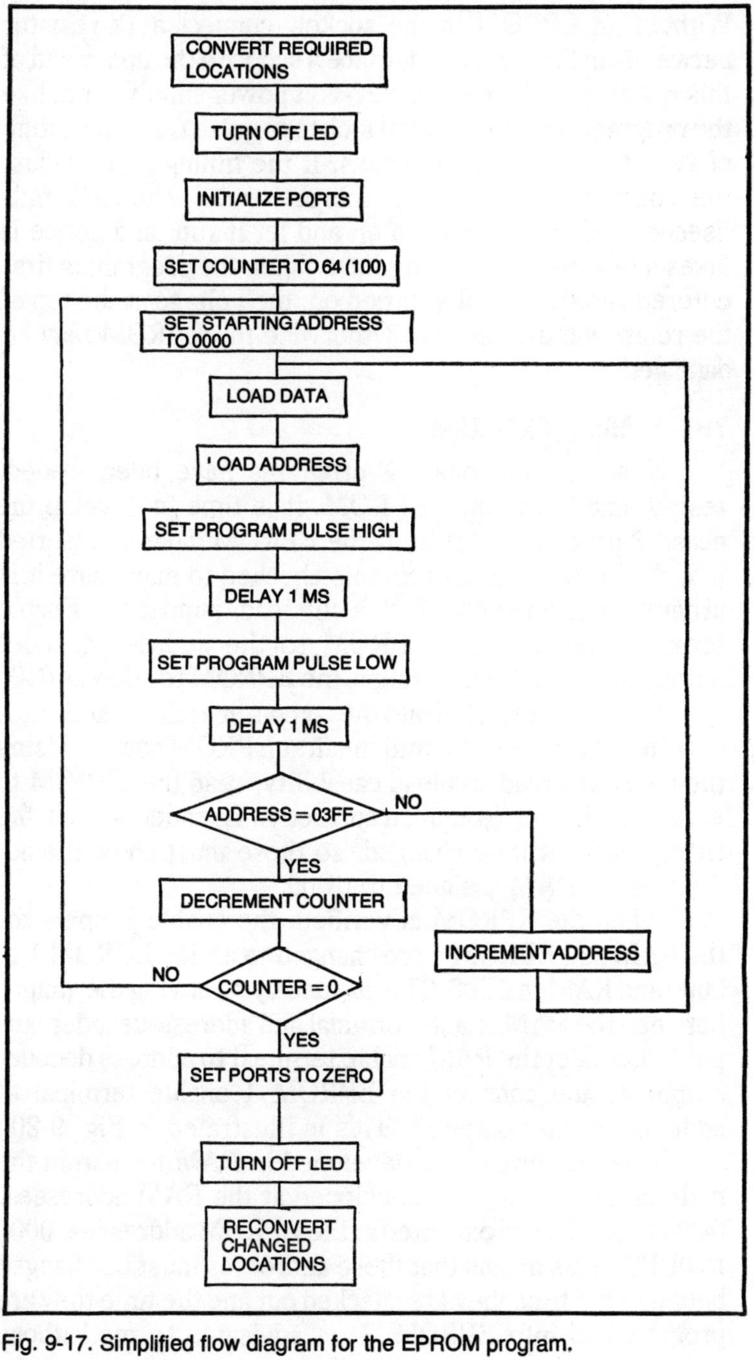

Fig. 9-17. Simplified flow diagram for the EPROM program.

Without an EPROM in the socket, connect a 1k resistor between pin 20 and ground. Place a scope to the upper end of this resistor, and turn on the 27-volt power supply. Initialize the programmer program and look for a pulse train consisting of 27-volt, 1-millisecond pulses. If the timing is off, adjust the constants in the delay subroutine to achieve 1 millisecond. Kick the program off and let it run, and notice it takes a few minutes to complete. When the program is first entered and the 27 volts turned on, the voltage at the top of the resistor must be zero. Otherwise the EPROM may be damaged.

THE PHASE-2 PROGRAM

Now that the phase-1 programs have been loaded, tested, and blown onto EPROM, it is time to develop the phase-2 programs. But first, the EPROM must be inserted into the system and its contents checked to make sure it is programmed correctly. With a clip lead, jumper the Enable terminal for the first EPROM to the address decoder output-terminal 2. This assigns the EPROM to address 0400 so that it can be inserted into the computer and checked out.

Insert the EPROM into the first EPROM socket. Using the hardware read and load capability, read the EPROM to verify that it is programmed correctly. The addresses in the change table will be changed, so these must show the addresses for RAM assigned to 0C00.

When the EPROM is verified, the enable jumpers for the RAM and EPROM 1 are changed to assign EPROM 1 to 0000 and RAM to 0C00. This is done by removing the jumper between the RAM enable terminal and address-decoder output 1. Connect the RAM enable terminal to address decoder output 4, and connect the EPROM 1 enable terminal to address-decoder output 1. This is illustrated in Fig. 9-20.

When programs are developed in RAM for use in the main program, they are developed at the RAM addresses, 0C00 to 0FFF, and executed at the EPROM addresses, 0000 to 0BFF. This means that these addresses must be changed between the time they are checked out and the time they are programmed into EPROM. It is advisable to mark those locations which require changing with a colored pencil on the program listing. This will highlight the locations to be changed when the time comes to change the addresses. The locations requiring changing are those which jump or transfer the program to locations within the program being developed. Any instruction which references an address in the program to be continued to EPROM must be changed.

CHANGE TABLE ADDRESS	DATA (ADDRESS OF HIGH ORDER ADDRESS BIT TO BE CHANGED	CHANGE TABLE ADDRESS	DATA
00A0	02	00B6	C0
00A1	00	00B7	01
00A2	10	00B8	CC
00A3	00	00B9	01
00A4	28	00BA	DE
00A5	00	00BB	01
00A6	40	00BC	E2
00A7	00	00BD	01
00A8	61	00BE	EE
00A9	00	00BF	01
00AA	64	00C0	08
00AB	00	00C1	02
00AC	43	00C2	0B
00AD	00	00C3	02
00AE	7F	00C4	29
00AF	00	00C5	02
00B0	4E	00C6	2C
00B1	01	00C7	02
00B2	66	00C8	4F
00B3	01	00C9	02
00B4	BD	00CA	53
00B5	01	00CB	02
		00CC	73
		00CD	02
		00CE	77
		00CF	02
		00DO	83
		00D1	02
		00D2	86
		00D3	02
		00D4	00
		00D5	00

Fig. 9-18. The change table.

```
ADDRESS  MNEMONIC      LOAD INTO COMPUTER
0000     LXI SP,03F0   31  SET STACK POINTER
0001                   F0
0002                   03
0003     MVI A,81      3E  INITIALIZE PORTS
0004                   81
0005     OUT 83        D3
0006                   83
0007     MVI A,80      3E
0008                   80
0009     OUT 87        D3
000A                   87
000B     CALL,0100     CD  INPUT ONE CHARACTER TO
000C                   00  DETERMINE TASK
000D                   01
000E     STA 03F1      32  STORE INPUT
000F                   F1
0010                   03
0011     CALL 0148     CD  DISPLAY CHARACTER
0012                   48
0013                   01
0014     CALL.019C     CD  TURN ON LED
0015                   9C
0016                   01
0017     CALL 0189     CD  READ SPECIAL KEYS
0018                   89
0019                   01
001A     ANI 0F        E6  MASK RESPONSE
001B                   0F
001C     CPI.02        FE  CHECK FOR S2
001D                   02
001E     JZ.000B       CA  IF DEPRESSED  RECYCLE FOR
001F                   0B  CHANGE
0020                   00
0021     CPI 01        FE  CHECK FOR EXECUTE
0022                   01
0023     JNZ.0017      C2  IF NOT. LOOK AGAIN
0024                   17
0025                   00
0026     LDA.03F1      3A  GET TASK NUMBER
0027                   F1
0028                   03
0029     CPI 01        FE  KEYBOARD READ LOAD
002A                   01
002B     JZ.0200       CA  IF YES. JUMP TO KEYBOARD
```

Fig. 9-19. Program listing for the monitor.

ADDRESS	MNEMONIC	LOAD INTO COMPUTER	
002C		00	PROGRAM
002D		02	
002E	CPI.03	FE	EPROM PROGRAM
002F		03	
0030	JZ.0300	CA	IF YES, JUMP TO EPROM
0031		00	PROGRAM
0032		03	
0033	CPI.02	FE	GO TO
0034		02	
0035	JNZ,000B	C2	IF NO, JUMP BACK FOR
0036		0B	NEW INPUT
0037		00	
0038	CALL,01A3	CD	START GO TO PROGRAM
0039		A3	TURN OFF LED
003A		01	
003B	CALL,01B9	CD	GET HIGH ORDER ADDRESS
003C		B9	
003D		01	
003E	STA 03F4	32	SAVE HIGH ORDER ADDRESS
003F		F4	
0040		03	
0041	STA 03F1	32	MOVE TO DISPLAY ADDRESS
0042		F1	
0043		03	
0044	CALL 0148	CD	CALL DISPLAY
0045		48	
0046		01	
0047	CALL 019C	CD	TURN OFF LED
0048		9C	
0049		01	
004A	CALL 0189	CD	READ SPECIAL KEYS FOR
004B		89	COMMAND
004C		01	
004D	ANI 0F	E6	MASK
004E		0F	
004F	CPI 02	FE	CHANGE COMMAND
0050		02	
0051	JZ,003B	CA	IF CHANGE, JUMP BACK
0052		3B	
0053		00	
0054	CPI 01	FE	EXECUTE COMMAND
0055		01	

ADDRESS	MNEMONIC	LOAD INTO COMPUTER
0056	JNZ 004A	C2 IF NO, LOOK AGAIN
0057		4A
0058		00
0059	CALL 01A3	CD TURN LED OFF
005A		A3
005B		01
005C	CALL,01B9	CD GET LOW ORDER ADDRESS
005D		B9
005E		01
005F	STA 03F3	32 SAVE LOW ORDER ADDRESS
0060		F3
0061		03
0062	STA 03F1	32 STORE IN DISPLAY ADDRESS
0063		F1
0064		03
0065	CALL 0148	CD CALL DISPLAY
0066		48
0067		01
0068	CALL 019C	CD TURN LED ON
0069		9C
006A		01
006B	CALL 0189	CD SPECIAL KEYS READ
006C		89
006D		01
006E	ANI 0F	E6 MASK
006F		0F
0070	CPI 02	FE CHANGE?
0071		02
0072	JZ,005C	CA IF CHANGE, JUMP BACK
0073		5C
0074		00
0075	CPI 01	FE EXECUTE?
0076		01
0077	JNZ,006B	C2 IF NO, LOOK AGAIN
0078		6B
0079		00
007A	CALL 01A3	CD TURN OFF LED
007B		A3
007C		01
007D	LHLD 03F3	2A LOAD GO TO ADDRESS
007E		F3
007F		03

Fig. 9-19. Program listing for the monitor. (Continued from page 217).

ADDRESS	MNEMONIC	LOAD INTO COMPUTER
0080	PCHL	E9 PUT IN PROGRAM COUNTER
0200	CALL 01A3	CD TURN LED OFF
0201		A3
0202		01
0203	CALL 01B9	CD KEY IN HIGH ORDER ADDRESS
0204		B9
0205		01
0206	STA 03F4	32 STORE
0207		F4
0208		03
0209	STA 03F1	32 STORE IN DISPLAY ADDRESS
020A		F1
020B		03
020C	CALL 0148	CD DISPLAY HIGH ORDER ADDRESS
020D		48
020E		01
020F	CALL 019C	CD TURN ON LED
0210		9C
0211		01
0212	CALL 0189	CD READ SPECIAL KEYS FOR
0213		89 COMMAND
0214		01
0215	ANI OF	E6 MASK
0216		0F
0217	CPI 02	FE CHANGE?
0218		02
0219	JZ,0203	CA IF CHANGE, JUMP BACK
021A		03
021B		02
021C	CPI 01	FE EXECUTE?
021D		01
021E	JNZ 0212	C2 IF NOT, LOOK AGAIN
021F		12
0220		02
0221	CALL 01A3	CD TURN OFF LED
0222		A3
0223		01
0224	CALL 01B9	CD GET LOW ORDER ADDRESS
0225		B9
0226		01
0227	STA C3F3	32 STORE
0228		F3

ADDRESS	MNEMONIC	LOAD INTO COMPUTER
0229		03
022A	STA 03F1	32 STORE IN DISPLAY ADDRESS
022B		F1
022C		03
022D	CALL 0148	CD DISPLAY LOW ORDER ADDRESS
022E		48
022F		01
0230	CALL 019C	CD LED ON
0231		9C
0232		01
0233	CALL 0189	CD READ SPECIAL KEYS
0234		89
0235		01
0236	ANI OF	E6 MASK
0237		0F
0238	CPI 02	FE CHANGE?
0239		02
023A	JZ 0224	CA IF CHANGE, JUMP BACK
023B		24
023C		02
023D	CPI 01	FE EXECUTE?
023E		01
023F	JNZ 0233	C2 IF NO, LOOK AGAIN
0240		33
0241		02
0242	IN 82	DB CHECK FOR SPECIAL KEY
0243		82 RELEASED
0244	CMA	2F
0245	ANI 0F	FE
0246		0F
0247	JNZ 0242	C2 IF NOT, JUMP BACK
0248		42
0249		02
024A	CALL 01A3	CD TURN OFF LED
024B		A3
024C		01
024D	LHLD 03F3	2A GET ADDRESS
024E		F3
024F		03
0250	MOV A,M	7E READ MEMORY LOCATION
0251	STA 03F1	32 STORE IN DISPLAY ADDRESS
0252		F1

Fig. 9-19. Program listing for the monitor. (Continued from page 219).

ADDRESS	MNEMONIC	LOAD INTO COMPUTER
0253		03
0254	CALL 0148	CD DISPLAY
0255		48
0256		01
0257	CALL 019C	CD TURN ON LED
0258		9C
0259		01
025A	CALL 0189	CD READ SPECIAL KEYS
025B		89
025C		01
025D	ANI OF	E6 MASK
025E		0F
025F	CPI 04	FE LOAD?
0260		04
0261	JZ 027B	CA JUMP TO LOAD IF YES
0262		7B
0263		02
0264	CPI 08	FE NEXT
0265		08
0266	JZ 0271	CA JUMP TO NEXT IF YES
0267		71
0268		02
0269	CPI 01	FE FINISHED
026A		01
026B	JNZ 025A	C2 IF NO, LOOK AGAIN
026C		5A
026D		02
026E	JMP 029D	C3 JUMP TO EXIT
026F		9D
0270		02
0271	LHLD 03F3	2A LOAD ADDRESS
0272		F3
0273		03
0274	INX H	23 INCREMENT ADDRESS
0275	SHLD 03F3	22 STORE ADDRESS
0276		F3
0277		03
0278	JUMP 0242	C3 JUMP BACK TO READ
0279		42
027A		02
027B	CALL 01A3	CD TURN LED OFF
027C		A3

ADDRESS	MNEMONIC	LOAD INTO COMPUTER	
027D		01	
027E	CALL 01B9	CD	GET DATA TO BE LOADED
027F		B9	
0280		01	
0281	STA 03F1	32	STORE IN DISPLAY ADDRESS
0282		F1	
0283		03	
0284	LHLD 03F3	2A	LOAD ADDRESS
0285		F3	
0286		03	
0287	MOV M,A	77	STORE DATA
0288	CALL 0148	CD	DISPLAY DATA
0289		48	
028A		01	
028B	CALL 0189	CD	READ SPECIAL KEYS
028C		89	
028D		01	
028E	ANI OF	E6	
028F		0F	
0290	CPI 02	FE	CHANGE?
0291		02	
0292	JZ 027E	CA	JUMP BACK IF YES
0293		7E	
0294		02	
0295	CPI 08	FE	NEXT?
0296		08	
0297	JZ 0271	CA	JUMP IF YES
0298		71	
0299		02	
029A	CIP 01	FE	FINISHED?
029B		01	
029C	JNZ 028B	C2	IF NO, LOOK AGAIN
029D		8B	
029E		02	
029F	JMP 0000	C3	EXIT TO MAIN
02A0		00	
02A1		00	
0300	LXI D,00A0	11	LOAD CHANGE TABLE
0301		A0	STARTING ADDRESS
0302		00	
0303	LDAX D	1A	LOAD LOW ORDER ADDRESS
0304	MOV L,A	6F	

Fig. 9-19. Program listing for the monitor. (Continued from page 221).

ADDRESS	MNEMONIC	LOAD INTO COMPUTER	
0305	INX D	13	
0306	LDAX D	1A	LOAD HIGH ORDER ADDRESS
0307	MOV H,A	67	
0308	INX D	13	
0309	CPI,00	FE	CHECK FOR END OF TABLE
030A		00	
030B	JNZ,0314	C2	CONVERT AND STORE
030C		14	
030D		03	
030E	MOV A,L	7D	
030F	CPI,00	FE	
0310		00	
0311	JZ,031B	CA	DONE
0312		1B	
0313		03	
0314	MOV A,M	7E	READ
0315	ADI,0C	C6	ADD 0C
0316		0C	
0317	MOV M,A	77	STORE
0318	JMP,0303	C3	JUMP BACK FOR NEXT
0319		03	
031A		03	
031B	CALL,019C	CD	TURN ON LED
031C		9C	
031D		01	
031E	MVI A,80	3E	LOAD CONTROL WORD
031F		80	
0320	OUT 87	D3	
0321		87	
0322	MVI A,00	3E	ZERO PORTS
0323		00	
0324	OUT 86	D3	
0325		86	
0326	MVI D,64	16	LOAD COUNTER FOR 100
0327		64	PASSES
0328	LXI H,0000	21	LOAD ADDRESS AT ZERO
0329		00	
032A		00	
032B	MOV A,M	7E	GET DATA
032C	OUT 84	D3	
032D		84	
032E	MOV A,L	7D	GET ADDRESS

ADDRESS	MNEMONIC	LOAD INTO COMPUTER	
032F	OUT 85	D3	OUTPUT LOW ORDER ADDRESS
0330		85	
0331	MOV A,H	7C	GET HIGH ORDER ADDRESS
0332	ANI,03	E6	MASK
0333		03	
0334	OUT 86	D3	OUT HIGH ORDER ADDRESS
0335		86	BITS
0336	NOP	00	DELAY FOR ADDRESS SET UP
0337	N0P	00	
0338	N0P	00	
0339	N0P	00	
033A	N0P	00	
033B	ORI 08	F6	SET PROGRAM PULSE
033C		08	
033D	OUT 86	D3	
033E		86	
033F	CALL 01AC	CD	DELAY
0340		AC	
0341		01	
0342	MVI A,00	3E	RESET PROGRAM PULSE
0343		00	
0344	CALL 01AC	CD	DELAY
0345		AC	
0346		01	
0347	MOV A,L	7D	CHECK FOR LAST ADDRESS
0348	CPI FF	FE	
0349		FF	
034A	JNZ	C2	JUMP IF NOT LAST
034B		53	
034C		03	
034D	MOV A,H	7C	CHECK H FOR LAST ADDRESS
034E	CPI 03	FE	
034F		03	
0350	JZ,03	CA	JUMP IF LAST
0351		57	
0352		03	
0353	INX H	23	
0354	JMP,032B	C3	JUMP BACK FOR NEXT ADDRESS
0355		2B	
0356		03	
0357	DCR D	15	DECREMENT COUNTER
0358	JNZ,0328	C2	JUMP BACK FOR NEXT LOOP

Fig. 9-19. Program listing for the monitor. (Continued from page 223).

ADDRESS	MNEMONIC	LOAD INTO COMPUTER
0359		28
035A		03
035B	MVI A,00	3E ZERO PORTS
035C		00
035D	OUT 84	D3
035E		84
035F	OUT 85	D3
0360		85
0361	OUT 86	D3
0362		86
0363	CALL 01A3	CD TURN LED OFF
0364	LXI D,00A0	11 LOAD CHANGE TABLE STARTING
0365		A0 ADDRESS TO CHANGE BACK
0366		00
0367	LDAX D	1A
0368	MOV L,A	6F
0369	INX D	13
036A	LDAX D	1A
036B	MOV H,A	67
036C	INX D	13
036D	CPI,00	FE CHECK FOR END
036E		00
036F	JNZ,0378	C2 NOT END
0370		78
0371		03
0372	MOV A,L	7D
0373	CPI,00	FE
0374		00
0375	JZ,0000	CA DONE
0376		00
0377		00
0378	MOV A,M	7E
0379	SUI 0C	D6
037A		0C
037B	MOV M,A	77
037C	JMP,0367	C3 JUMP BACK FOR NEXT
037D		67
037E		03

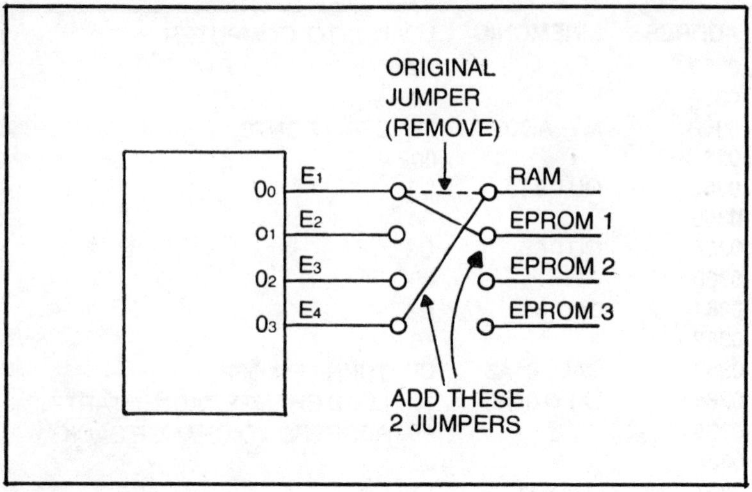

Fig. 9-20. Changing address decoder jumpers to change RAM address assignment.

Figure 9-21 shows the simplified flow diagram for the phase 2 main program. The function of the Keys are identified below:

Key	Program
1	Keyboard read and load
2	GOTO
3	EPROM program
4	EPROM test for FF
5	Compare EPROM
6	Move
7	Fill
8	Compare

The keyboard read and load program and the GOTO program are identical to those in phase 1, except for the location of the table. The EPROM program is considerably more versatile than the phase-1 program. The EPROM test and compare EPROM software can actually assist in programming EPROMs. The EPROM test program tests the EPROM for all FFs. This indicates that the EPROM is completely erased. The compare EPROM routine compares a selected portion (or all of the EPROM) against a selected portion of memory.

Figure 9-22 shows the flow diagram for the EPROM programmer software. This program allows the operator to specify the starting and ending address of data and the EPROMs starting address. This allows programming part of the EPROM at one time, then programming another part of it at a later time. For this software, it isn't necessary to change addresses in the program, such as was done in phase 1 with the change table.

A new subroutine, shown in Fig. 9-23, inputs two bits, displays them, and checks for an execute or change command. This subroutine is used to enter the addresses involved, 2 hexadecimal bits at a time.

The flow diagram, Fig. 9-22, shows the sequence of events required to program the EPROM. First you enter,

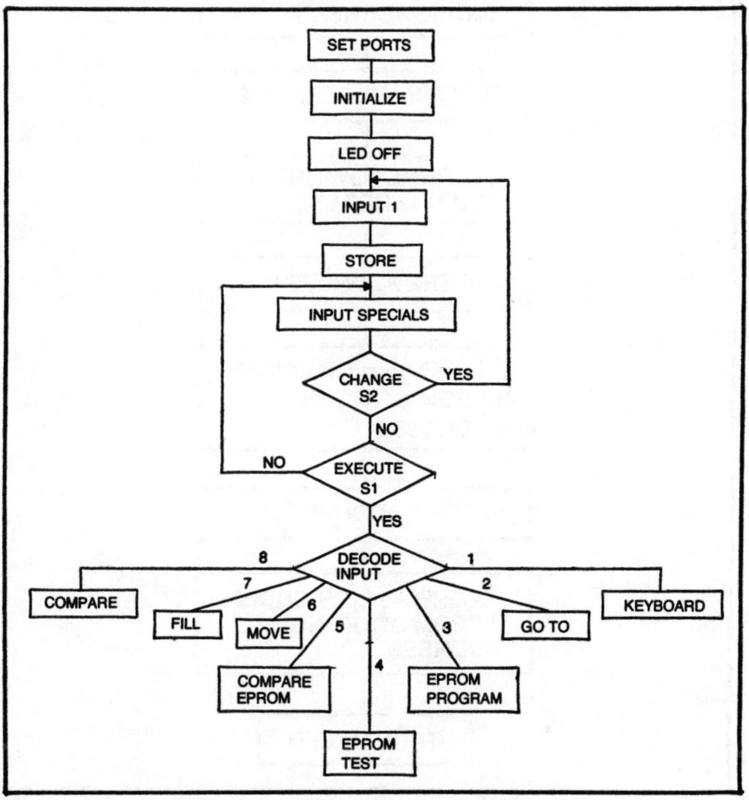

Fig. 9-21. Phase 2 main program simplified flow diagram.

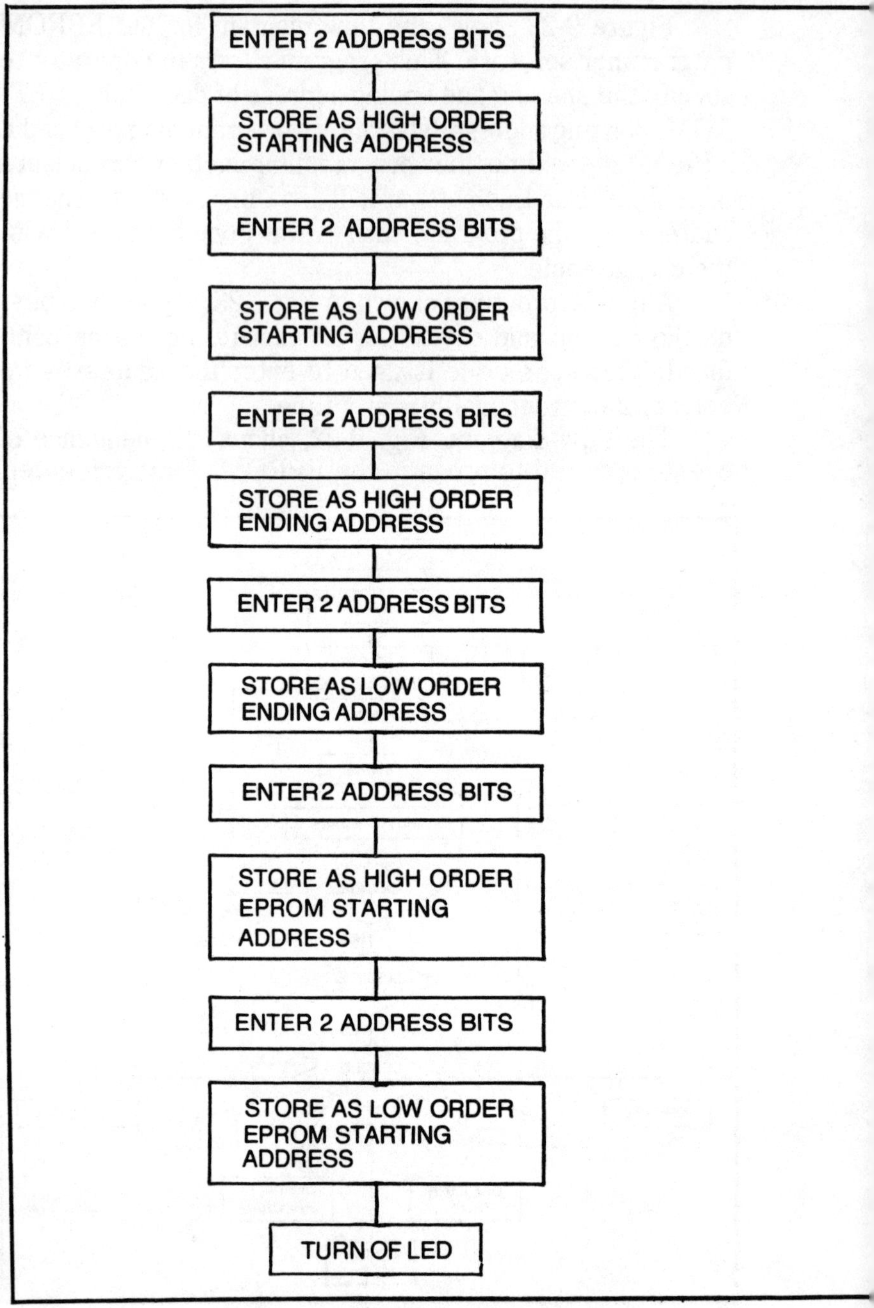

Fig. 9-22. Phase 2 EPROM programmer simplified flow diagram.

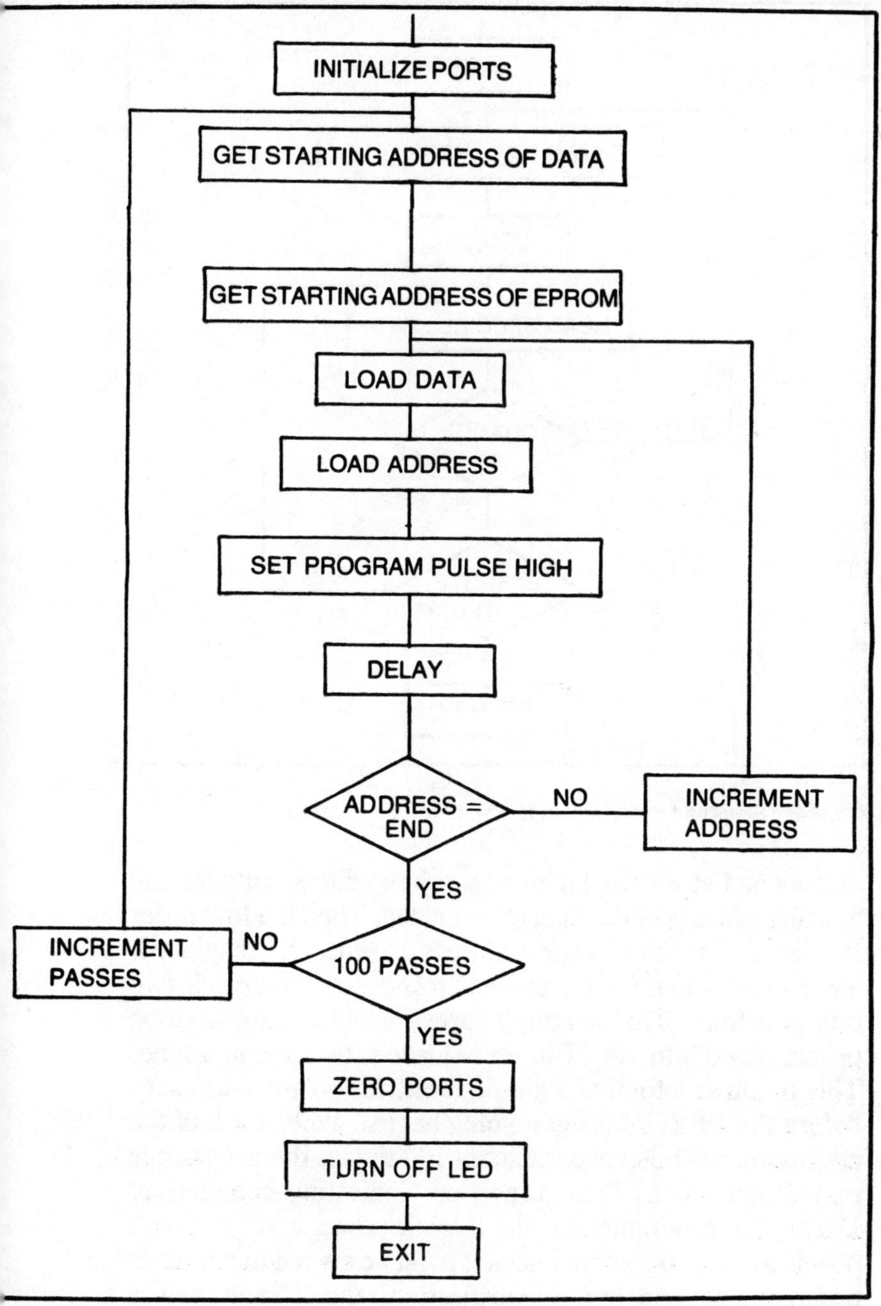
INITIALIZE PORTS
GET STARTING ADDRESS OF DATA
GET STARTING ADDRESS OF EPROM
LOAD DATA
LOAD ADDRESS
SET PROGRAM PULSE HIGH
DELAY
ADDRESS = END
NO
INCREMENT ADDRESS
YES
INCREMENT PASSES
NO
100 PASSES
YES
ZERO PORTS
TURN OFF LED
EXIT

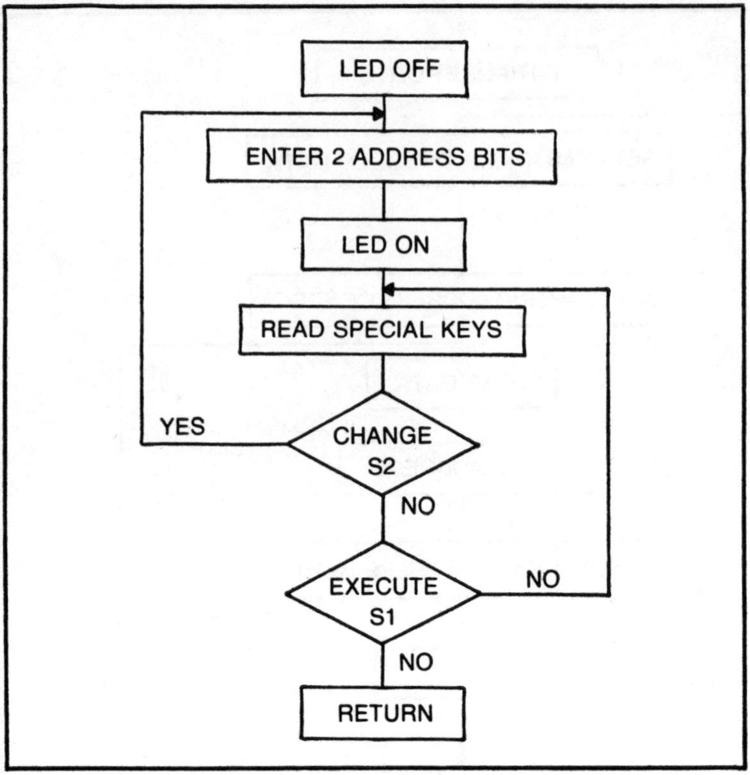

Fig. 9-23. Simplified flow diagram for the Enter 2 subroutine.

display and store the high-order 2 hex address bits for the starting address of the data to be loaded. Then the low-order two hex bits for the starting address are entered, displayed, and stored. Then the data's ending address is entered, two bits at a time. The starting address that the data is to be programmed into the EPROM is loaded, two bits at a time. This requires a total of six 2-digit entries for the addresses before the EPROM programming begins. When each of the addresses has been programmed 100 times, the program is exited and the LED is turned off, indicating completion. During the programming, the 27-volt power and the 5-volt power to the programmer socket must be switched on. After programming and before verification, the 27-volt power should be turned off.

Address	Mnemonic	Load into computer	
0000	CALL 01A3	CD	Turn LED off
0001		A3	
0002		01	
0003	CALL 01B9	CD	Input 2 from keyboard
0004		B9	
0005		01	
0006	STA OFF1	32	Store at display address
0007		F1	
0008		0F	
0009	CALL 0148	CD	Display
000A		48	
000B		01	
000C	CALL 019C	CD	Turn on LED
000D		9C	
000E		01	
000F	CALL 0189	CD	Read special keys for
0010		89	command
0011		01	
0012	ANI OF	E6	Mask
0013		0F	
0014	CPI 02	FE	Change?
0015		02	
0016	JZ,0003	CA	Ifchange, jump back
0017		03	
0018		00	
001A	CPI 01	FE	Execute?
001B		01	
001C	JNZ,000F	C2	If not, look again
001D		0F	
001E		00	
001F	CALL 01A3	CD	Turn off LED
0020		A3	
0021		00	
0022	RET	C9	Exit

Fig. 9-24. Program listing for the Enter 2 subroutine.

Address	Old Mnemonic	New Mnemonic
014C	LDA 03f1	LDA OFF1
0164	LDA 03F1	LDA OFF1
01BB	STA 03F2	STA OFF2
01BE	STA 03F1	STA OFF1
01CA	STA 03F2	STA OFF2
01DC	LDA 03F2	LDA OFF2
01EO	STA 03F2	STA OFF2
01EC	LDA 03F2	LDA OFF 2

Fig. 9-25. Addresses requiring change for phase 2 subroutines.

The subroutines used in the phase-1 program must be retained and a few new ones added. These will be represented and discussed as they are added. Figure 9-24 gives the program listing for the input 2 digits with the command subroutine shown in Fig. 9-23. The data ends up in the display address, 0FF1, and can be retrieved from this address.

When using the subroutines given in phase 1, the changed addresses, listed in the change table shown in Fig. 9-18, are changed as shown in Fig. 9-25. This gives the addresses and their new contents. These are already changed in the EPROM.

Several of the programs require the entering of a starting address, ending address, and secondary starting address, as shown in the top 12 blocks of Fig. 9-22. These should be committed to a subroutine, as shown in Fig. 9-26, with the program listing shown in Fig. 9-27. Part of this subroutine can be used if only a starting address and ending address are required. To enter only a starting address and ending address, call the subroutine between the fourth and fifth blocks of Fig. 9-26, and use the information as starting address and ending address. The data is stored in the addresses shown below. The definition is given for the addresses for both

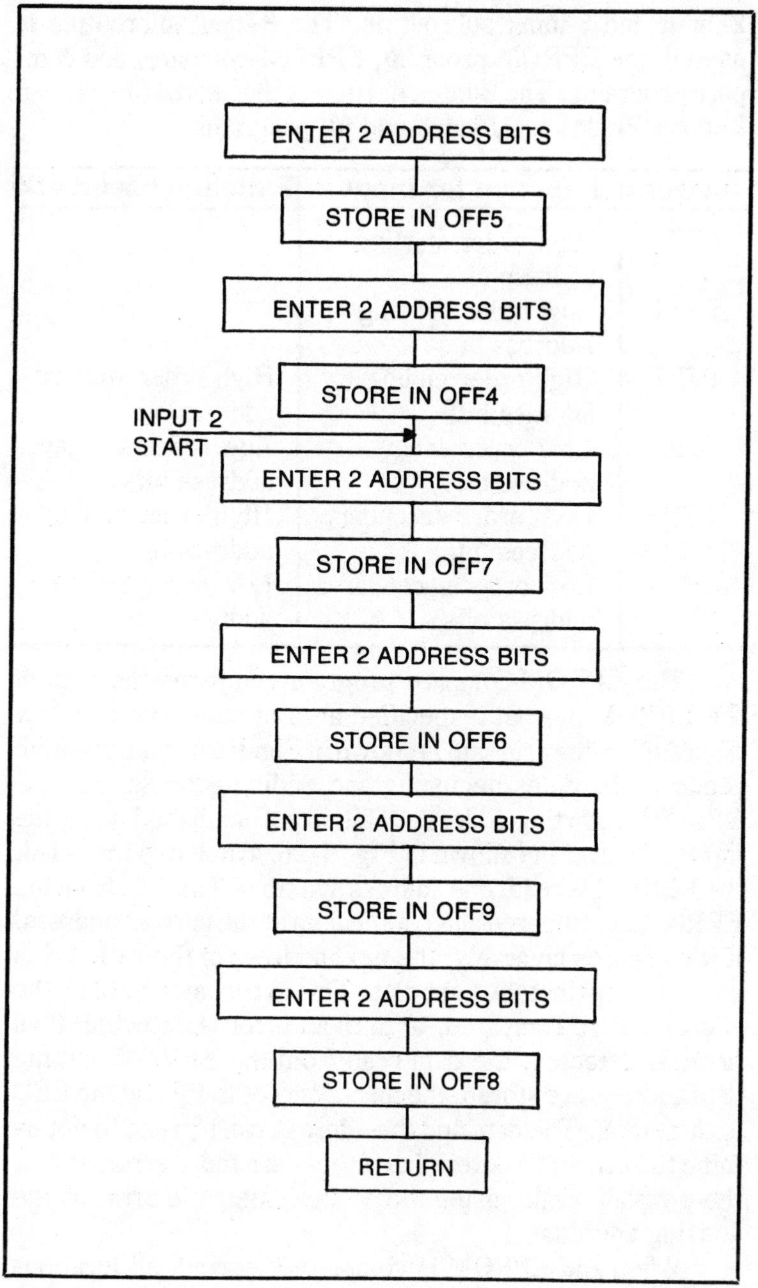

Fig. 9-26. Input 3 addresses subroutine flow diagram.

2-input and 3-input subroutine. The 3-input subroutine is used in the EPROM program, EPROM-compare, and compare programs. The 2-input portion of the subroutine is used in the EPROM test, move and fill programs.

Address	Function for input 3	Function for input2
0FF5	High order starting address bits	
0FF4	Low order starting Address bits	
0FF7	High order ending address bits	High order starting address bits
0FF6	Low order ending address bits	Low order starting address bits
0FF9	High order secondary address bits	High order ending address bits
0FF8	Low order secondary address bits	Low order ending address bits

The EPROM-compare program compares the data of the EPROM against a specified area of memory. The flow diagram for this program is shown in Fig. 9-28. This program requires the datas beginning and ending address, and the EPROM's starting address. This is accomplished using the input-3 subroutine shown in Fig. 9-26. When this is loaded, the EPROM is read, one address at a time. The data from the EPROM is compared against the data at the current address. If it compares favorably, the next address of the EPROM is compared against the next data. This is repeated until all the addresses are compared, or until an error is detected. If an error is detected, the data read from the EPROM and the data address are stored, the display is set to FF and the LED is turned off. The data and the address can be read to determine the error. To determine if there are more errors, enter the program again, using the address after the error as the starting address.

When and EPROM is completely erased, all locations are HIGH, or FF. The EPROM-programming routine, therefore, selected addresses and data bits to zero. The EPROM

ADDRESS	MNEMONIC	LOAD INTO COMPUTER	
0000	CALL ENTER2	CD	ENTER HIGH ORDER
0001		XX	BITS OF FIRST ADDRESS
0002		XX	
0003	LDA OFF1	3A	GET DATA
0004		F1	
0005		OF	
0006	STA OFF5	32	STORE
0007		F5	
0008		OF	
0009	CALL ENTER 2	CD	ENTER LOW ORDER BITS
000A		XX	OF FIRST ADDRESS
000B		XX	
000C	LDA OFF1	3A	GET DATA
000D		F1	
000E		OF	
000F	STA OFF4	32	STORE
0010		F4	
0011		OF	
0012	CALL ENTER 2	CD	ENTER HIGH ORDER BITS
0013		XX	OF SECOND ADDRESS
0014		XX	
0015	LDA OFF1	3A	GET DATA
0016		F1	
0017		OF	
0018	STA OFF7	32	STORE
0019		F7	
001A		OF	
001B	CALL ENTER 2	CD	ENTER LOW ORDER BITS
001C		XX	OF SECOND ADDRESS
001D		XX	
001E	LDA OFF 1	3A	GET DATA
001F		F1	
0020		OF	
0021	STA OFF6	32	STORE
0022		F6	
0023		OF	
0024	CALL ENTER 2	CD	ENTER HIGH ORDER BITS
0025		XX	OF THIRD ADDRESS
0026		XX	
0027	LDA OFF1	3A	GET DATA
0028		F1	
0029		OF	
002A	STA OFF9	32	STORE
002B		F9	
002C		OF	
002D	CALL ENTER 2	CD	ENTER LOW ORDER BITS
002E		XX	OF THIRD ADDRESS
002F		XX	
0030	LDA OFF1	3A	GET DATA
0031		F1	
0032		OF	
0033	STA OFF8	32	STORE
0034		F8	
0035		OF	
0036	RET	C9	EXIT

NOTE: XXXX INDICATES THE ADDRESS FOR THE ENTER TWO SUBROUTINE(Fig 9-24)

Fig. 9-27. Program listing for the input 3 addresses subroutine.

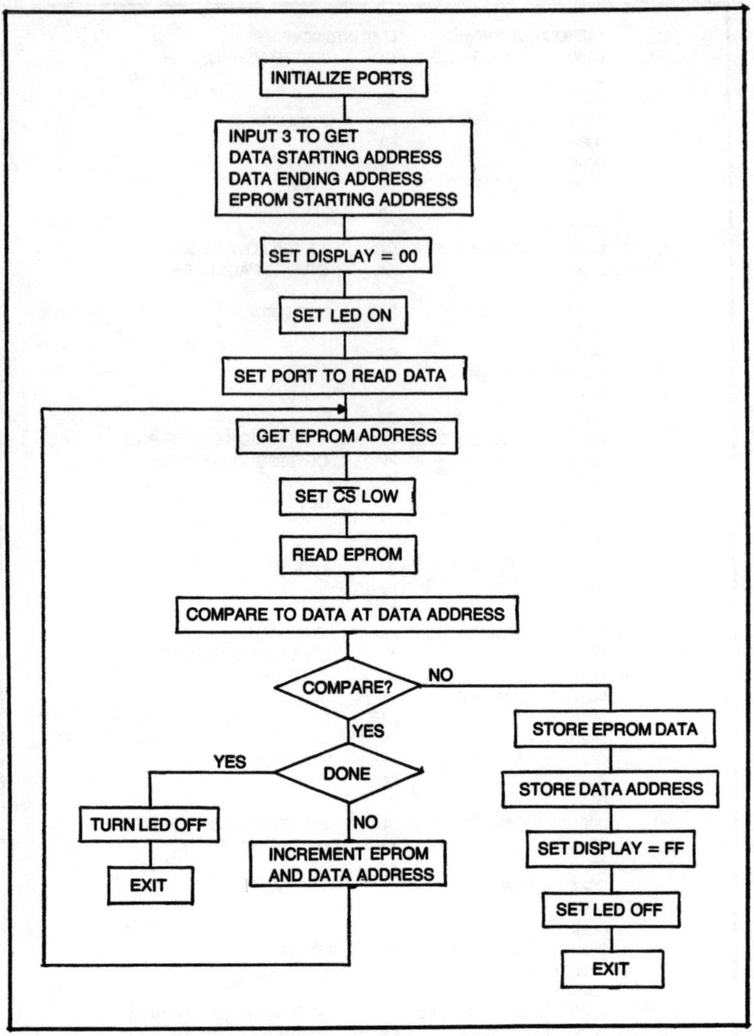

Fig. 9-28. Flow diagram for the EPROM compare function.

test program tests for all locations HIGH (FF) indicating a completely erased EPROM. This program can only be used on completely erased EPROMs, and not on partially programmed EPROM's. The flow diagram for this program is shown in Fig. 9-29.

Both the EPROM test and the compare-EPROM programs require reading the EPROM while it's in the programmer socket (Fig. 9-30). The requirements to read the EPROM are:

- Set the program pulse to zero by setting port C's bit 3 to zero.
- Set the low-order address bits through port B hits 0 through bit 7.
- Set address bits A_8 and A_9 port C bits 0 and 1.
- Set CS low by setting port C bit 2 low.
- Read the data at the selected address using port A.

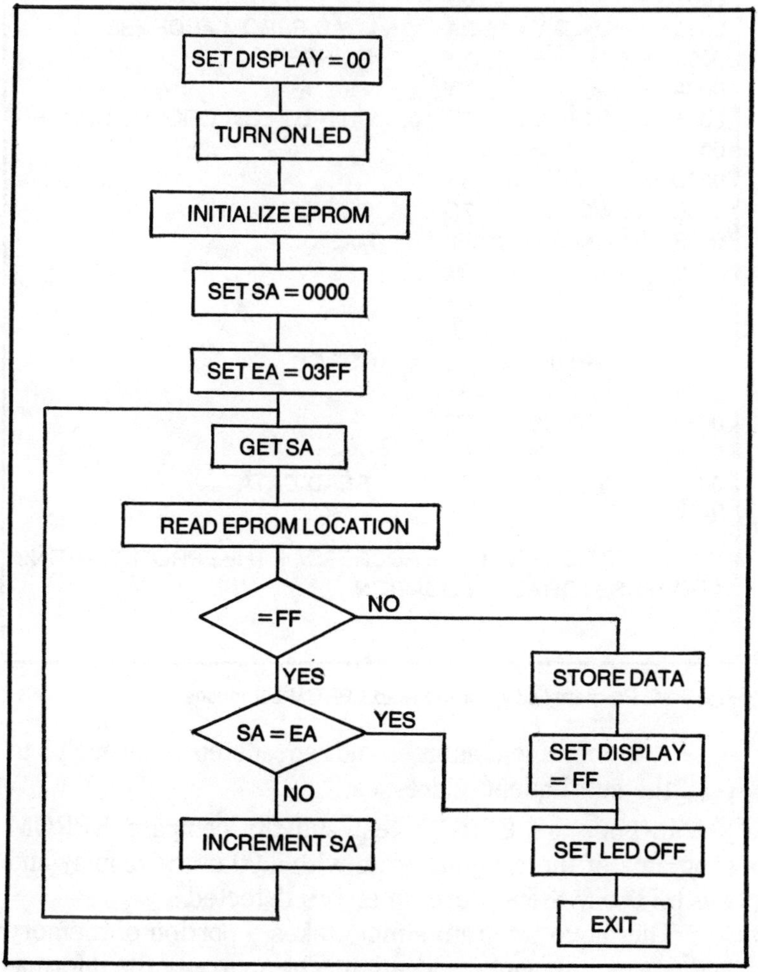

Fig. 9-29. Flow diagram for the EPROM test program.

ADDRESS	MNEMONIC	LOAD INTO COMPUTER	
0000	MVI A,90	3E	LOAD CONTROL WORD TO
0001		90	READ DATA
0002	OUT 87	D3	
0003		87	
0004	MVI A,00	3E	SET PORT C
0005		00	
0006	OUT 86	D3	
0007		86	
0008	LHLD,YYYY	2A	LOAD EPROM ADDRESS
0009		YY	POINTER
000A		YY	
000B	MOV A,L	7D	OUTPUT LOW ORDER ADDRESS
000C	OUT 85	D3	
000D		85	
000E	MOV A,H	7C	OUTPUT A_8 AND A_9
000F	ANI 03	E6	MASK
0010		03	
0011	OUT 86	D3	
0012		86	
0013	ORI 04	F6	SET CS
0014		04	
0015	OUT 86	D3	
0016		86	
0017	IN 84	DB	READ DATA
0018		84	

YYYY SITHE STOR-AGE ADDRESS OF THE EPROM STARTING ADDRESSSTORAGE LOCATION.

Fig. 9-30. Program listing for the read EPROM subroutine.

- Increment address and repeat steps 2 through 5 to read the subsequent addresses.

In both the EPROM test and the compare EPROM programs, if the program exits with a 00 in the display and the LED off, there were no errors detected.

The move program simply takes a portion of memory and moves it to another location. The source of the information to be moved can be memory location, but the destination address must be in RAM—this is the only memory area which can be written into. Note that the program-flow chart, shown in Fig. 9-31, shows that the move can start from either the high-order address or the low-order address, depending if the move is to a higher address or a lower address. This must be done if the move is only a few addresses, and the resulting moved locations occupy some of the original memory locations. If the directional test is not made, it is possible to overwrite some of the information before it is moved.

The fill program allows the operator to fill a selected portion of memory with a selected data word. The flow diagram for this program is shown in Fig. 9-32. The starting address and ending address are entered using the input 2

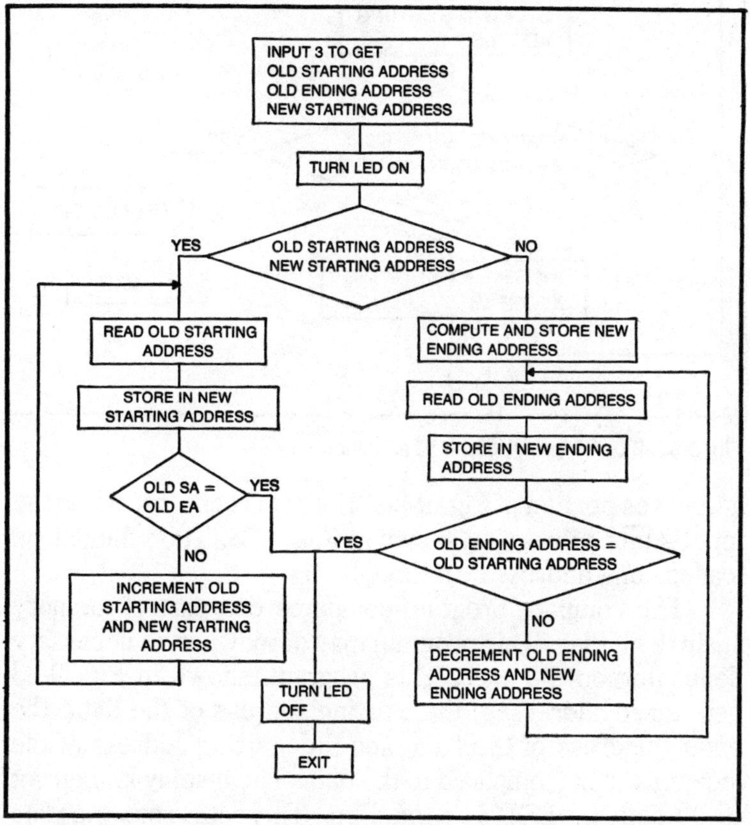

Fig. 9-31. Flow diagram for the move function.

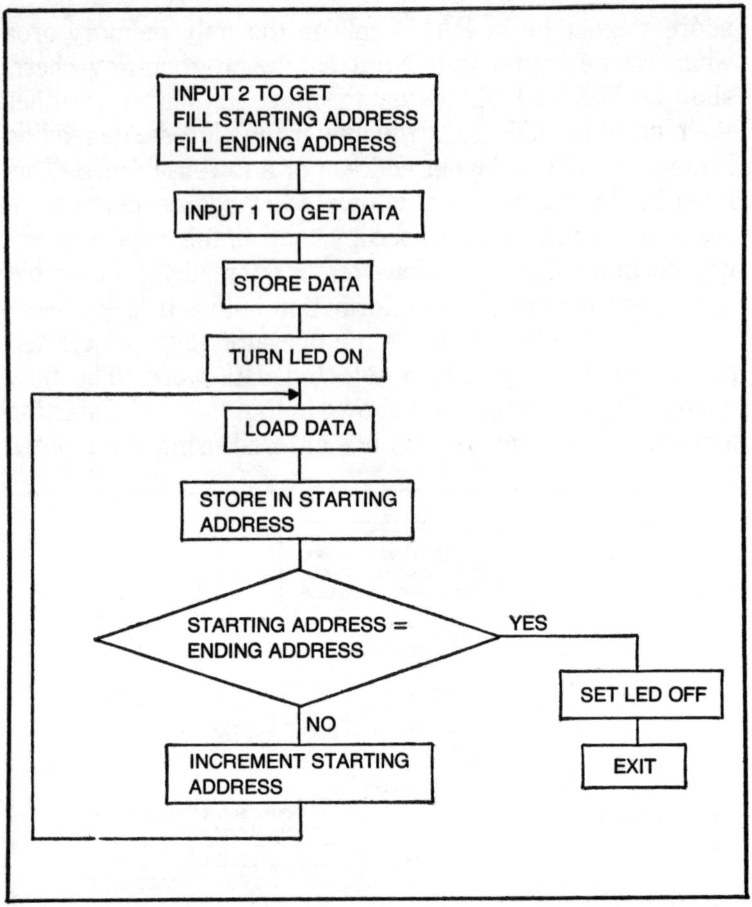

Fig. 9-32. Flow diagram for the fill function.

addresses portion of Fig. 9-26. The data is entered using the input 2 bits subroutine shown in Fig. 9-23. Then the data is loaded, one address at a time.

The compare program compares one part of memory against another. This program may or may not be necessary depending on the user. This program, shown in Fig. 9-33 gets three addresses, the starting address of the data, the ending address of the data, and the starting address of the locations to be compared to the data. The display is then set to 00 and the LED is turned on. The data from the data addresses and the compare addresses are read, one address at a time, and compared. If an address does not compare, the display is set to FF, the compare address stored, and the program is exited. When this happens, the data and addresses can be read and the error examined. If there is no error, the addresses are incremented until the data address is equal to the data ending address.

The program listings shown in this section all show 0000 as the origin of the program. This is because it is up to

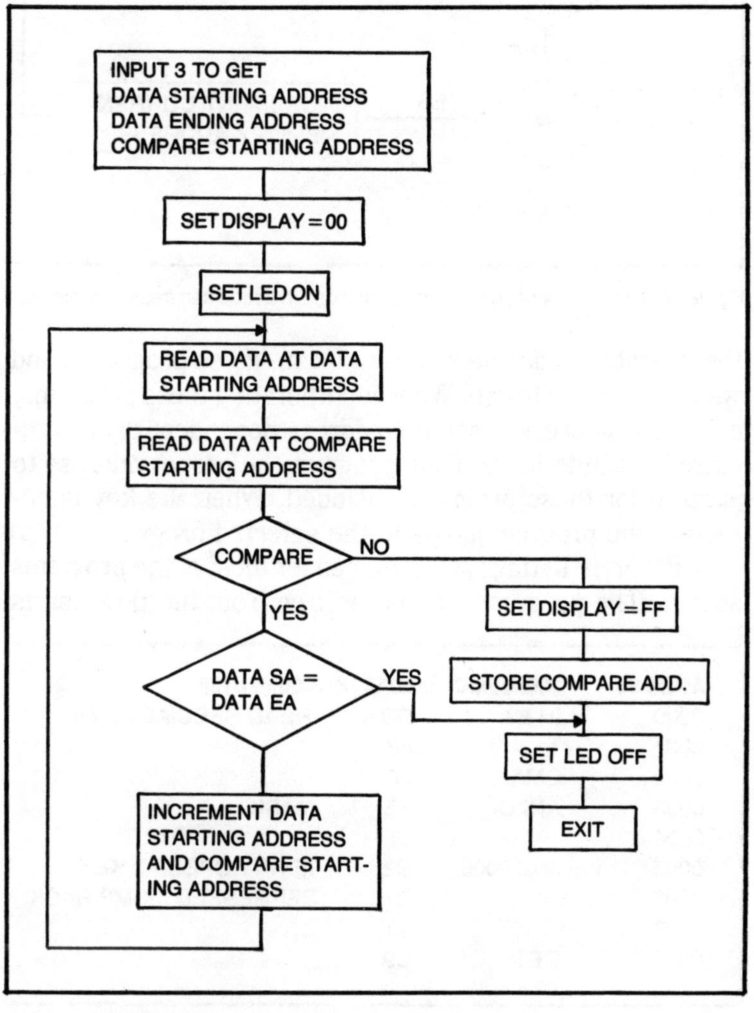

Fig. 9-33. Flow diagram for the compare function.

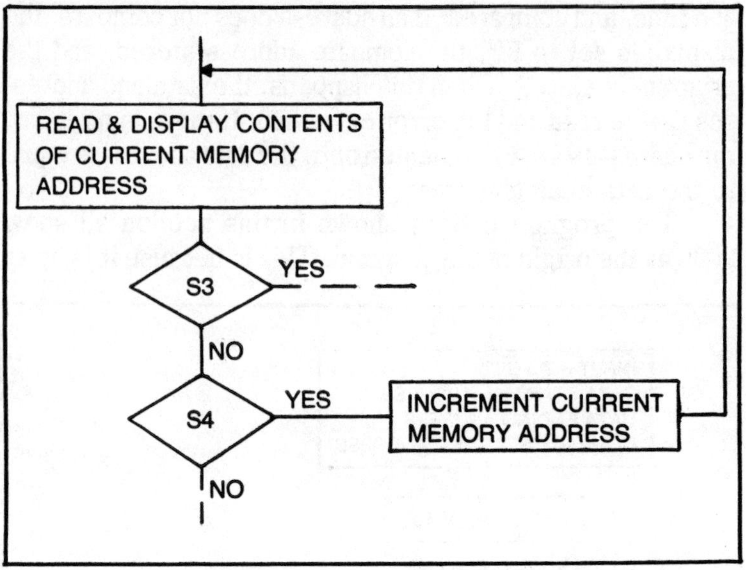

Fig. 9-34. Two consecutive command functions in a loop can cause problems.

the operator to decide where to locate these programs, and which programs to use. When incorporating these programs, adjust the addresses and the address-dependent data as required. Include in the main program the proper address to jump to for those programs included. When the key is detected, the program jumps to the selected program.

Program listings are not given for most of the programs shown. The programs can be written from the flow charts

ADDRESS	MNEMONIC	LOAD INTO COMPUTER	
0000	IN 82	DB	READ SPECIAL KEYS
0001		82	
0002	CMA	2F	
0003	ANI OF	FE	MASK
0004		OF	
0005	JNZ 0000	C2	IF ANY SPECIAL KEY
0006		00	DEPRESSED, JUMP BACK
0007		00	
0008	RET	C9	

Fig. 9-35. Program listing to check for special key released.

ADDRESS	MNEMONIC	LOAD INTO COMPUTER	
0000	MVI A,FO	3E	ENABLE ALL HORIZONTALS
0001		FO	
0002	OUT 82	D3	OUTPUT ENABLES
0003		82	
0004	IN 82	DB	READ KEYBOARD
0005		82	
0006	CMA	2F	
0007	ANI OF	E6	MASK
0008		OF	
0009	ORA A	B7	SET FLAGS
000A	JNZ 0004	C2	JUMP BACK IF ANY DATA
000B		04	KEY DEPRESSED
000C		00	
000D	RET	C9	EXIT

Fig. 9-36. Program listing for keyboard key released.

given, using a little logic, and the instruction information. And this, after all, is one of the objectives of the book, to teach the user programing, and how to do it.

When using the keyboard in new programs, care must be taken to make sure one key depression cannot be sampled by the program as two successive commands. For example, in the loop shown in Fig. 9-34, if special key S4 is depressed, it is possible to pass through the loop several times before the key is released. After all, the computer operates in microseconds and few of us can even comprehend a mechanical action that fast, much less respond that quickly.

Thus, a set of instructions must be inserted which will detect if the switch or key is released. Figure 9-35 shows the flow chart for a program to detect if the special keys are released. Figure 3-36 gives the program to detect if all the data keys are released. These programs are not required every time the keys are used, but they are required when you input commands without data between the commands, or when inputting more than one keystroke in a sequence without a command between. The program of Fig. 9-35 assumes H5 is enabled.

Chapter 10
Expanding the System

When the system is up and running it makes for a useful tool. But there are several things which can be done to improve the system and its usefulness. Several such improvements are discussed in this chapter to improve the system. The four major topics are:

Cassette Recorder. Connecting a cassette recorder to the system allows storing of the RAM's contents. This allows you to develop parts of a program in RAM, and to save it on tape and load it back into the computer at a later date. This recorder also allows recording of data, so that such things as the checkbook balance can be put in the computer and recorded. You can update it periodically to change the stored data.

Adding 4 More Displays. Four more hexadecimal displays lets the system display all 4 address digits and the two data digits at the same time. This makes it easier to use the keyboard load and read program, and gives the capability of displaying 6 hex digits at the same time.

Adding More Memory. Adding more RAM memory expands the memory capability of the computer. The memory capacity can be doubled with little effort.

RS 232 Interface. An RS-232 interface allows the computer to talk to a standard display terminal.

In addition, several minor topics are discussed. This chapter does not give all the details required to incorporate the functions—only the hardware and program requirements are discussed. It is up to the operator to incorporate these into the computer. They can be added easily because the computer was laid out with expansion in mind.

CASSETTE RECORDER

Cassette recorders operate in the audio region, with very little high-frequency response. For this reason, an effective I/O rate is about 500 bits-per-second for a simple approach using a HIGH to represent a 1 and a LOW to represent a 0. But each bit position should contain at least one transition in order to provide clocking of the signal. Figure 10-1 shows the pulse train representing the serial data. The generation of the pulse train requires only two timing loops (to generate T1 and T3), while the reading requires only one timing loop to generate T2.

The total pulse time is T1 plus T3, where T3 equals at least twice T1. For an alternating series of ones and zeros, all pulses will be T3 plus T1 long, while for a series of ones or

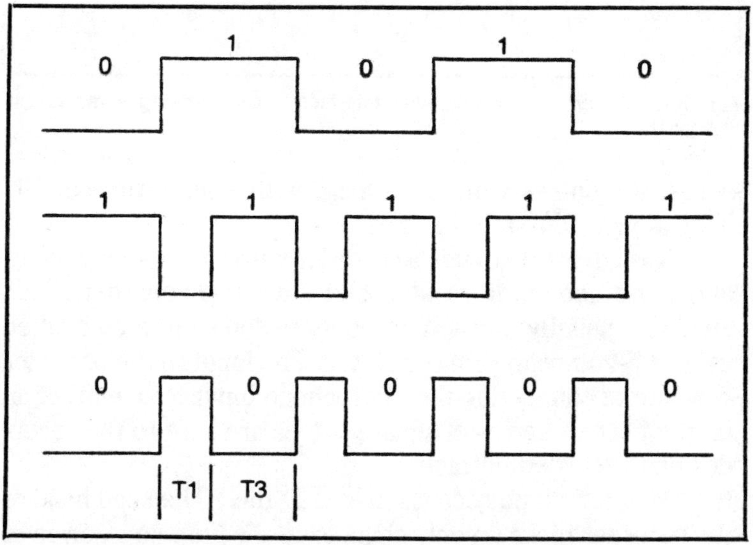

Fig. 10-1. Serial FSK data to the recorder, showing different bit patterns.

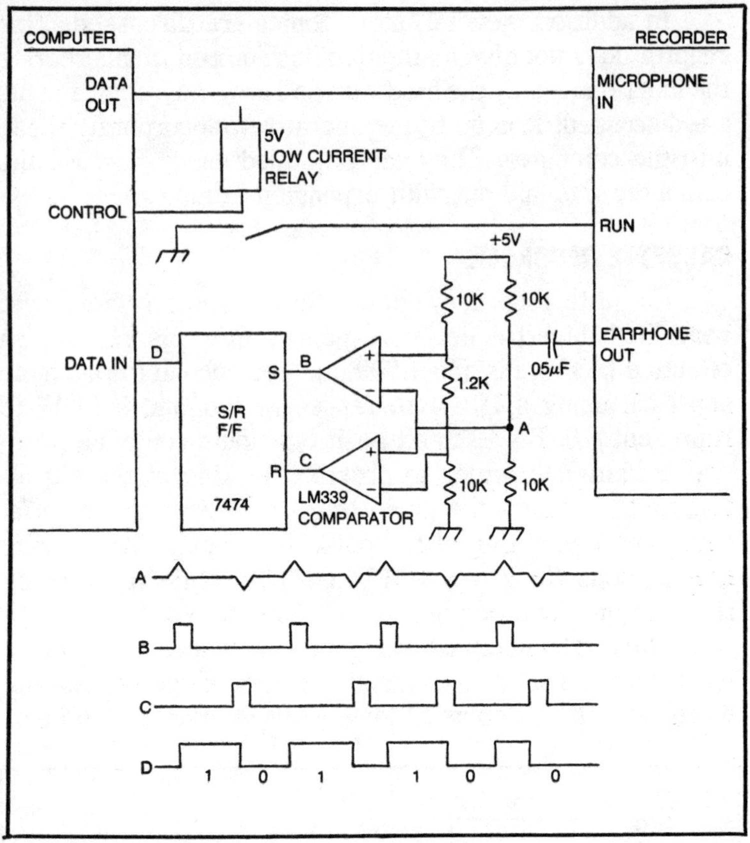

Fig. 10-2. Recorder microcomputer interface circuit showing some circuit waveshapes.

zeros, the pulses will be T3 long, with a reset time of T1. This is also illustrated in Fig. 10-1.

It is advisable to use a recorder with a remote switch to allow the computer to stop and start the recorder. This switch is usually on the microphone, and can be controlled using a 5-volt relay or a transistor. The input to the recorder consists of connecting the microphone input to one bit of an output port. A series of square waves are sent to the recorder and recorded on tape.

Magnetic tape records magnetic flux. The read head of the recorder picks up only changes in the flux, so a series of blips is recorded on tape. This series of blips must be reconstructed into a pulse train to be useful to the computer. This is accomplished using a pair of comparators and a flip/flop.

The recorder interface is shown in Fig. 10-2, along with the waveshapes. The earphone output connects to the comparator inputs through an RC network. The comparators set

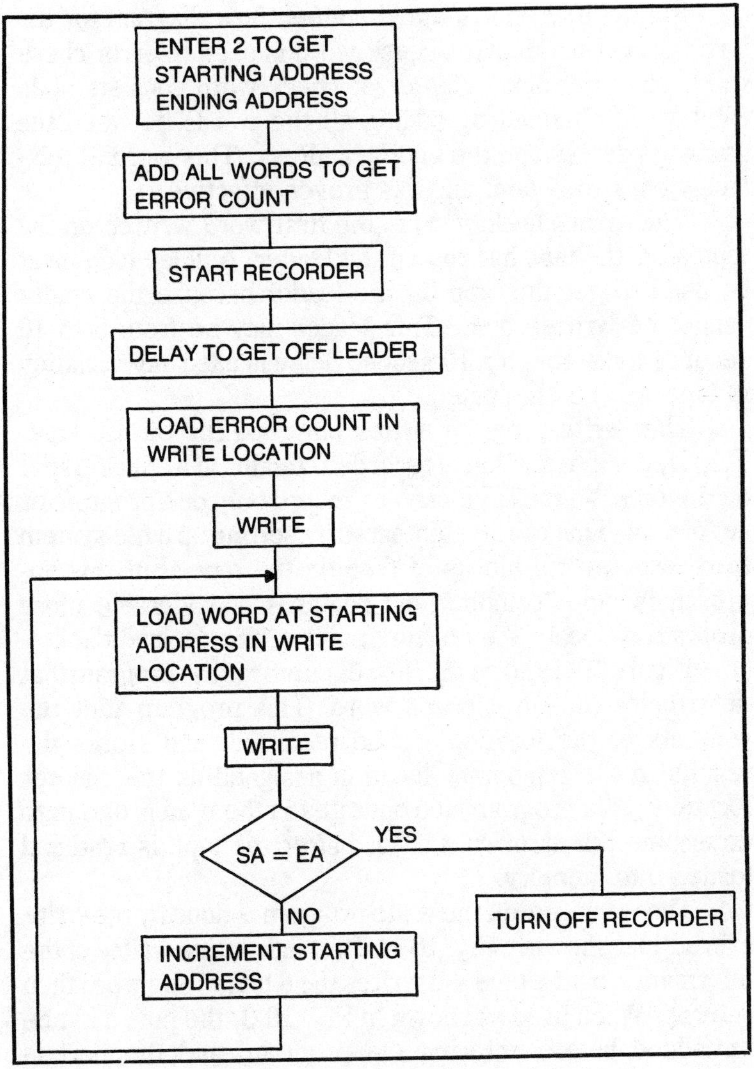

Fig. 10-3. Tape write simplified flow diagram.

and reset the flip/flop to provide a pulse train at the computer. As shown, three bits are required at the I/O to service the interface. The data output and the control bits must be the latching type, such that once they are set they will stay set until reset. If there are three bits available on an 8255 interface chip, they can be used. Otherwise a new interface must be created using some interface chip.

Figure 10-3 shows the simplified flow diagram for the write program. An error-check word is used to error check the read of the tape. This error check word consists of an 8-bit word obtained by adding all the words between the starting address and the ending address. This word is relatively easy to obtain, and has proven effective.

The error-check word is the first word written on the tape after the tape has run off the leader. A delay loop must be used to get the tape off the leader because the leader cannot be written onto. This leader may be from 5 to 10 seconds long, and, if a 10-second delay is used any variation in tape will be eliminated.

This write program writes only one file on the tape. That is, the information is recorded starting at a specific spot on the tape, so it can be used to record only one program or set of data. This can be eliminated by setting up a file system to record several blocks of data on the tape. But this approach is quite complex and requires considerable more program to locate the starting point of the desired data.

Figure 10-4 shows the flow diagram for the program that determines the error check word. This program adds the contents of the locations to be recorded, and stores the results in the temporary location assigned as the counter location. This program also operates in the read program to determine the error-check word after the tape is read and loaded into memory.

The work done in the write program is done by the write subroutine, shown in Fig. 10-5. This subroutine writes of the information on the tape—it writes the 8 bits of one word then returns. When used as shown in Fig. 10-3, the port must be initialized before entering the program, and the port is turned off by the recorder off block.

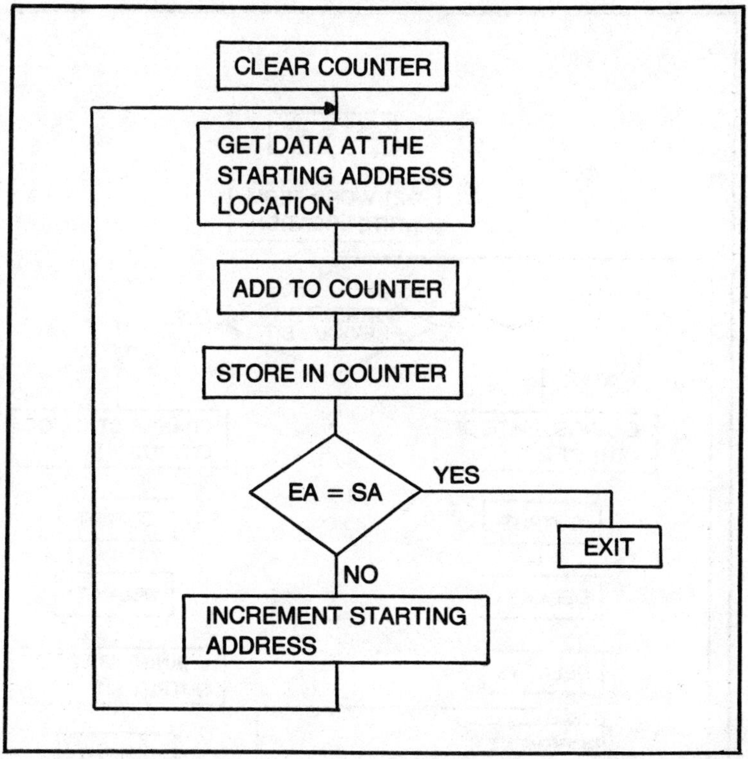

Fig. 10-4. Flow diagram for the program to calculate the error check number.

The state of the previous bit must be remembered to determine if the consecutive pulses are the same (either both ones or zeros). This can be accomplished in several ways; one is to remember the state of the last pulse; another easy method is to read the port to determine its state. The 8255 ports can be read by simply commanding a read to an output port. The control word does not need to be changed. No matter what method is used, the previous bit for the first bit to be written is a zero.

To read data that is written on the tape, the first data transition is detected, a time delay (T2) is executed, then the data is sampled. The next data transition is detected and the data is sampled at T2 time later. Every bit is timed from the original data transition on the bit being read. The timing is shown in Fig. 10-6.

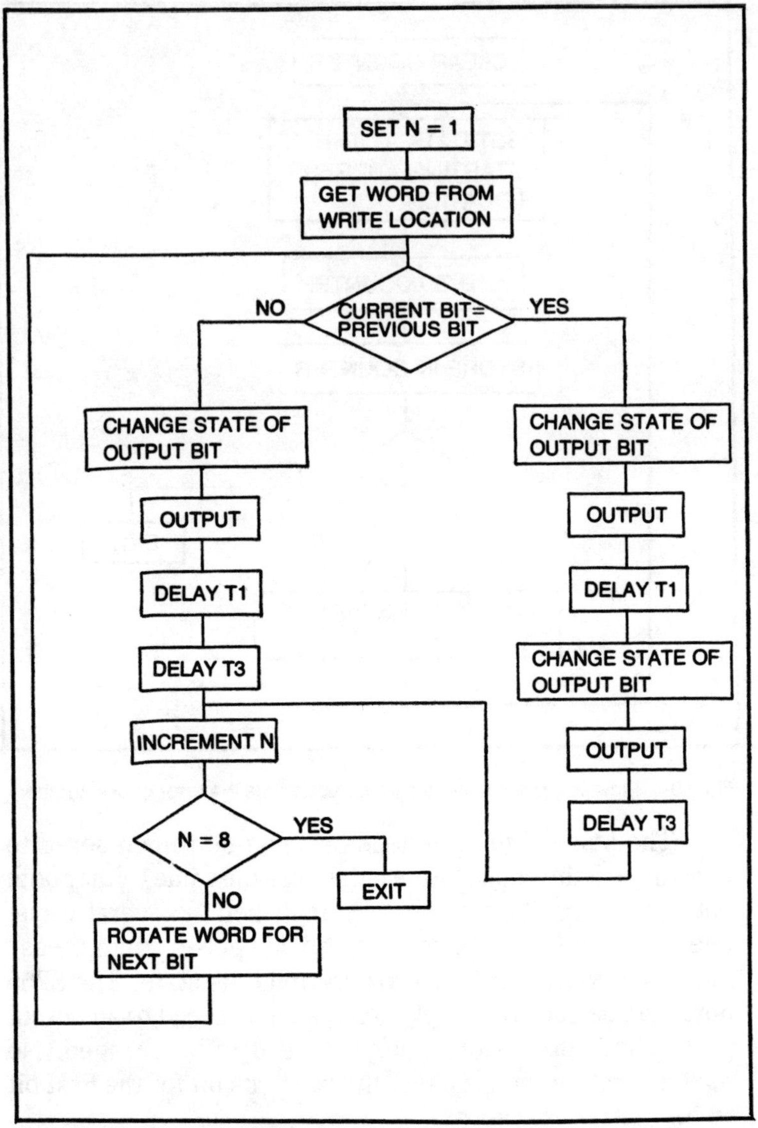

Fig. 10-5. Flow diagram for the tape write subroutine.

Figure 10-7 shows the read program. The initial delay to allow the recorder to get past the leader should be a second or so less than it was for the write program. The routine looks for the first data transition, from LOW to

HIGH, and it reads the input after a delay of T2 time. The bit read is moved into the bit position and the word checked to see if it is complete. If it is not, the program is looped back for the next bit after the program logic is set up to receive the bit.

If the word is complete, it is checked to see if it is the first, or error-check, word. If it is, it is stored in the error-check temporary location. If it isn't the first word, the word is stored in the address contained in the starting-address pointer, and this pointer is incremented. Then the program loops back for the next word, if that word wasn't the last word.

When designing and constructing the interface circuitry, it must be determined if the switch on the microphone is on the ground or power line. Typically they are on the ground line so that the same ground can be used for the microphone and the switch. The relay may also be replaced by a transistor or an SCR, if desired. If a relay is used, it must be a low-current device so that the current capability of the port is sufficient to energize it. Otherwise a current driver may be required to increase the current drive capability.

When determining the time delays, times T1 plus T3 determine the tape's bit-packing density. This time must not exceed 500 bits-per-second, so the time T1 plus T3 should

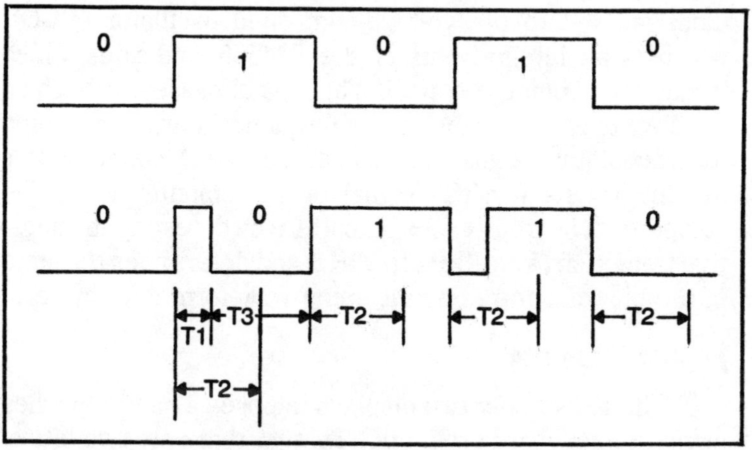

Fig. 10-6. Read timing waveshapes.

be about 2 milliseconds. T2 should be about 1 millisecond. These times are generated by delay loops in the program.

When recording information, the recorder must be placed in the record mode, running in the forward direction, before the program is entered. The computer actually controls the start of the tape. When the recording is finished, the tape must be manually rewound. In the read mode, place the recorder in the read or play mode, with the tape rewound. The computer will start the tape, but the recorder switches must be in the correct position.

Figure 10-8 shows another approach to a recorder interface. This circuit uses the frequency-shift-keying (FSK) recording mode. To write data, the computer generates an FSK signal that alternates between 2000 and 4000 Hz. When a logical zero os written on the tape, 2000 Hz appears for two-thirds of the bit time and 4000 Hz for one-third of the bit time. When a logical 1 is written, 2000 Hz appears for one-third of the bit time and 4000 Hz for two-thirds of the bit time. These signals are generated by the computer program and output to the recorder through a one-bit data-output port. An inverter drives the RC network which converts the pulse train to an alternating waveform of either 4000 Hz or 2000 Hz. The bit rate should be about 166 bits-per-second.

To read data, an LM565 phase-lock loop with a free-running frequency of 3000 Hz locks on the input signal. The input voltage to the voltage-controlled oscillator (VCO), which is an integral part of the LM565, indicates which frequency is being received. This signal passes through an RC filter to eliminate the carrier frequencies, while retaining the modulating signal. A comparator (811) converts this low-level signal to a TTL signal for the computer input. The computer synchronizes the bit pattern by detecting the negative transition (from 4kHz to 2kHz) and determines the state of the bit transmitted by incoming waveform duty cycle.

ADDING DISPLAYS

The use of only two displays imposes a handicap when using the keyboard programs. That is, that only two bits of information can be displayed at one time. Adding four more

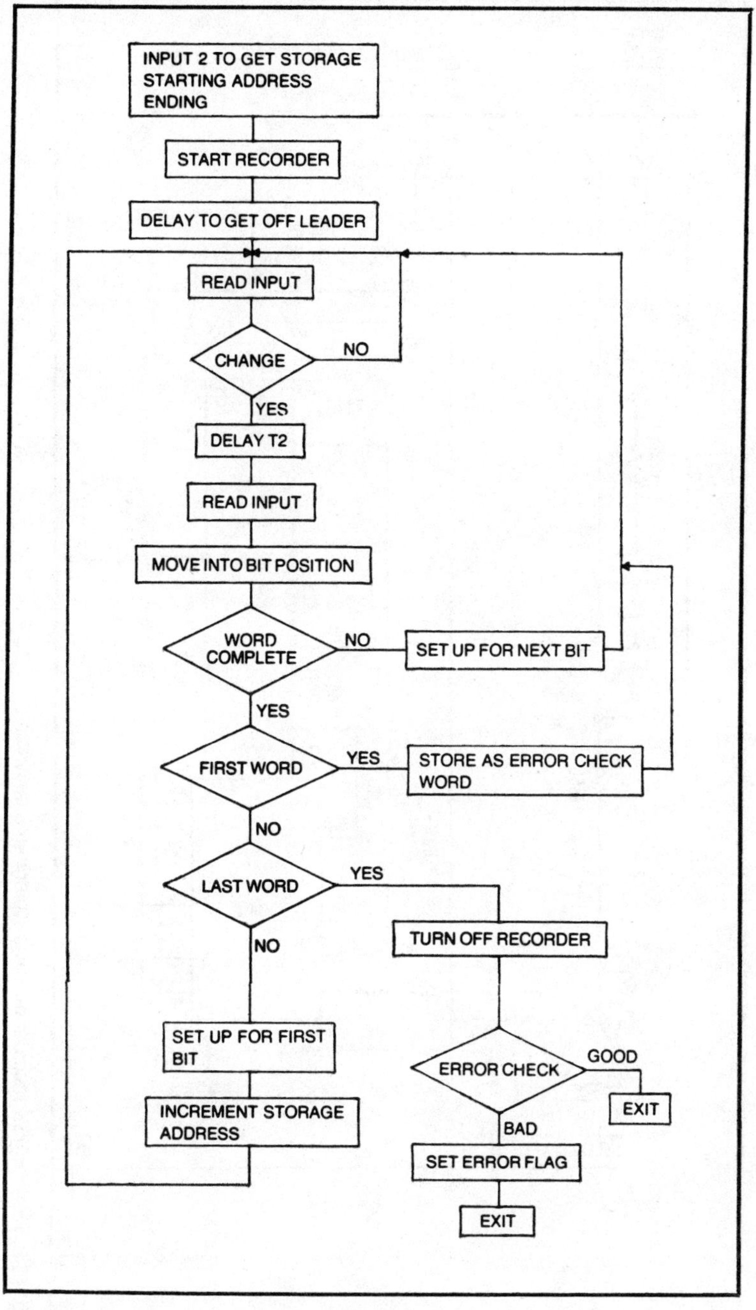

Fig. 10-7. Read tape program flow diagram.

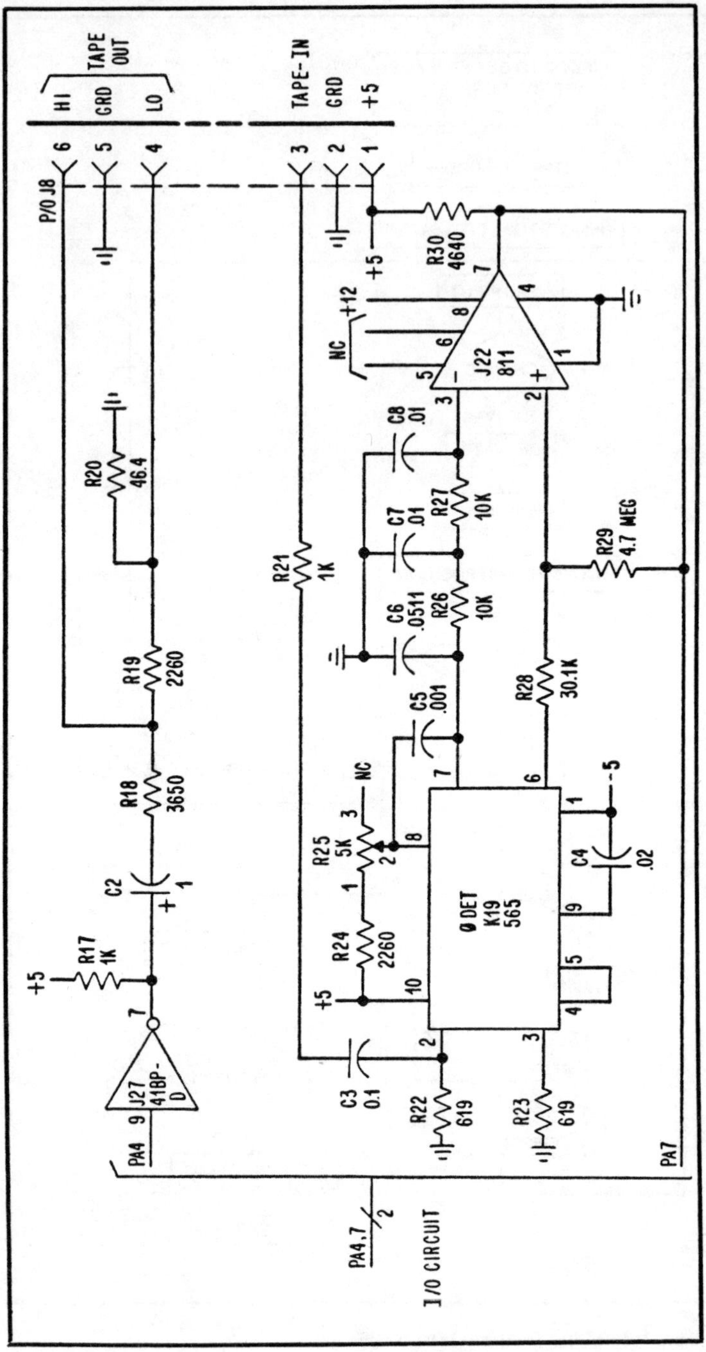

Fig. 10-8. Another FSK recorder microcomputer interface circuit.

displays allows the operator to display six bits of information at once. Typically this is the four hex bits required to display one 16-bit address, and the two hex digits to display the 8-bit data. But, since the displays will operate under program control, they can be used to display any desired information.

Figure 10-9 shows the connection of the 4 displays to output ports. Four 7-bit output ports are required, taking one and one-third 8255 interface chips. Alternatively, individual chips, such as the 7093, can be used. If the port connections to the keyboard are changed to a different port than originally

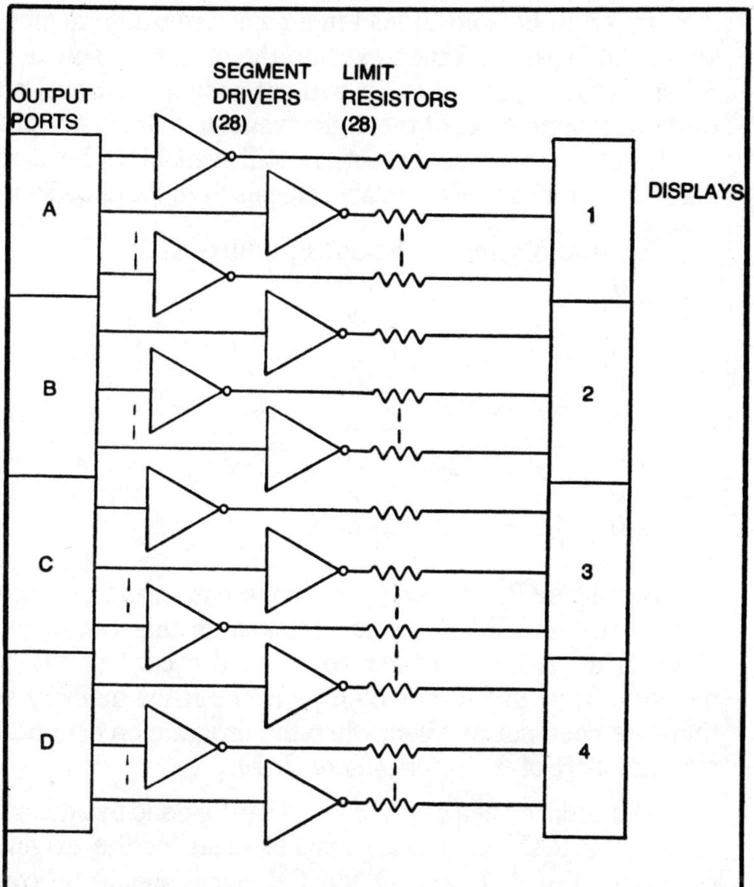

Fig. 10-9. Adding 4 LED displays to the microcomputer.

shown, the fourth port can be the vacated port of the 8255. This will assign the six displays to two 8255s, and make them easier to program.

To program these displays, expand the display to cover these output ports in a manner similar to the original display subroutine. Assign consecutive addresses as the data-storage locations for these displays.

ADDING MEMORY

One of the restrictions of this computer is the limited amount of memory available. Typically, more RAM memory is required to be able to load in a complete program along with a data base, and then execute the program. The 1k of RAM can be expanded to 5k without adding additional address decoders. Four of the eight available outputs are presently used, and the upper four are still available. The starting address for each of the enable signals from the decoder is:

Enable signal	Starting address
0_0	0000
0_1	0400
0_2	0800
0_3	0C00
0_4	1000
0_5	1400
0_6	1800
0_7	1C00

Any added RAM should be in consecutive address location so that the RAM memory makes up one continuous block. This makes it easier to use and record the RAM memory. This also leaves no gaps in the RAM memory so that care need not be taken when the program on data base occupies part of both portions of RAM.

The addition of a block of RAM can be done by adding 8 more 2102 RAM chips in a manner used for the original computer, Fig. 3-1, except the $\overline{CE}$ signal should be connected to 0_4 of the address decoder. This requires the addition of 8 RAM chips for each block of 1k of RAM desired.

Any of the 1k RAM chips can be used, provided that the total block ends up as a 1k by 8-bit block. Although there are available 1k by 8 RAM chips, they are expensive and hard to get. The 2102 series is the most prominent RAM available which is 1k wide.

If you use different-size blocks, you'll need two-level address decoding. One level decodes the existing 1k blocks

A block of memory consists of a memory with 8 bits and the number of addresses used by the individual memory chips. For instance, eight 1k by 1 memory chips make up a block of memory 1k by 8 bits. This block of memory uses a common chip-select signal, and is addressed as one block. Sixteen 512 by 1-bit chips cannot be connected as one block of 1k by 8-bit memory. Instead it will be 2 blocks of memory each 512 by 8-bits.

AN RS-232 INTERFACE

One of the largest advances in the usefulness of any computer comes when you connect it to a video display and keyboard. This allows the display of many lines of information at the same time, and allows using a standard keyboard input, with many keys. This is especially useful when using the computer for such applications as recipe retrieval, text display, and checkbook balancing. Yet, a video display and keyboard can cost more than the rest of the computer together, and can be complex to connect. A few words will be presented here about the requirements to interface with a display and keyboard.

Most terminals operate over an RS-232 interface. This is a 3-wire interface with some optional handshaking. The three wires consists of a transmit line, receive line, and a common-ground line. The pulses normally range from −9 volts to +9 volts, and are usually handled by a line transmitter and a line receiver chip, such as the 1488 and the 1489. The information is transmitted in ASCII code. This is a code which uniquely defines each possible key in 7-bits. Figure 10-10 gives the ASCII coding chart. When the code for the character is transmitted to the display, that character appears on the screen.

HEX	FUNCTION (CHARACTER)
00	NULL
01	SOH
02	STX
03	ETX
04	EOT
05	ENG
06	ACK
07	BELL
08	BACK SPACE
09	HT
0A	LINE FEED
0B	VT
0C	FORM FEED
0D	CARRIAGE RETURN
0E	SO
0F	SI
10	DELETE
11	DC1
12	DC2
13	DC3
14	DC4
15	NAK
2C	"
2D	-
2E	.
2F	/
30	0
31	1
32	2
33	3
34	4
35	5
36	6
37	7
38	8
39	9
3A	:
3B	;
3C	<
3D	=
3E	>
3F	?

HEX	FUNCTION (CHARACTER)
16	SYN
17	ETB
18	CAN
19	EM
1A	SUB
1B	ESCAPE
1C	FORWARD SPACE
1D	GS
1E	RS
1F	US
20	SP
21	!
22	"
23	#
24	$
25	%
26	&
27	'
28	(
29	)
2A	*
2B	+
42	B
43	C
44	D
45	E
46	F
47	G
48	H
49	I
4A	J
4B	K
4C	L
4D	M
4E	N
4F	O
50	P
51	Q
52	R
53	S
54	T
55	U

HEX	FUNCTION (CHARACTER)
40	@
41	A
58	X
59	Y
5A	Z
5B	[
5C	\
5D	]
5E	∧
5F	—
60	/
61	A
62	B
63	C
64	D
65	E
66	F
67	G
68	H
69	I
6A	J
6B	K
6C	L
6D	M

HEX	FUNCTION (CHARACTER)
56	V
57	W
6E	N
6F	O
70	P
71	Q
72	R
73	S
74	T
75	U
76	V
77	W
78	X
79	Y
7A	Z
7B	{
7C	|
7D	}
7E	~
7F	DELETE

Fig. 10-10. ASCII code table.

Notice that only the hex numbers 0 through F are useful as computer information. The remaining characters may be stored and used for such programs as letter writing, text editing, and checkbook balancing. When performing operations which require entering information for use by the computer, such as writing computer programs, the hexadecimal numbers must be decoded from the ASCII input to their hex equivalent. The converse is true when transferring information from the computer to the display. This requires the generation of two conversion programs, ASCII-to-hex, and hex-to-ASCII.

All data on the RS232 interface is transmitted at a given baud rate which is simply the bit rate for the 7 bits required to define one character. Since the computer and the keyboard and display are not synchronized with timing pulses, the baud rate generators must be accurate. Typically, the baud rate is generated from a crystal-controlled baud-rate generator, with several different standard baud rates available. The standard baud rates and the bit times are shown in Fig. 10-11.

Figure 10-12 shows the interface, using the 1488 and the 1489 line transmitter and receiver chips, in the full duplex mode. This means that the information displayed on the screen comes from the computer, not the keyboard. Although the computer may just turn the data around and send it to the display.

USING A CALCULATOR CHIP

It is the simplicity of the microcomputer which makes it so popular. But it is also this simplicity that limits the amount

Fig. 10-11. Baud rates versus bit times.

BAUD RATE	BIT TIME (MS)
110	9.1
150	6.4
300	3.2
600	1.6
1200	.8
2400	.4
4800	.2
9600	.1

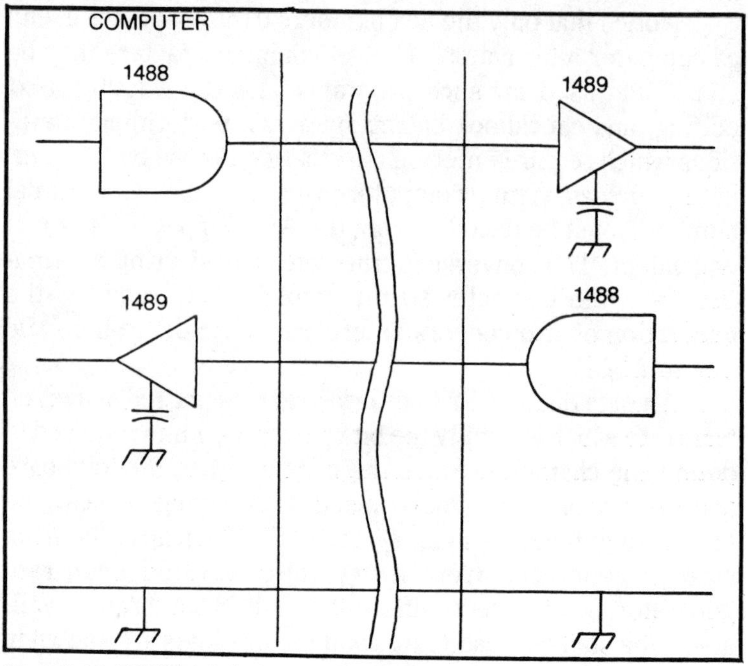

Fig. 10-12. RS232 full duplex interface circuit.

of mathematical operations it can perform—it offers a limited repertoire of instructions. Most microcomputers can only add and subtract, while others can do limited multiply and divide. This is all done in hex format, while most of its inputs, such as checkbook analysis and financial analysis are decimal. This means that input and output conversion routines are required.

Most complex mathematical operations, such as X^Y and sine functions can be conducted using specialized subroutines. But in a small computer this can take up most of the available memory space. One relatively inexpensive and simple method around this is to incorporate a calculator chip in the computer. After all, the calculator is a special purpose microcomputer, with a simple keyboard input and display output. Depending on the chip used, several complex functions can be performed with simple programming and simple hardware. Furthermore, the calculator is a decimal chip usually with floating-point arithmetic, with several digits of accuracy.

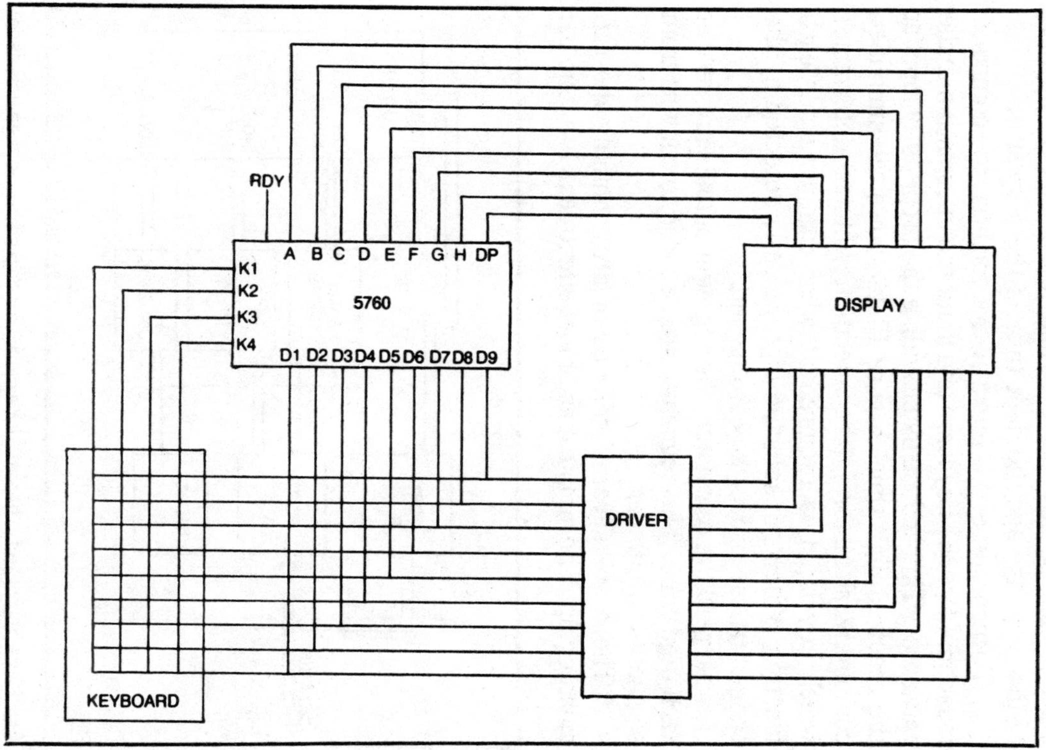

Fig. 10-13. Typical calculator diagram.

Figure 10-13 shows a typical calculator, using a 5760 chip and a LED display. The segment outputs are connected to the display, and the digits are selected for the segment signals by the digit signals D1 through D9. The calculator generates these digit signals using an internal clock. It is these digit signals which provide the system timing and tell the calculator which key is depressed. This is accomplished by scanning the Key inputs, K1 through K4, for each digit signal. The closure is detected and decoded for the key line of the response and the digit time of the response.

To incorporate this into a microcomputer, the computer must simulate the keyboard and input the information to the calculator. This is done by providing the proper key input at the required digit time. Figure 10-14 shows the simplified computer/calculator interconnection. A table determines which key input is required at what digit time for each function. When the selected digit pulse is detected by the computer, the proper key is enabled.

To read the calculator, the segment outputs are read at each digit time. The segments are decoded to convert from segments to numbers.

There are several methods of programming the calculator chip. The simplest and most effective is to set up the

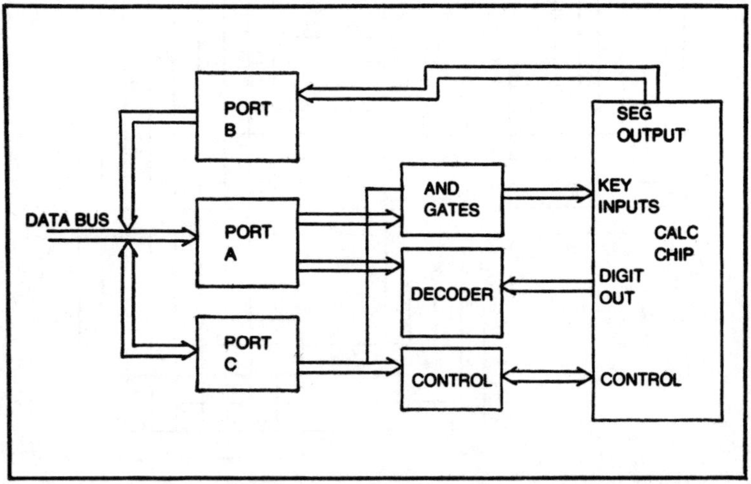

Fig. 10-14. Simplified schematic for a calculator chip microcomputer interface.

desired mathematical operation in a table, and to execute the table. This requires table-handling routines which decode the information in the table and provide the proper commands to the calculator. Incorporated into this routine can be the capability of defining memory locations where to get the information for the mathematical operation. The definition and development of this program is beyond the scope of this book.

Glossary

A/D conversion: Analog-to-digital conversion, the process of converting a continuous voltage usually on the range (of 0 to 10 volts) into a discrete digital number (frequently an 8-bit binary number used in microcomputers).

absolute decoding: The decoding of a binary number to produce a unique pulse to select a certain memory address, etc.

access, random: A method of accessing data without regard to the sequence in which they are stored.

accumulator: The register and associated digital electronics circuitry in arithmetic/logic unit (ALU) of a computer in which arithmetic and logical operations are preformed.

accumulator I/O: A term associated with 8080A-based micro systems. The I/O instructions are IN and OUT and the data transfer occurs between the I/O device and the accumulator within the 8080A chip.

addend: A quantity which, when added to another quantity (called the augend), produces a result called the sum.

adder: A device that is capable of forming the algebraic or arithmetic sum of two or more quantities.

address: A group of bits that identify a specific memory location or I/O device. An 8080A micro uses sixteen bits to identify a specific memory location and eight bits to identify an I/O device.

address bus: A unidirectional bus over which digital information appears to identify either a particular memory location or a particular I/O device. The 8080A address bus is a group of sixteen lines.

address select pulse: A software-generated clock pulse from a microcomputer that is used to strobe the operation of a memory mapped I/O device.

alphanumeric: Data in the form of letters, decimal numbers, and the ASCII symbols (as opposed to binary or graphical information).

analog: Data represented in an analog form by variables such as voltage, current and resistance.

analog-to-digital (A/D) converter: A circuit that changes a continuously varying voltage or current into a digital output.

AND gate: A binary circuit with two or more inputs and a single output, in which the output is logic 1 only when all inputs are logic 1, and the output is logic 0 if any of the inputs is a logic 0.

ASCII code: The American Standard Code for Information and Interchange. A seven-bit character code without the primary bit or an eight-bit character code with the parity bit.

assembler: A software or firmware program to convert programs written in assembly language into executable machine code.

assembly language: An intermediate-level, mnemonic representation of machine level code.

astable element: A two-state element that has no stable state.

asynchronous inputs: Those input pins in a flip-flop that can affect the output state of the flip-flop independent of the clock. Called preset, and reset or clear.

augend: In an arithmetic addition, the number increased by having another number, called the addend, added to it.

auxiliary device: Any separate or outboard device required to make the system operational.

BASIC: A high-level, interactive language developed at Dartmouth College and now in widespread use on microcomputers and time-shared systems.

baud: A unit of the modulation pulse rate for the Baudot code.

bidirectional data bus: A data bus in which digital information can be transferred in either direction. With reference to an 8080A-based micro, the bidirectional data path by which data is transferred between the CPU, memory, and input/output devices.

binary: A numbering system using a base number of 2. There are two digits (0 and 1) in the binary system.

binary code: A code in which each code element is one of two distinct states. These states are usually given the symbols 0 and 1.

binary coded decimal: Abbreviated BCD. A system of number representation in which each decimal digit of a number is expressed by binary numbers. Also known as the 8 4 2 1 code.

binary counter: An interconnections of flip-flops having a single input and so arranged to permit binary counting. Each time a pulse appears at the input, the counter changes state and tabulates the number of input pulses for readout in binary number form.

binary signal: Typically a voltage or current that carries information in the form of changes between two different states that are a discrete invertal apart. One of these states is called the logic 0 state, and the other, the logic 1 state.

bistable element: Another name for flip-flop. A circuit in which the output has two stable states and can be caused to go to either of these states by input signals, but remains in that state after the input signals are removed.

bit: Abbreviation for BInary digiT. A unit of information equal to one binary decision, or the designation of one or two values of states such as (0 or 1).

bit check: A binary digit (within a group of bits) used for checking digital pulse information data.

black box: A device that performs a specific function or action, but whose detailed operation is not specified or known.

boolean algebra: A system of mathematical logic dealing with operators such as AND, OR, NOT, NOR..... etc., which allows logic computations. Named after George Boole.

boolean symbol: A symbol used to represent a specific Boolean operation.

bootstrap: A procedure for a machine routine whose first few instructions are sufficient to bring the rest of the program into the machine.

breadboard: A device used to temporarily wire together various components to prove the feasibility of a circuit or complete system.

buffer: A digital circuit element that may be used to handle a large fan-out or to invert input and output levels.

buffer gate: A digital circuit that increases the power or current-handling capability of a binary circuit. Also known as a driver stage.

bus: A path over which digital information is transferred, from any of several sources to any of several destinations. Only one transfer of information can take place at any one time. While such transfer of information is taking place, all other sources that are tied to the bus must be disabled.

bus monitor: A binary, octal, or hexadecimal display that monitors and displays the data that appears on the bidirectional data bus.

byte: A group of eight contiguous bits that are operated on as a unit or occupy a single memory location.

cassette: Tape recorder used with inexpensive cassette tapes for mass storage of software.

central processing unit (Main Frame): Also called the central processor (CPU). That part of a computer system which contains the main storage, arithmetic unit, and special register groups. Performs arithmetic operations, controls instruction processing, and provides timing signals and other housekeeping operations.

central processing unit (Microprocessor): A single integrated chip that performs data transfer, control, input/output, arithmetic, and logical instructions by executing all basic instructions obtained from memory.

clock: Any device that generates one or more clock (square wave) pulses.

clock input: That terminal on a flip-flop whose condition or change of condition controls the admission of data into a flip-flop through the synchronous inputs, and thereby controls the output state of the flip-flop. The clock signal performs two functions: (1) it permits data signals to enter the flip-flop, and (2) after entry, it directs the flip-flop to change states accordingly.

clock, master: A pulse generator that controls the timing of clocked logic devices and regulates the speed at which such devices operate. It serves to synchronize all operations in a digital system.

clock pulse: A complete logic cycle from logic 0 to logic 1 and back to logic 0 (positive clock pulse).

COBOL: Common Business Oriented Language. This is a computer language used for business data processing.

code conversion: The changing of the bit grouping for a character in one code into the corresponding bit grouping in another code.

communication: The imparting, conveying, or exchange of ideas knowledge, information, etc. Whether by speech, writing, signs, or signals.

compiler: A computer program that prepares a machine language from another kind of programming language.

complement: To form the complement of a binary number. The complement of 1 is 0, and the complement of 0 is 1. The complement of 100101 is 011010.

computer: Refer to digital computer.

Computer program: A sequence of instructions which, taken as a group, allow the computer to accomplish a desired task.

control: Those parts of a computer which carry out instructions in proper sequence, interpert instructions, and apply proper signals.

control bus: A set of signals that regulate the operation of microcomputer system, including I/O devices and memory. They function much like traffic signals or commands. They may also originate in the I/O devices, generally to transfer to or receive signals from the CPU. A unidirectional set of signals that indicate the type of activity-memory read, memory write, I/O read, I/O write, or interrupt acknowledge-in current process.

controller: An instrument that holds a process or condition at a desired level or status as determined by comparison of the actual value with the desired value.

counter: A device capable of changing states in a specified sequence upon receiving proper input signals. The output of the counter indicates the number of pulses that have been applied. A counter is made from flip-flops and some gates. The output of all flip-flops is accessable to indicate the exact count at all times.

CPU: Central processing unit. The functional unit of a computer (usually the microprocessor in the case of minicomputers) which performs the arithmetical, logical, and control operations of the computer.

cross-talk: The unwanted energy transferred from one circuit, the disturbing circuit, to another circuit, the disturbed circuit. This could be digital pulses from one control line crossing over to another signal control line.

D/A conversion: The process of converting a digital number (usually an 8-bit binary word) to an analog voltage.

data byte: For the 8080A micro, this is the eight-bit binary number that is transferred over the bidirectional data bus.

data logger: An instrument that automatically scans data produced by another instrument or process, and records readings of the data for future use.

decade counter: A logic device that has ten stable states and may be cycled through these states by the application of ten clock or pulse inputs. A decade counter usually counts in a binary sequence from state 0 through 9 and then cycles back to state 0. Also called a divide-by-ten counter.

decode: To use a code to reverse a previous encoding. To determine the meaning of a set of pulses or logic signals that describe an instruction, a command, or an operation to be carried out.

decoder: A device capable of decoding a group of coded signals and thereby producing the original information.

delay line: A device used for introducing time lag in the transmission of data information.

device code: For an 8080A micro, the 8-bit code for a specific input or output device.

device select pulse Q: A software-generated clock pulse from a microcomputer that is used to strobe the operation of an accumulator I/O device.

digital code: A system of symbols that represent data values and make up a special language that a computer or digital circuit can understand and use.

digital computer: An electronic device that is capable of accepting, storing, and arithmetically manipulating information, which includes both data and controlling program. The information is handled in the form of coded binary digits (0 and 1) that are represented by dual voltage levels.

digital device: Any device that operates on or manipulates binary, or two-state, information.

digital signals: Discrete or discontinuous signals whose various states are discrete intervals apart.

digital-to-analog converter: A circuit that changes a digital input into a continuously varying voltage or current.

digital waveform: A graphical representation of a digital signal, showing the varations in logic state as a function of time. This type of representation is also known as a timing diagram.

diode: A two-electrode semiconductor device that makes use of the rectifying properties of a PN junction or a point contact diode. Also called crystal diode, rectifier diode, and semiconductor diode.

dip: A common method of packaging IC chips (dual, in-line, package).

disable: To prevent the passage of digital signals by the application of the proper signal to the disable terminal of a digital device.

display: A device that provides a visual presentation of an electron signal, such as a scope or video terminal.

DMA: Direct memory access. The ability to access memory without going through the CPU.

driver: A digital circuit element coupled to the output stage of a circuit to increase the power or current handling capability, or fanout, of the stage. For example, a clock driver is used to supply the current necessary for a clock line.

DTL logic: Abbreviation for diode transistor logic.

dumb: Terminals like TTYs and video monitors which do not attempt to format or process the data as it is transmitted or received.

dump: To hardcopy the contents of data that is stored in the memory of a microcomputer.

edge-triggered flip-flop: A type of flip-flop in which some minimum clock signal rate of change, in Volts/second, is one necessary condition for an output change to occur.

electric pencil: A character oriented word processing system that may be used as a text editor. Program is usually loaded into the memory of the microcomputer from a cassette recorder.

enable: To permit the passage of a digital signal into or through a digital device or circuit.

encode: To use a code, frequently one composed of binary numbers, to represent individual characters or groups of characters in a message. To change from one digital code to another. If the codes are a lot different, the process is called code conversion.

encoder: A device capable of translating from one form of data to another form of data. The decoder may have the appearance of a matrix.

exclusive-OR gate: A binary circuit with two inputs and a single output, in which the output is logic 1 when the inputs are at different logic states, and the output is logic 0 if both inputs are at the same logic states.

fall time: The time required for the negative trailing edge of a pulse to decrease from 90% to 10% of its initial value. In digital electronics, the measured length of time required for an output voltage of a digital circuit to change from a high level to a low level.

fan-in: The input load requirements of a digital input to an integrated circuit chip.

fan-out: The number of parallel loads within a given logic family, such as TTL, that can be driven from one output of a logic circuit.

fetch: One of the two functional parts of an instruction cycle. The collective actions of acquiring a memory address and then an instruction or data byte from memory.

firmware: Software systems, often supplied by ROM. Also referred to as monitor programs.

flag: Some sort of digital register or device that is used to indicate the state or status of a device. It can be cleared or set in response to an operation.

flip-flop: A circuit having two stable states and the capability of changing from one state to another with the application of a control signal, and remaining in that state even after the signal has passed.

floppy disk: A flexible magnetic disk used for mass storage of information.

flowchart: A graphical representation for the definition, analysis, or solution of a computer problem, in which symbols are used to represent operations, data, flow, or equipment.

gate: To control the passage of a digital signal through a digital circuit.

gate (gating device): A circuit having two or more inputs and one output. One of the inputs can be clearly identified as a data input, with the remaining inputs being gating inputs. The logic state of the gating inputs determine whether or not the input data can appear at the output.

gate (logic device): A circuit having two or more inputs and one output, the output of which depends upon the combination of the logic signals at the inputs. There are four basic gates, called AND, OR, NAND, and NOR.

gate circuit: A circuit that passes a signal only when a gating is present. An electronic circuit with one or more inputs and one output with the property that a pulse goes out on the output line if and only if some specified combination of pulses occurs on the input lines.

gate pulse: A pulse that enables a gate circuit to pass a signal. The gate pulse generally has a longer duration then the signal to ensure time coincidence.

gate signal: See gate pulse. A signal that permits a gate circuit to pass a signal.

gated buffer: A low-impedance driver circuit that may be used as a line driver for pulse differenfiation or in multivibrators. In general, a buffer that is gated.

gated driver: In general, a driver that is gated.

gated circuit: A circuit that operates as a selective switch and allows conduction only during selected time intervals or when the signal magnitude is within specified limits.

gating pulse: A pulse that modifies or controls the operation of a gate circuit.

gating signal: A digital signal that modifies or controls the operation of a gate circuit.

general-purpose register: For the 8080A micro, this would be the 8-bit registers that can participate in arithmetic and logical operations with the contents of the accumulator.

general-purpose registers: For an 8080A-based micro, a six eight-bit registers that temporarily store signal bytes of information. The registers are called B, C, D, E, H, and L.

glitch: An unwanted pulse or logic state, usually caused by poor design and/or propagation delays.

hardware: The mechanical, magnetic, electronic, and the electrical devices from which a computer is built. The parts that make up a microcomputer.

hex: Hexadecimal (base 16) number system comprized of the numbers and letters 0123456789 ABCDEF. An 8-bit word may be represented by two hex numbers.

hi address byte: The eight most significant bits in the 16-bit memory address word for the 8080A micro chip.

hierarchy: A series of items classified according to rank or order.

I/O: Input/Output, the functions required to communicate with computers. Generally classified into serial or parallel ports. Devices include toggle switches, keypads, keyboards TTYs, video terminals, lineprinters and graphics.

immediate byte: A data byte that is contained within a multibyte computer instruction.

inclusive masking: A masking technique in which one leaves unaltered all bits not operated upon.

inclusive-OR: See OR gate.

increment: To increase the value of a binary word by one.

input/output: A general term for the device used to communicate with a computer and the data involved in the communication.

integrated circuit (IC): (1) A combination of interconnected circuit elements inseparably associated on or within a continuous substrate: (2) Any electronic device in which both active and passive elements are contained in a single package. In digital electronics, the term chiefly applies to circuits containing semiconductor elements.

interface: The linkage of various computer components. Thus, the term that the computer must be interfaced with the outside world.

interrupt: In a digital computer, a break in the normal execution of a computer program such that the program can be resumed from that point at a later time.

interrupt instruction register: An external 8-bit register that permits an instruction to be jammed into the instruction register within an 8080A chip during an interrupt.

inverter: A digital device that complements an input digital signal.

k: kilobyte or 1024 bytes as in 1k, 8k, 16k or 65k memory.

keypad: A small keyboard with usually 16 to 24 buttons to enter programs, data, and control functions.

language (computer): The whole body of words and/or methods of combination of words used to program a computer.

latch: A simple logic storage element. A feedback loop used in a symmetrical digital circuit, such as a flip-flop, to retain a logic state.

LED: Light Emitting Diodes use as discrete indicators, in seven-segment readouts or in dot matrix displays.

led lamp monitor: A light-emitting diode (LED) that is lighted in the logic 1 state and unlighted in the logic 0 state.

lo address byte: The eight least significant bits in the 16-bit memory address word for an 8080A micro chip.

logic switch: A mechanical device that applies either a logic 0 or a logic 1 state at its output terminal.

logical instructions: A logic operation that is performed on a pair of multi-bit data words, in which ten corresponding bits of each word participate in two-bit logic operation, such as AND, OR and Exclusive-OR.

machine code: A binary representation of a computer instruction.

machine cycle: A subdivision of an instruction cycle during which time a related group of actions occur within the microprocessor chip. All instructions are combinations of one or more machine cycles.

machine language: The set of binary numbers instructing the CPU to perform specific operations.

masking: A logical technique in which certain bits of a multi-bit word are blanked out or inhibited.

memory: Any device that can store logic 0 and logic 1 bits in such a manner that a single bit or group of bits can be accessed or retrived.

memory address: The storage location of a memory word.

memory mapped I/O: A term associated with 6800, 8080A and other microcomputer sustems. The I/O instructions are memory reference instructions and the data transfer occurs, in the case of the 8080A chip, between the I/O device and any of the general purpose registers within the chip.

microcomputer: A microprocessor with associated memory, I/O circuitry, and power supplies.

microprocessor: Usually a discrete integrated circuit chip containing a CPU, register, flags, and associated control circuitry.

mnemonic: Computer instructions written in a form the programmer can easily remember, but which must be converted into machine code later by a computer or by the user.

mnemonic instructions: Computer instructions that are written in a meaningful notation. As an example, ADD, SUB, DIV, etc.

mnemonic language: A programming language that is based upon easily remembered symbols and that can be assembled into machine code by a computer.

mode: A type or kind of operation. A status. As an example, a manner or method of doing something.

modulo: The number of distinct states a counter goes through before repeating.

monitor: A firmware system for monitoring and controlling computer operations, sometimes called an operating system.

monostable multivibrator: A digital circuit that has only one stable state, from which it can be triggered to change the state, but only for a predetermined time interval, after which it returns to the original state. Also called a one-shot multivibrator, single shot multivibrator, or a start-stop multivibrator.

multilevel interrupt: Several independent interrupt lines are provided, each of which causes a specific action. Polling is not needed unless multiple devices are ORed to one of the inputs.

multiplexer: A digital device that can select one of a number of inputs and pass the logic state of that input on to the output.

NAND gate: A combination of a NOT function and an AND function in a binary circuit that has two or more inputs and one output. The output is logic 0 only if all inputs are logic 1 and it is logic 1 if any input is logic 0.

negative edge: The transition from logic 1 to logic 0 in a clock pulse.

nibble: A group of four contiguous bits that are operated on as a unit or occupy a single memory location.

node: Nodes are used to designate a state, an event, or a time coincidence. A node could be referred to as the state of the gate.

NOR gate: An OR gate followed by an inverter to form a binary circuit in which the output is logic 0 if any of the inputs is logic 1, and is logic 1 only if all the inputs are logic 0.

NOT gate: A binary circuit with a single output that is always the opposite of the single input. Also called an inverter circuit.

octal: Base eight number system, sometimes used to represent instructions and data in computers.

octal code: Pertaining to a binary coded numbering system with the radix 8, in which the natural binary values 0 through 7 are used to represent octal digits with values from 0 to 7.

OEM (original equipment manufacturer): Applications in which the computer is usually built into a larger instrument or machine.

open collector output: An output from an integrated circuit device in which the final pull-up resistor in the output transistor for the device is missing and must be provided by the user before the circuit is complete.

operation: A specific action which a computer will perform whenever an instruction calls for it, such as addition, OR, subtraction, AND, etc.

operation code: For an 8080A-based micro, the eight-bit code for the specific action that the 8080A micro-chip will perform.

parallel: Data or communications channels in which a full word is transmitted. In microcomputers this usually requires an eight-wire conductor to handle eight bits simultaneously.

polling: A periodic checking of input/output or control devices to determine their condition or status, such as full/empty, on/off, busy/ready, done/not done, etc.

positive edge: The transition from logic 0 to logic 1 in a clock pulse.

preset: An asynchronous input that is used to control the logic state of the Q output of a flip-flop. Signals entered through this input cause the Q output to go logic 1. The preset input cannot cause the Q output to go to logic 0.

priority interrupt: Interrupts that are ordered in importance so that some interrupting devices take precedence over others.

program counter: The 16-bit register in the 8080A chip that contains the memory address of the next instruction byte that must be executed in a computer program.

PROM: programmable read only memory. Programmed by the manufacturer or user, for the permanent storage of programs or data.

propagation delay: A measure of the time required for a logic signal to travel through a logic device or series of logic devices forming a logic string. It occurs as a result of four types of circuit delays—storage, rise, fall and turn-on delay—and is the time between when the input signal crosses the threshold-voltage point and when the responding output voltage crosses the same voltage point.

PSW: Abbreviation for processor status word. The contents of the accumulator and the five status flags in the 8080A microprocessor chip.

pulser: A logic switch that generates a single clock pulse.

race: The condition that occurs when changing the state of a system requires a change in two or more state variables. If the final state is affected by which variable changes first, the condition is a critical race. Also, the condition that exists when a signal is propagated through two or more memory elements during the same clock period.

RAM: Random access memory. Any location that can be read from and written into in a nonsequential manner.

read: To transmit data from a specific memory location to some other digital device. A synonym for retrieve.

read-only memory (ROM): A semiconductor memory from which digital data can be repeatedly read-out, but cannot be written into as in the case of a RAM.

read/write memory A semiconductor memory into which logic 0 and logic 1 states can be written (stored) and read out (retrieved) again. Also referred to as RAM memory.

real-time clock: This refers to a device that provides interrupts at regular time intervals, frequently twice the AC line frequency. It allows maintence of an accurate time of day clock and the measurement of elasped time.

register: A short-term digital electronic storage circuit the capacity of which is usually one computer word or byte.

reset: An asynchronous input that is used to control the logic state of the Q output of a flip-flop. Signals entered through this input cause the Q output to go to logic 1.

resistor: A device connected into an electrical circuit to introduce a specified resistance.

rise-time: The time required for the positive leading edge of a pulse to rise from 10% to 90% of its final value. It is proportional to the time constant and is a measure of the steepness of the wavefront. In digital electronics, the very measured length of time required for an output voltage of a digital circuit to change from a low voltage level (logic 0) to a high voltage level (logic 1).

ROM: Read-only memory. A memory which is fixed (often by the manufacturer) and typically stores the operating system for the microcomputer.

RS232C: An industry standard definined logic levels, control signals and connector configuration for serial peripheral interfaces.

RTL logic: This is an abbreviation for resistor-transistor logic.

S-100: A 100-pin bus system that is now a standard used by many computer manufacturers.

schematic diagram: A printed drawing of electronic devices that are wired to form a useful electronic circuit.

serial: Transmission of data in a sequential manner, bit-after-bit on one data line. An example of a serial device is a TTY.

service routine: A computer subroutine that services an interrupting device.

single-byte instruction: An instruction consisting of eight contiguous bits that occupy a single memory location.

single-line interrupt: An interrupt signal that is input to the computer on a single line and causes a well defined action to take place. Multiple devices must be ORed onto this line and a polling routine must be determined which device caused the interrupt.

smart: As in a smart terminal. This is a terminal that is able to format and process data.

software: Programs (such as on tape or punch cards) that must be loaded into memory to control a computer.

stack pointer: The 16-bit register in the 8080A microprocessor chip that stores the memory address of the top of the stack, which is a region of read/write memory that stores temporary information.

strobe: To activate or enable a digital circuit.

symbol: A written character or mark used to represent a device on a circuit diagram.

sync: Short for synchronous and synchronization.

synchronization pulses: Pulses originated by the transmitting equipment and introduced into the receiving equipment to keep the two units at each location operating in step or proper phase.

synchronize: To lock one part of a system into step with another one.

synchronous: Operation of a clocked logic system with the aid of a clock pulse generator. All actions take place synchronously with the clock.

synchronous computer: A digital computer in which all ordinary operations are controlled by a master clock.

synchronous inputs: Those terminals on a flip-flop through which data can be entered but only upon command of the clock. These inputs do not have direct control of the outputs such as those of a gate, but only when the clock permits and commands. Called JK inputs and D inputs.

synchronous logic: The type of digital logic used in a system in which logical operations take place in synchronism with clock pulses.

synchronous operation: Operation of a system under the control of clock pulses.

text editor: An electronic method for editing text on the video terminal screen before the data is transmitted.

three-byte instruction: An instruction consisting of information that occupies three successive memory locations.

three-state device: A semiconductor logic device in which there are three possible output states: (1) a logic 0 state; (2) a logic 1 state; and (3) a state in which the output is, in effect, disconnected from the rest of the circuit and has no influence upon it.

timing loop: A software loop that requires a precise period of time for its execution.

tri-state device: See three-state device.

trigger: A pulse that starts an action. It may also be the edge of a pulse. Also refer to enable.

truth table: A tabulation that shows the relationship of all output logic levels of a digital circuit to all possible combinations of input logic levels in such a way as to characterize the circuit functions completely.

TTL logic: Abbreviation for transistor-transistor logic.

two-byte instruction: An instruction consisting of information that occupies two successive memory locations.

VDM (video display monitor): A software package for displaying data on a video monitor screen.

vectored interrupt: Each device points, or vectors, the control of the computer to specify software routines for the interrupting devices.

video monitor: A device which accepts video information and displays it on a television screen.

word: The number of bits that a computer can manipulate simultaneously.

write: To transmit data from some other digital device into a specific memory location. A synonym for store.

XOR: See Exclusive-OR gate.

Appendix A
Pin Configurations for Several Chips

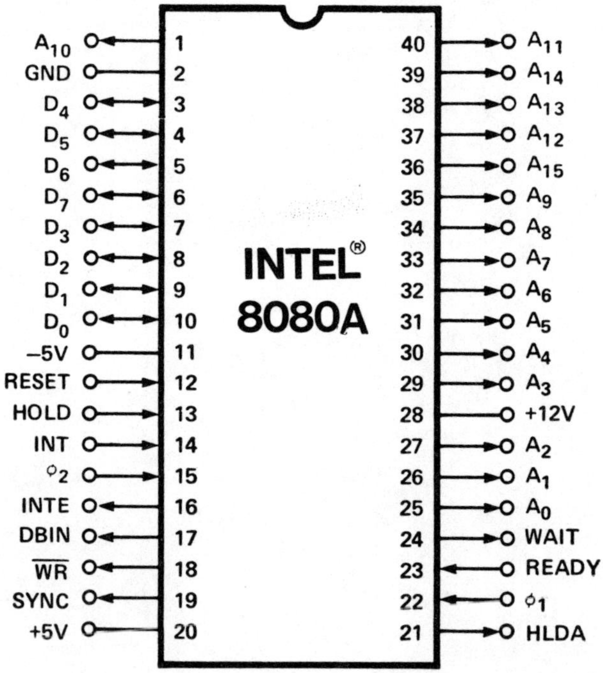

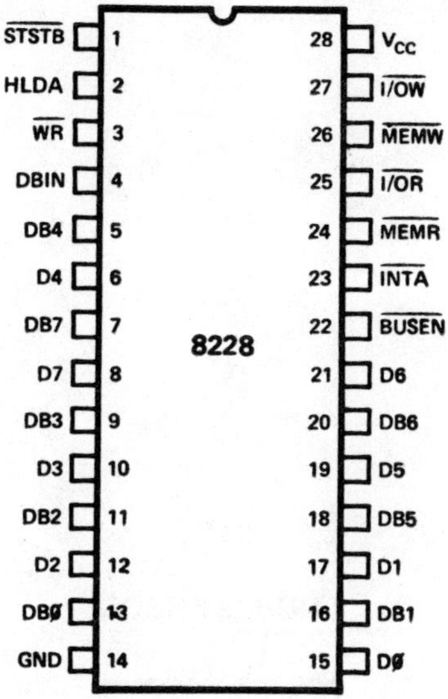

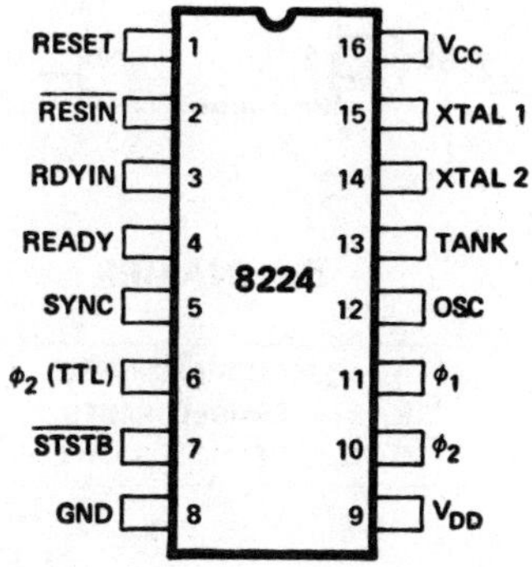

PIN NAMES

$\overline{RESIN}$	RESET INPUT
RESET	RESET OUTPUT
RDYIN	READY INPUT
READY	READY OUTPUT
SYNC	SYNC INPUT
$\overline{STSTB}$	STATUS STB (ACTIVE LOW)
ϕ_1	8080 CLOCKS
ϕ_2	

XTAL 1	CONNECTIONS FOR CRYSTAL
XTAL 2	
TANK	USED WITH OVERTONE XTAL
OSC	OSCILLATOR OUTPUT
ϕ_2 (TTL)	ϕ_2 CLK (TTL LEVEL)
V_{CC}	+5V
V_{DD}	+12V
GND	0V

PIN NAMES

D7-D0	DATA BUS (8080 SIDE)
DB7-DB0	DATA BUS (SYSTEM SIDE)
$\overline{I/OR}$	I/O READ
$\overline{I/OW}$	I/O WRITE
$\overline{MEMR}$	MEMORY READ
$\overline{MEMW}$	MEMORY WRITE
DBIN	DBIN (FROM 8080)

INTA	INTERRUPT ACKNOWLEDGE
HLDA	HLDA (FROM 8080)
$\overline{WR}$	WR (FROM 8080)
$\overline{BUSEN}$	BUS ENABLE INPUT
$\overline{STSTB}$	STATUS STROBE (FROM 8224)
V_{CC}	+5V
GND	0 VOLTS

PIN CONFIGURATION

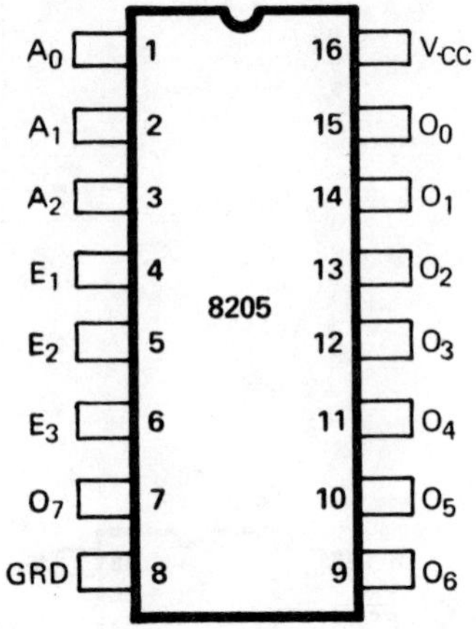

LOGIC SYMBOL

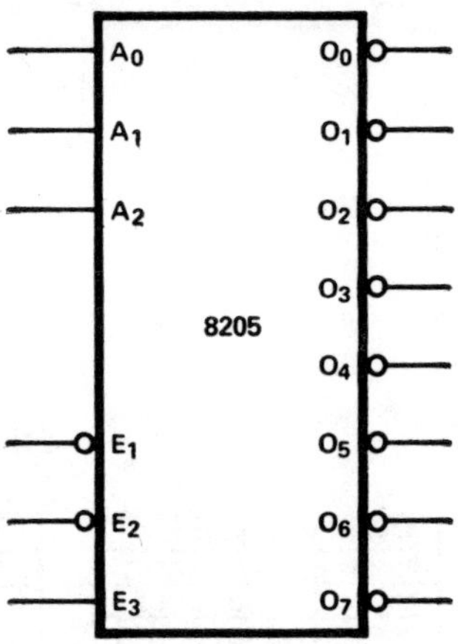

PIN NAMES

A_0- A_2	ADDRESS INPUTS
$\overline{E_1}$- $\overline{E_3}$	ENABLE INPUTS
$\overline{O_0}$- $\overline{O_7}$	DECODED OUTPUTS

ADDRESS			ENABLE			OUTPUTS							
A_0	A_1	A_2	E_1	E_2	E_3	0	1	2	3	4	5	6	7
L	L	L	L	L	H	L	H	H	H	H	H	H	H
H	L	L	L	L	H	H	L	H	H	H	H	H	H
L	H	L	L	L	H	H	H	L	H	H	H	H	H
H	H	L	L	L	H	H	H	H	L	H	H	H	H
L	L	H	L	L	H	H	H	H	H	L	H	H	H
H	L	H	L	L	H	H	H	H	H	H	L	H	H
L	H	H	L	L	H	H	H	H	H	H	H	L	H
H	H	H	L	L	H	H	H	H	H	H	H	H	L
X	X	X	L	L	L	H	H	H	H	H	H	H	H
X	X	X	H	L	L	H	H	H	H	H	H	H	H
X	X	X	L	H	L	H	H	H	H	H	H	H	H
X	X	X	H	H	L	H	H	H	H	H	H	H	H
X	X	X	H	L	H	H	H	H	H	H	H	H	H
X	X	X	L	H	H	H	H	H	H	H	H	H	H
X	X	X	H	H	H	H	H	H	H	H	H	H	H

PIN CONFIGURATION

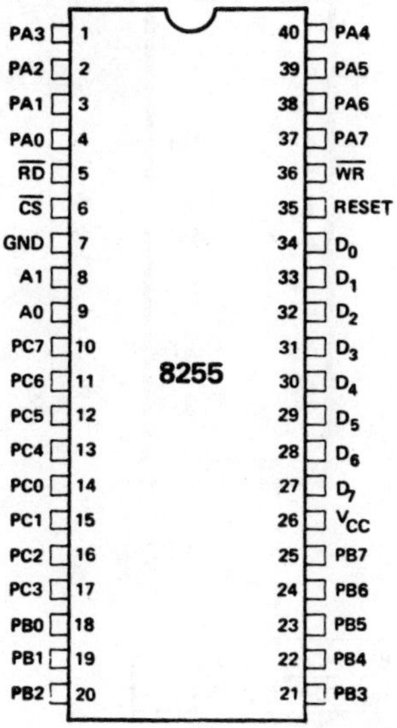

PIN NAMES

D_7–D_0	DATA BUS (BI-DIRECTIONAL)
RESET	RESET INPUT
$\overline{CS}$	CHIP SELECT
$\overline{RD}$	READ INPUT
$\overline{WR}$	WRITE INPUT
A0, A1	PORT ADDRESS
PA7-PA0	PORT A (BIT)
PB7-PB0	PORT B (BIT)
PC7-PC0	PORT C (BIT)
V_{CC}	+5 VOLTS
GND	Ø VOLTS

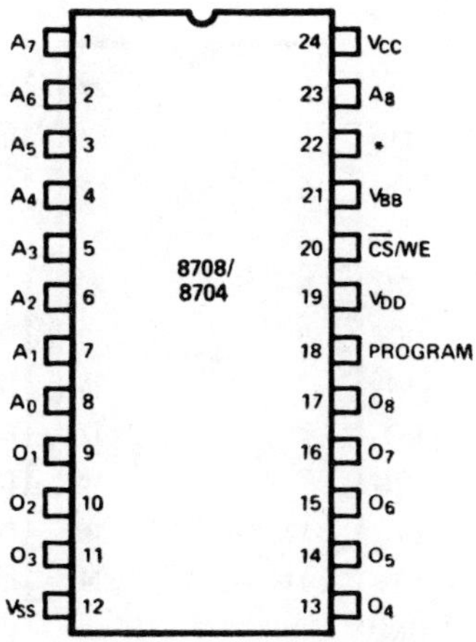

*8704 = V_{SS}
8708 = A_9

PIN NAMES

A_0-A_9	ADDRESS INPUTS
O_1-O_8	DATA OUTPUTS
$\overline{CS}$/WE	CHIP SELECT/WRITE ENABLE INPUT

PIN CONFIGURATION

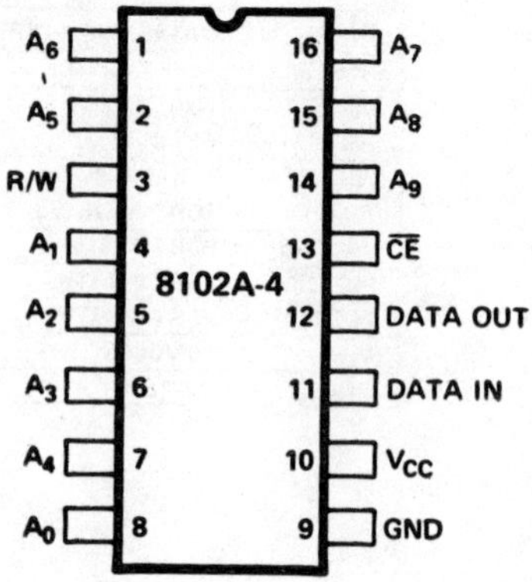

LOGIC SYMBOL

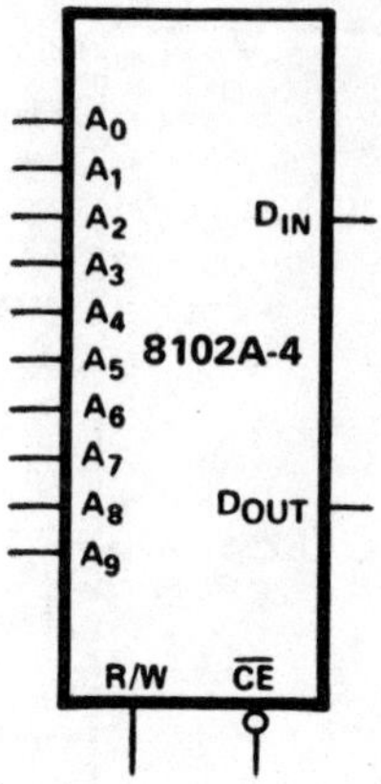

PIN NAMES

D_{IN}	DATA INPUT	$\overline{CE}$	CHIP ENABLE
A_0-A_9	ADDRESS INPUTS	D_{OUT}	DATA OUTPUT
R/W	READ/WRITE INPUT	V_{CC}	POWER (+5V)

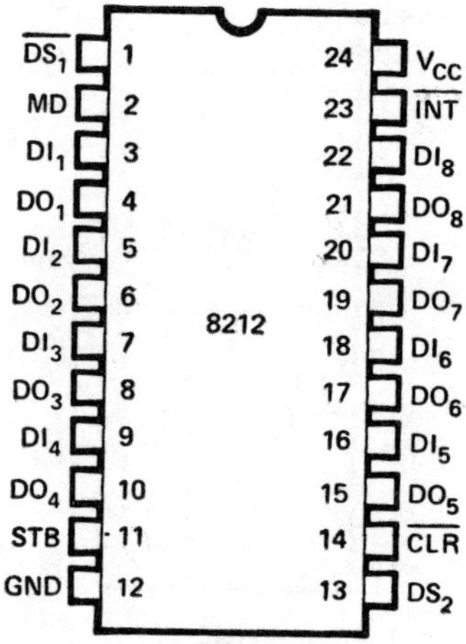

PIN NAMES

DI_1-DI_8	DATA IN
DO_1-DO_8	DATA OUT
$\overline{DS_1}$-DS_2	DEVICE SELECT
MD	MODE
STB	STROBE
$\overline{INT}$	INTERRUPT (ACTIVE LOW)
$\overline{CLR}$	CLEAR (ACTIVE LOW)

PIN CONFIGURATION

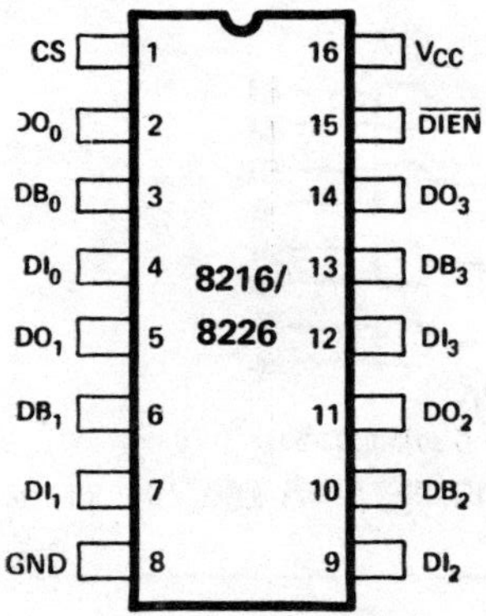

LOGIC DIAGRAM 8216

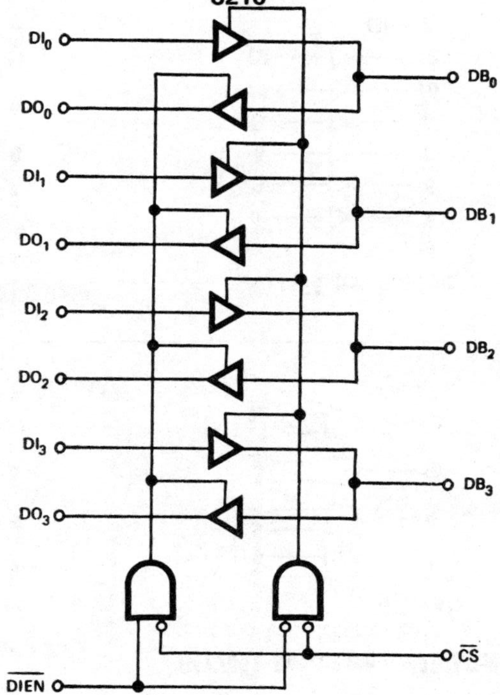

LOGIC DIAGRAM 8226

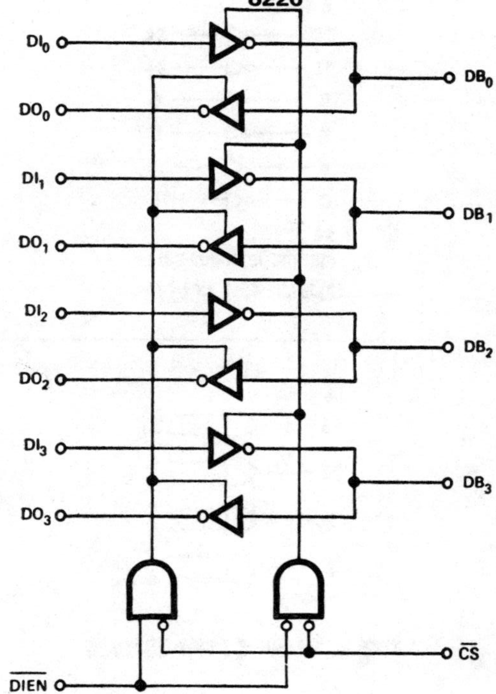

PIN NAMES

DB_0-DB_3	DATA BUS BI-DIRECTIONAL
DI_0-DI_3	DATA INPUT
DO_0-DO_3	DATA OUTPUT
$\overline{DIEN}$	DATA IN ENABLE DIRECTION CONTROL
$\overline{CS}$	CHIP SELECT

54/7400 Quad 2-input NAND Gate

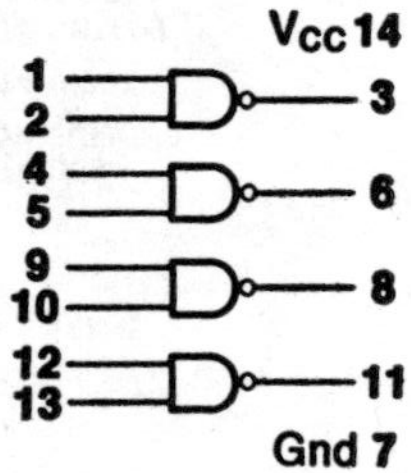

54/7401 Quad 2-input NAND Gate

Free-collector outputs

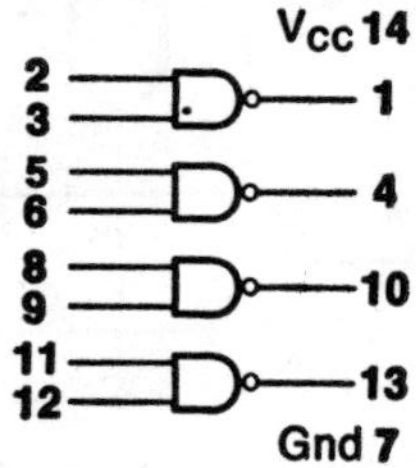

54/7402 Quad 2-input NOR Gate

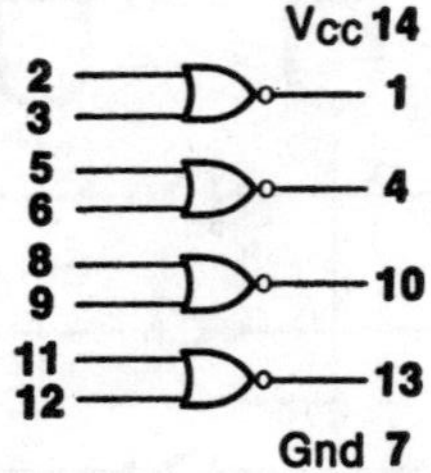

54/7403 Quad 2-input NAND Gate

Free-collector outputs

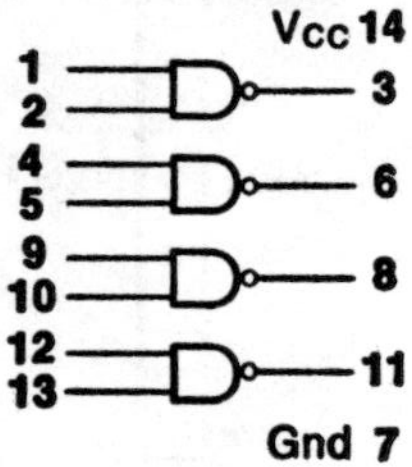

54/7404 Hex Inverter

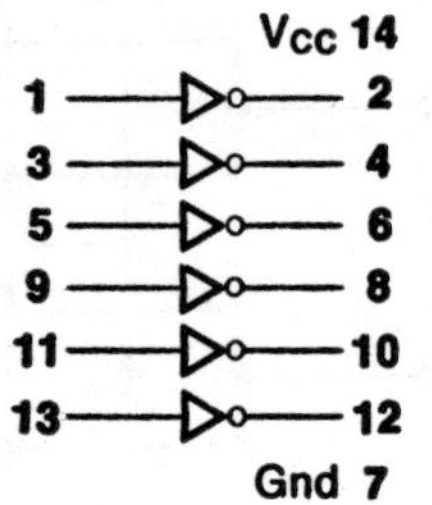

54/7405 Hex Inverter

Free-collector outputs

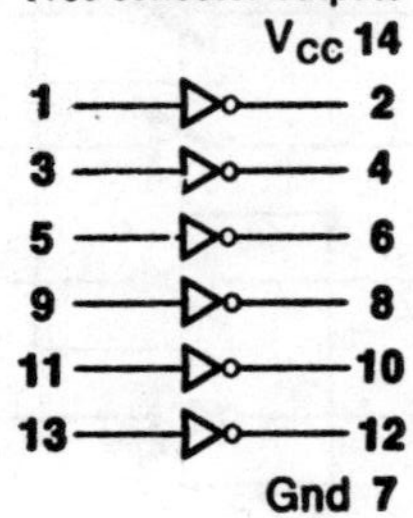

54/7406 Hex Inverting Buffer

Free-collector outputs, 30V rating

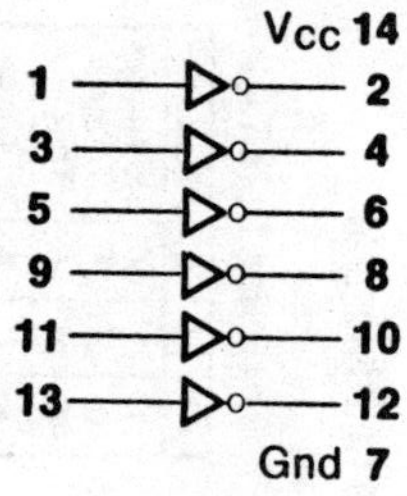

54/7407 Hex Buffer

Free-collector outputs, 30V rating

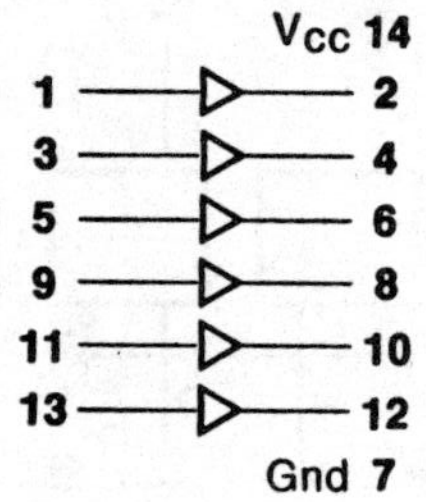

54/7408 Quad 2-input AND Gate

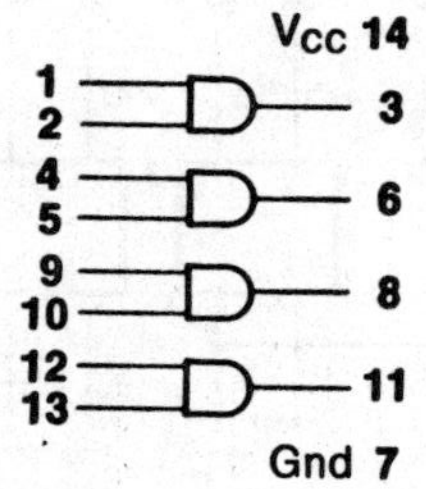

54/7409 Quad 2-input AND Gate

Free-collector outputs

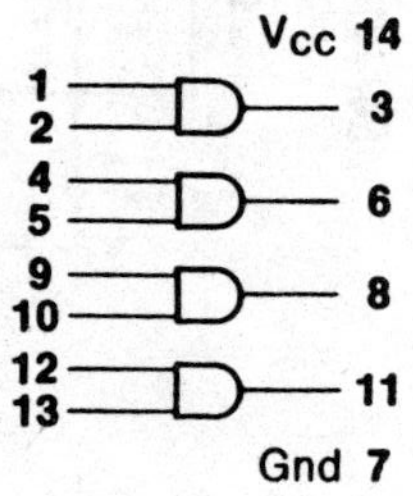

54/7410 Triple 3-input NAND Gate

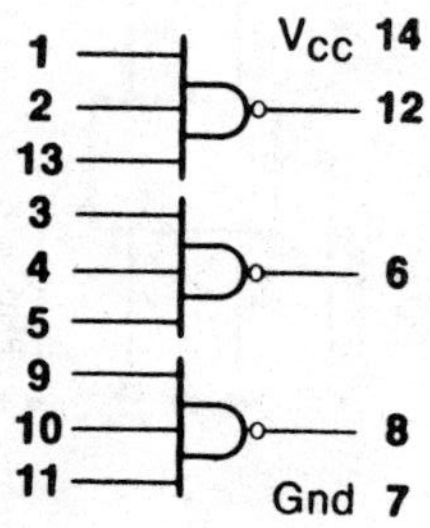

54/7412 Triple 3-input NAND Gate

Free-collector outputs

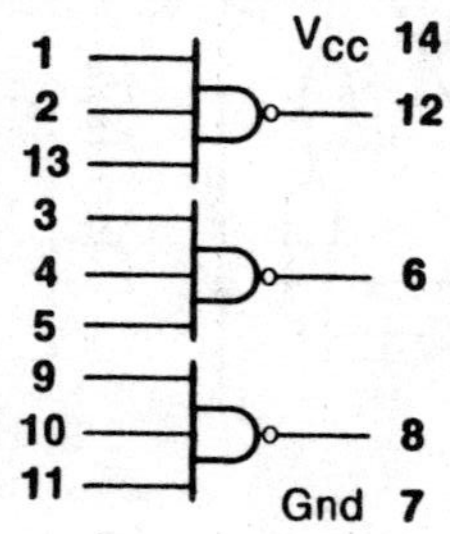

latch logic

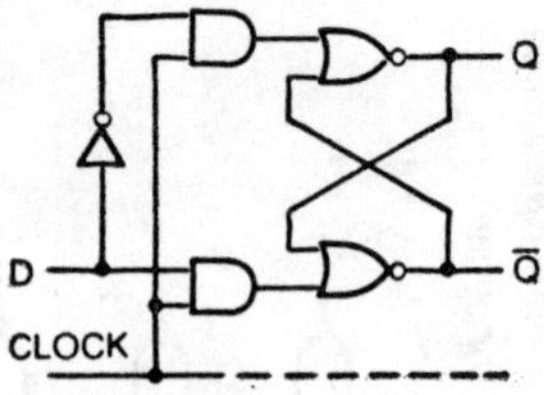

Truth Table

C	D	Q	$\overline{Q}$
Low	Low	No Change	
Low	High	No Change	
High	Low	Low	High
High	High	High	Low

54/7475 Quad Latch

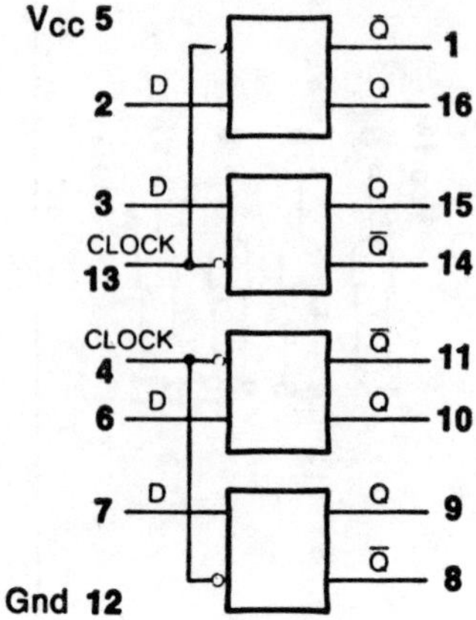

54/7476 Dual J-K Flip-Flop

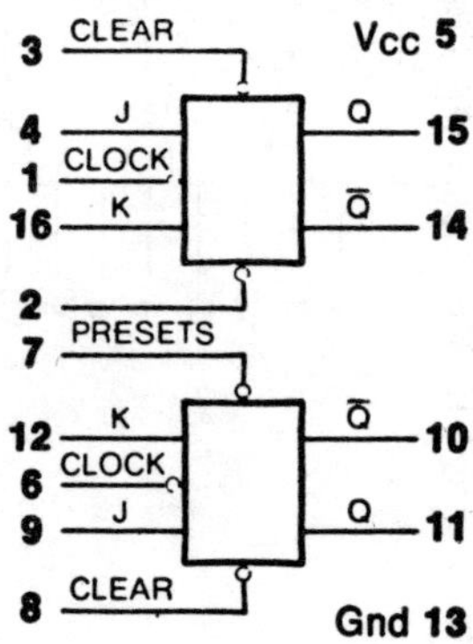

54/7477 Quad Latch*

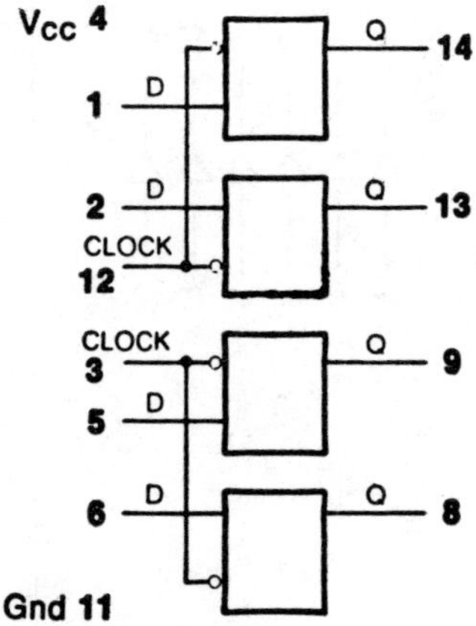

54/74121 Monostable Multivibrator

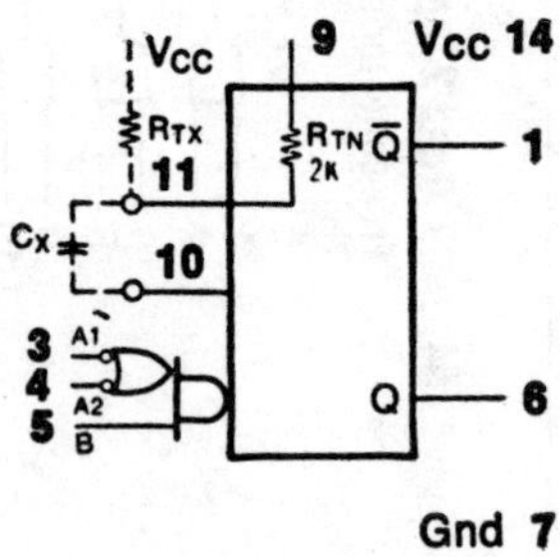

Triggering Truth Table

A1	A2	B	RESPONSE
1	1	↑	No Trigger
0	X	↑	Trigger
X	0	↑	Trigger
↓	0	X	No Trigger
↓	X	0	No Trigger
↓	1	1	Trigger
0	↓	X	No Trigger
X	↓	0	No Trigger
1	↓	1	Trigger

X = immaterial

54/74122 Retriggerable Multivibrator

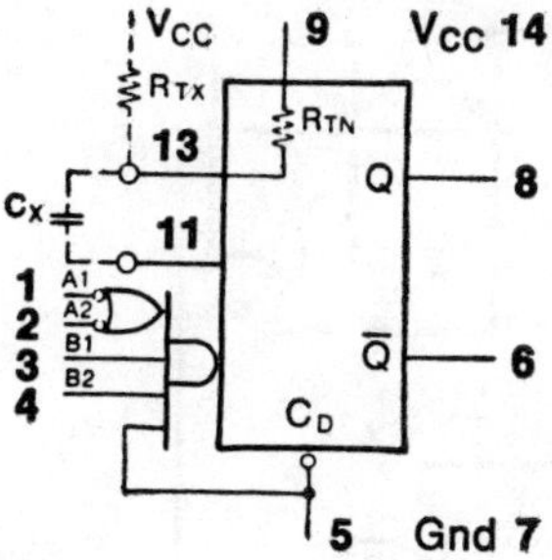

Triggering Truth Table

A1	A2	B1	B2	C_D	RESPONSE
X	X	X	X	0	No Trigger
↓	0	X	X	X	No Trigger
↓	X	0	X	X	No Trigger
↓	1	1	1	1	Trigger
X	X	↑	0	X	No Trigger
1	1	↑	X	X	No Trigger
0	X	↑	1	1	Trigger

*A1 & A2 are logically interchangeable, as are B1 & B2
X = immaterial

54/74123 Dual Retriggerable Multivibrator

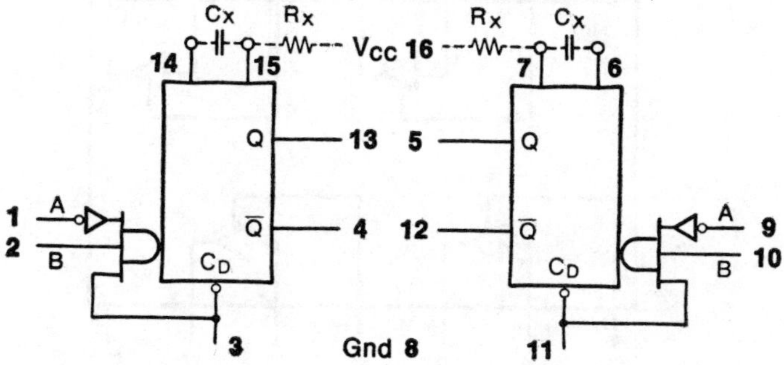

Triggering Truth Table

A	B	C_D	*RESPONSE
X	X	0	No Trigger
↓	0	X	No Trigger
↓	1	1	Trigger
1	↑	X	No Trigger
0	↑	1	Trigger

X = immaterial

Connection Diagrams

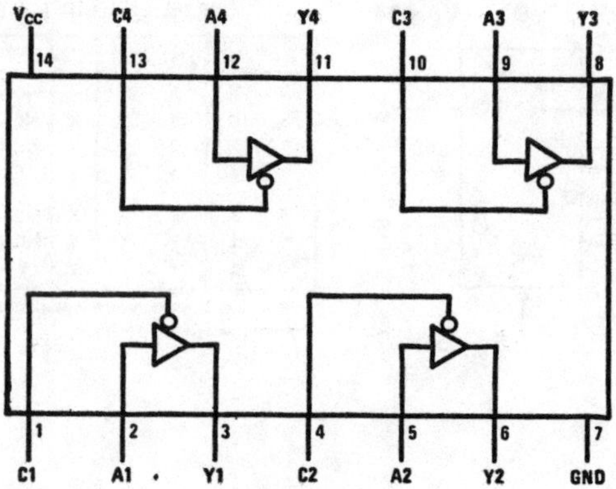

7093/8093(J), (N), (W)

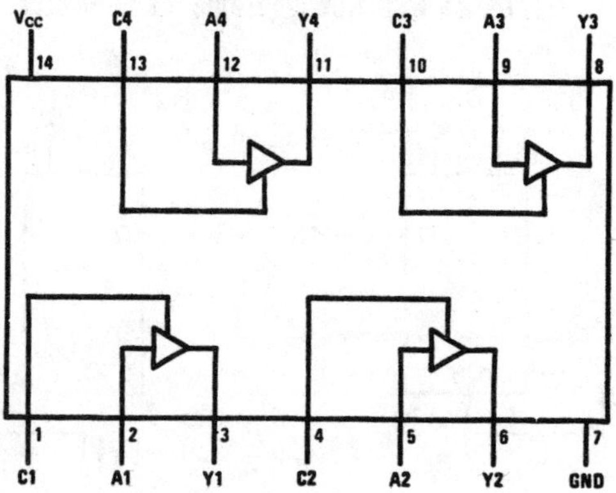

7094/8094(J), (N), (W)

Truth Tables

DM7093/DM8093

DATA	CONTROL	OUTPUT
H	L	H
L	L	L
X	H	Hi-Z

DM7094/DM8094

DATA	CONTROL	OUTPUT
H	H	H
L	H	L
X	L	Hi-Z

Connection Diagrams

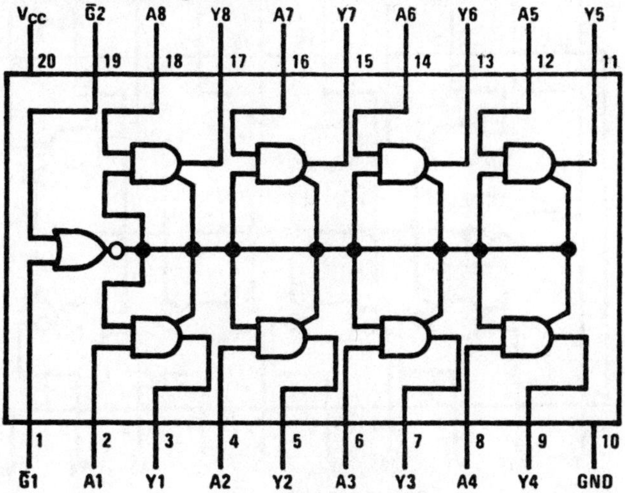

71LS95/81LS95(N)

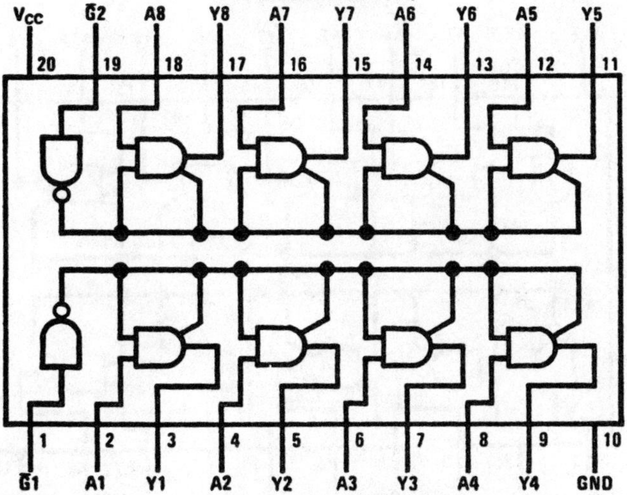

71LS97/81LS97(N)

Truth Tables

LS95

INPUTS			OUTPUT
$\overline{G}1$	$\overline{G}2$	A	Y
H	X	X	Z
X	H	X	Z
L	L	H	H
L	L	L	L

LS96

INPUTS			OUTPUT
$\overline{G}1$	$\overline{G}2$	A	Y
H	X	X	Z
X	H	X	Z
L	L	H	L
L	L	L	H

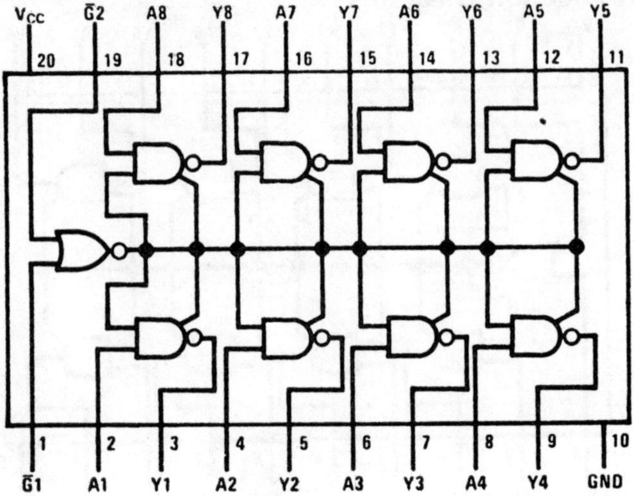

71LS96/81LS96(N)

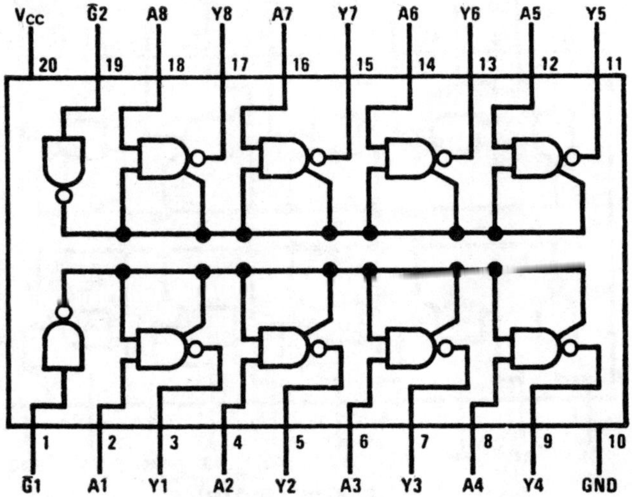

71LS98/81LS98(N)

LS97

INPUTS		OUTPUT
$\overline{G}$	A	Y
H	X	Z
L	H	H
L	L	L

LS98

INPUTS		OUTPUT
$\overline{G}$	A	Y
H	X	Z
L	H	L
L	L	H

Connection Diagrams

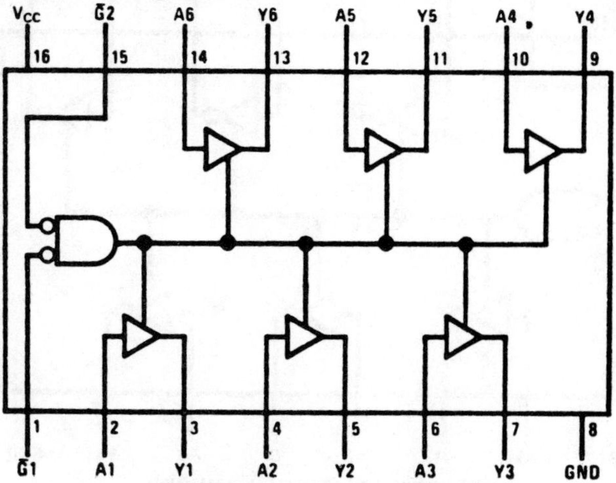

7095(J), (W); 8095(J), (N), (W); 70L95/80L95(J), (N), (W)

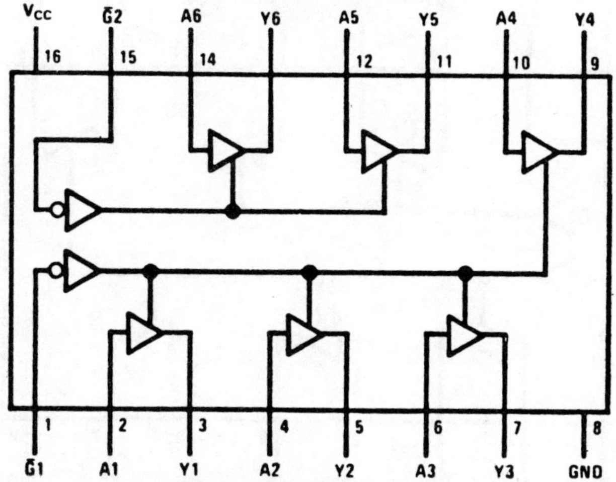

7097(J), (W); 8097(J), (N), (W); 70L97/80L97(J), (N), (W)

Truth Tables (Each Driver)

95, L95

INPUTS			OUTPUT
$\bar{G}1$	$\bar{G}2$	A	Y
H	X	X	Hi Z
X	H	X	Hi-Z
L	L	H	H
L	L	L	L

96, L96

INPUTS			OUTPUT
$\bar{G}1$	$\bar{G}2$	A	Y
H	X	X	Hi-Z
X	H	X	Hi Z
L	L	H	L
L	L	L	H

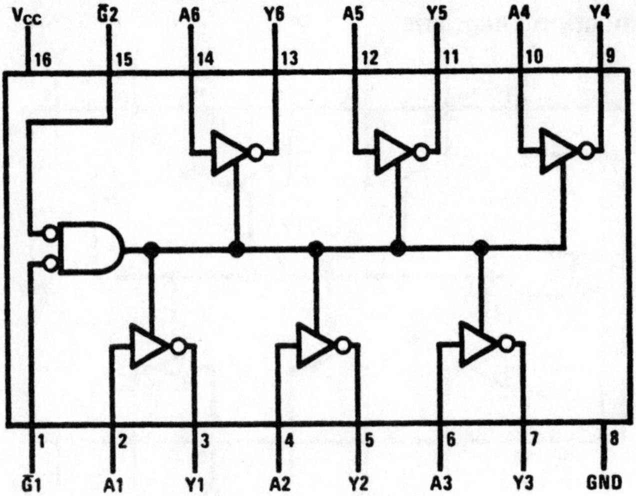

7096(J), (W); 8096(J), (N), (W); 70L96/80L96(J), (N), (W)

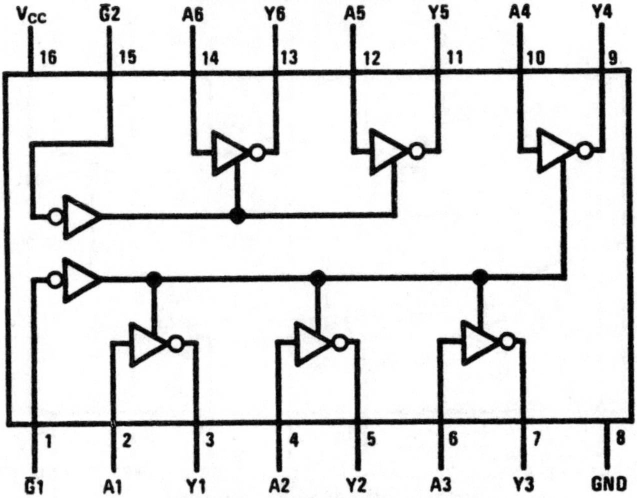

7098(J), (W); 8098(J), (N), (W); 70L98/80L98(J), (N), (W)

97, L97

INPUTS		OUTPUT
$\overline{G}$	A	Y
H	X	Hi-Z
L	H	H
L	L	L

98, L98

INPUTS		OUTPUT
$\overline{G}$	A	Y
H	X	Hi-Z
L	H	L
L	L	H

Dual-In-Line Package

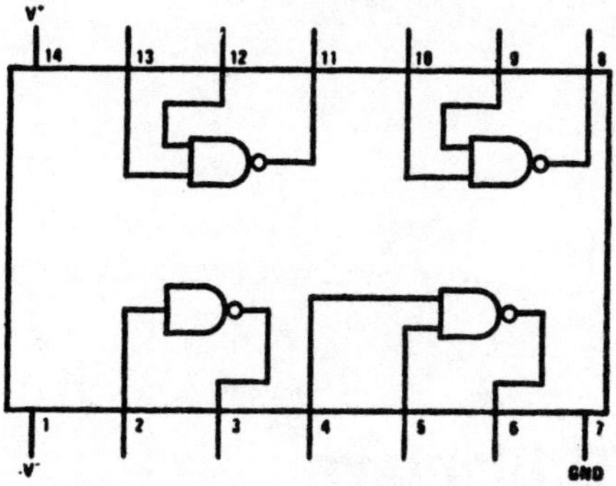

Dual-In-Line Package

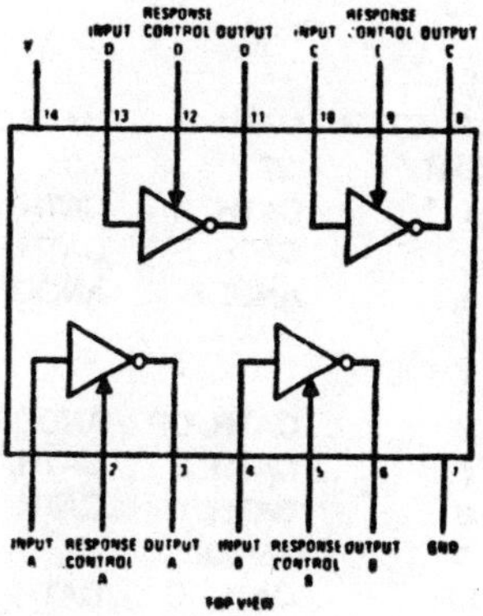

RS232C Data Transmission

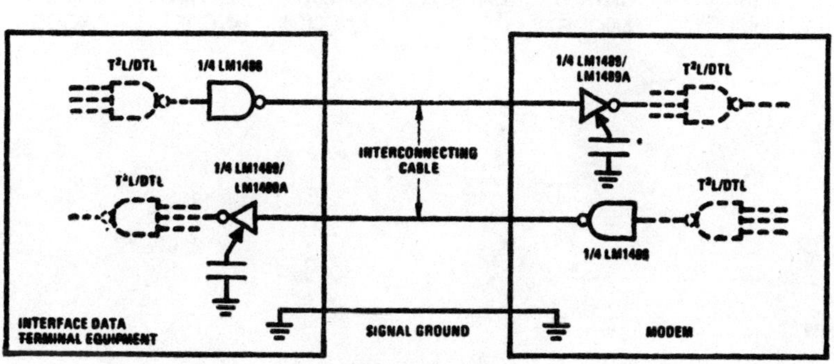

*OPTIONAL FOR NOISE FILTERING

Appendix B
7-Segment LED Displays

TYPE				MAN50/70	5082-
CHARACTER	MAN1	MAN6A	MAN10	80 SERIES	7730
HEIGHT	.27	.60	.27	.3	.3
PIN 1	CATH. A	CATH. A	CATH. A	CATH. A	CATH. A
2	CATH. F	CATH. F	CATH. F	CATH. F	CATH. F
3	ANODE	ANODE	ANODE	ANODE	ANODE
4					
5					
6	CATH. DP	ANODE DP	CATH. DP	CATH. DP	CATH. DP
7	CATH. E	CATH. E	CATH. E	CATH. E	CATH. E
8	CATH. D	CATH. D	CATH. D	CATH. D	CATH. D
9	ANODE		ANODE	ANODE	
10	CATH. C	CATH. C	CATH. C	CATH. C	
11	CATH. G	CATH. G	CATH. G	CATH. G	CATH.C
12					CATH. G
13	CATH B	CATH. B	CATH. B	CATH. B	CATH. B
14	ANODE		ANODE	ANODE	ANODE

Appendix C
Drawing Symbols

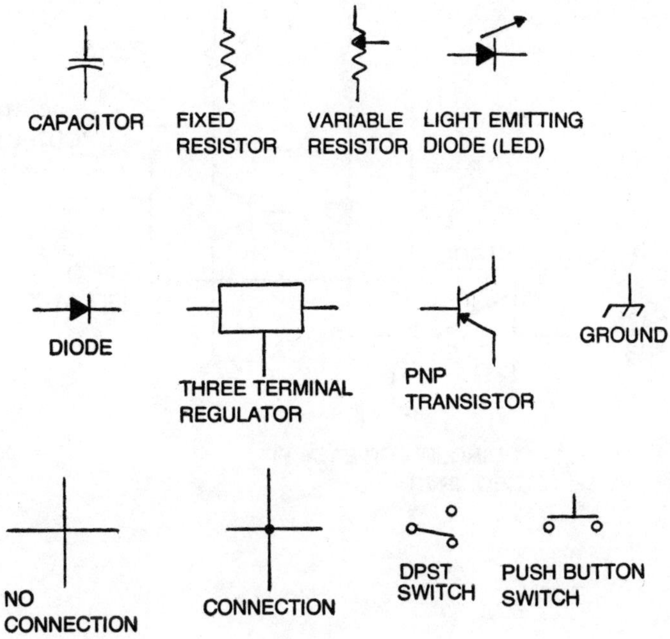

Appendix D
Using an Opto-Isolator as an Output Device

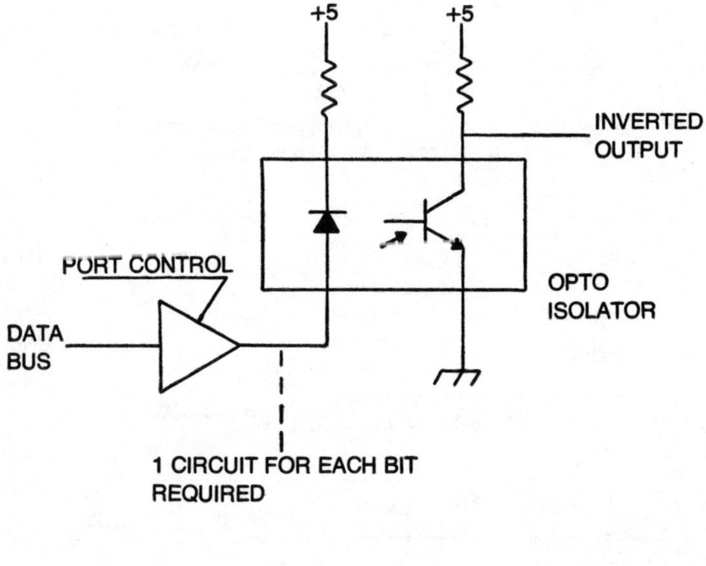

Index

Index